THE EMANCIPATORY PROMISE
OF CHARTER SCHOOLS

THE EMANCIPATORY PROMISE OF CHARTER SCHOOLS

Toward a Progressive Politics of School Choice

Edited by
Eric Rofes
and
Lisa M. Stulberg

FOREWORD BY
HERBERT GINTIS

State University of New York Press

Cover Photo: Sandie McDade-Allen

Published by
State University of New York Press, Albany

For information, address State University of New York Press,
90 State Street, Suite 700, Albany, NY 12207

Production by Judith Block
Marketing by Fran Keneston

Library of Congress Cataloging-in-Publication Data

The emancipatory promise of charter schools : toward a progressive politics of school
    choice / edited by Eric Rofes & Lisa M. Stulberg
        p. cm.
    Includes bibliographical references and index.
    ISBN 0-7914-6235-8 — ISBN 0-7914-6236-6 (pbk.)
    1. Charter schools—Political aspects—United States.   2. School choice—Political
    aspects—United States.   3. Educational equalization—United States.   I. Rofes,
    Eric E., 1954-   II. Stulberg, Lisa M.

LB2806.36.E42 2004
371.01—dc22
                                                                        2003068663

                    10   9   8   7   6   5   4   3   2   1

Contents

PART II: Frameworks for Progressive School Choice Analysis

F o r e w o r d

HERBERT GINTIS

Progressives who deal with American education on the grassroots level have long awaited an intelligent, persuasive, and visionary defense of school choice. *The Emancipatory Promise of Charter Schools: Toward a Progressive Politics of School Choice* perfectly fits the bill. It has been more than a quarter century since Samuel Bowles and I published *Schooling in Capitalist America*. We there claimed that capitalism generates a high degree of within- and across-generational inequality, that IQ and other test scores account only for a small portion of that inequality, that schooling reproduces rather than ameliorates that inequality, and that schools contribute to worker productivity in considerable part via the personality traits and behaviors they foster, rather than cognitive skills alone. Contemporary research has strengthened the empirical evidence underlying our analysis (Bowles, Gintis, & Groves, 2003; Bowles, Gintis, & Osborne, 2001). We are also no less committed today than we were when we conceived of and wrote *Schooling* to the vision of making a better, more democratic society in which all have the material and social prerequisites for developing their personal capacities to the fullest. But neither there nor elsewhere have we offered concrete steps toward a more progressive educational system. This volume provides a long stride in this direction.

When I wrote "The Political Economy of School Choice" for *Teachers College Record* some ten years ago, my progressive friends thought I had lost my sense of reason. Everyone knew that school choice was a conservative plot to finance the private education of the well-to-do, to bleed the public schools of needed revenue, and to add one more roadblock against the struggle for social equality. Indeed, when I started writing about education in the 1970s, I shared this view. Not that I had ever really thought about the matter. I just knew that if Milton Friedman (the conservative University of Chicago economist) was for it, and if the teachers unions were against it, I must be against it, too.

Well, we were all very wrong. If school choice is *fully funded*, so that choice schools financed with government funds are not permitted to impose tuition charges on families of students, as is the case with charter schools, then school choice can be an extremely progressive institution.

Perhaps the most important attraction of school choice—and I use the admittedly broad term in this piece to mean those choice plans that allow for significant autonomy in curriculum and governance—is that a creative and dedicated group of teachers can set up their own school without being beholden to rich donors or to unresponsive school boards. This sort of creative experimentation is likely to improve both the average quality of schooling and the diversity of types of educational experience.

A second major attraction of school choice is that parents will have much more influence over their children's education than under the current system. In general, public institutions work best when their constituents can control institutional behavior (*voice*) and when they can vote with their feet by moving to a competitive supplier (*exit*). The public schools give parents very little voice and no exit. In traditional public schools, principals and teachers are beholden first and foremost to school boards, who hire and fire them, rather than parents, who have no more power than the average voter in making and changing school policy and determining school personnel. By contrast, school choice options, like charter schools, directly empower parents, yet citizens retain general control over the choice system by regulating and accrediting the educational institutions that they fund.

A third attraction of school choice is that poorly performing teachers, and indeed poorly performing schools, need not be tolerated by parents intent on improving their children's education. The competition among schools for students will make it easier to eliminate deadwood and ineffective management is replaced.

Many progressive educators are wary of "competition," which they equate with the cutthroat capitalist marketplace. It is certainly true that cooperation is often more effective than competition, but in general, cooperation itself is enhanced in a competitive system. School choice allows teachers and administrators to cooperate voluntarily, subject only to the competitive restraint that parents and students must be satisfied with the results of their cooperative efforts. Indeed, competition itself is problematic only when it leads to inequality. If choice schools are fully funded, an unequal distribution of financial resources cannot occur. Financial equality will not, of course, guarantee that better teachers will not prefer to work with more affluent students, but it will allow the many teachers who are dedicated to improving the lot of the less affluent to do so much more effectively. Nor will financial equality redress the fact that advantaged families are more likely to have the time and energy to shop wisely for their children's schools than are disadvantaged families. But social service agencies and faith-based groups can be drawn upon to advise poor families how best to use their right to choose their children's schools.

A fourth attraction of school choice is that in choice schools, the influence of less-well-off parents will be heightened. In traditional school, only parents who have the time, energy, and resources to devote to affecting school policy and the school's treatment of the children have an attentive audience with school staff. With school choice, the simple threat of withdrawing one's children and sending them elsewhere is enough to make school personnel stand up and listen.

It is not surprising, then, that parents, students, and teachers find charter schools a highly positive experience, and that urban minorities are the strongest supporters of this choice alternative.

What about the downside of school choice? Why have so many progressive educators rejected this alternative? I think the answer is very simple: they have taken the workers' point of view instead of the consumers', or, in this case, that of the teachers unions rather than the students. Organized teachers have a vested interest in the traditional school system because its monopoly position in controlling educational funds allows teachers' organizations to bargain effectively, in a centralized framework, for higher wages.

There are two weaknesses in these arguments for rejecting school choice. First, in many states and communities teachers are extremely well paid, and where they are not, it is unlikely that school choice will leave teachers less well off than they are now. Indeed, since dedicated and creative teachers are a basic prerequisite for charter school success, a widespread choice system might well raise average salaries, both because high salaries will be needed to draw teachers from competing professions, and because the less capable teachers will be weeded out of the system, thus raising average teacher productivity. Second, while the United States might be better served by a strong labor movement, this end must be achieved by labor legislation on the federal level that is applicable to all industries. The school choice movement should not be asked to shoulder the brunt of the burden of achieving worker representation for the country as a whole.

The bottom line is that defenders of the monopoly public school system are simply throwing up smokescreens to hide the simple fact that teachers are loathe to submit themselves to the United States labor market—a market that most Americans are obliged to live with and that has turned out to strongly benefit consumers.

In defending school choice, you will hear the objection that parents are really incapable of choosing for their children, and education will be turned into a popularity contest. Nonsense! Parents choose their health care providers quite effectively. Why should they be any less capable of choosing their educational providers?

You will hear that charter schools bleed the traditional schools of needed funds. Well, that's what they are supposed to do! If the traditional schools want to compete effectively, they will simply have to improve their service delivery. Indeed, one of the most important effects of choice schools is the improvement of the performance of the nonchoice schools with which they are in competition.

You will hear that choice schools will teach whatever parents happen to want, thus lowering educational standards. However, if credentialing standards are up to snuff, this cannot happen. Once again, the American health care system, where people choose their providers, shows how such a system can work.

You will hear that choice schools represent one more step toward the privatization of American society through the atrophy of public spirit. However, accepting school choice does not imply a lesser role for the public sector, but only a different role. By regulating and accrediting choice schools (for example, by requiring participation in a national standardized testing system, or by prohibiting discrimination based on race, ethnicity, or religion), government will play the same role in a choice educational system that it now plays in most spheres of economic life: the government makes the rules of the game, but is not itself a player.

You will hear that choice schools will promote racial and ethnic segregation by accepting only certain kinds of students. Again, this can be prevented by the appropriate regulatory standards, prohibiting discrimination on the basis of race and ethnicity.

You will hear that choice schools do not perform better than standard schools in raising student reading and math scores. In fact, however, they do raise cognitive performance, although not generally by a huge amount. This is because most choice schools are quite young and are often harassed by the traditional educational establishment when they attempt to acquire the educational resources to which they are entitled. Moreover, test scores are not everything. Indeed, my work with Samuel Bowles has shown that test scores are not the major way schools affect the future wages and life chances of their students. It is likely that such factors as good citizenship, ability to take orders and complete tasks, and having a long time horizon are what schools really pass on to their charges in addition to cognitive skills. The more positive, community-oriented attitude of many choice schools is likely to do as much to help children control their lives as will their higher test scores.

School choice is a creative experiment. We don't know that it will work. The fact that the well-off parents (including teachers) prefer to send their children to private schools, involving a very high material sacrifice, is some indication of the value of being able to choose. Let's extend this privilege to the rest of our citizens.

References

Bowles, S., & Gintis, H. (1976). *Schooling in capitalist America: Educational reform and the contradictions of economic life.* New York: Basic Books.

Bowles, S., Gintis, H., & Groves, M. (Eds.). (2003). *Unequal chances: Family background and economic success.* Princeton, NJ: Princeton University Press.

Bowles, S., Gintis, H., & Osborne, M. (2001). The determinants of individual earnings: Skills, preferences, and schooling. *Journal of Economic Literature, 39(4),* 1137–1176.

Gintis, H. (1995, Spring). The political economy of school choice. *Teachers College Record, 96*(3), 492–511.

Acknowledgments

The editors acknowledge the following publishers who gave us permission to quote from previously published works:

Sage Publications, Ltd., for permission to quote from *Reproduction in Education, Society and Culture*, by Pierre Bourdieu and Jean-Claude Passeron, 1996.

Education Policy Analysis Archives for permission to use portions of "To Learn and Belong: Case Studies of Emerging Ethnocentric Charter Schools in Hawai'i," by N. K. Buchanan and R. A. Fox, which appeared February 23, 2003, in *EPPA*, retrieved from http://epaa.asu.edu/epaa/v11n8/.

Quotations from *Distinction: A Social Critique of the Judgment of Taste* by Pierre Bourdieu, translated by Richard Nice, are reprinted by permission of Harvard University Press and Taylor and Francis. Copyright © 1984 by the President and Fellows of Harvard College and Routledge and Kegan Paul, Ltd.

Introduction

ERIC ROFES AND LISA M. STULBERG

I t is time for progressive educational leaders to rethink their positions on school choice. For the past four decades, scholars of the political Left have offered insightful, cutting-edge analyses of the social reproductive function of schooling in the United States. They have successfully illustrated the many ways that attempts to utilize public schools to transform the life chances of poor and working-class children are resisted, undermined, and blatantly opposed. These scholars have identified the formidable social forces that lock public schools into their role of reproducing race and class inequities.

At the same time, these researchers have resisted or opposed almost all initiatives proposing alternatives to the current organization of schooling in America. While they have indicted various reform efforts, they generally have neglected to offer their own alternative, potentially liberatory, school reforms. It often feels as if the Left has given up on schooling as a force for social change. The Left's position on school choice demonstrates this precise dynamic.

Today, choice can take many forms: from the de facto school choice that comes with residential choice, to the choices involved in tracking and track placement within schools, to district-wide "controlled choice" plans in which every public school student participates, to magnet schools, to charter schools, and finally to public subsidy of private schools in the form of tuition tax credits and educational vouchers. The ideologies driving school choice vary widely. Some call for market competition to force public schools to better and more efficiently address the needs of their so-called clients, while others argue that providing schooling options for a variety of student needs and wants is a matter of educational equity, equal opportunity, and even educational self-determination.

School choice also has different meanings for different communities, and this fact has been repeatedly overlooked by the institutionalized Left. For middle-class white suburban families, for instance, choice may offer opportunities for smaller schools, special pedagogies, or a whiter, more affluent peer group. For low-income families of color in urban areas, choice may offer opportunities for safe schools, smaller classes, and more affirming curricula. For poor rural families, choice may offer the only opportunity in their area for specialized alternative curricula and instruction. School choice proposals, therefore, must be understood as situated reforms linked very closely to particular locations, communities, and political moments.

Public debate and research on current school choice options is increasingly abundant and is usually quite polarized. For instance, many choice proponents recklessly dismiss legitimate research that is critical of a choice reform's effect on underserved student populations or that questions the efficacy of particular choice plans. Similarly, choice opponents often lump together those who support charter schools, vouchers, and other forms of school choice as either naïve, market-driven reformers, elitists, or antidemocratic threats to public education. As charter schools proliferate, private "scholarship" programs expand and gain more corporate support, and public voucher plans push First Amendment bounds, research and public attention to school choice will continue to grow.

For this reason, as choice becomes a larger part of the American education reform agenda, critical and nuanced looks at school choice are increasingly important. The lived reality of school choice plans is more complicated than many supporters and critics would have us believe. The Left is often encouraged to oppose choice as a threat to racial integration, a party to the maintenance of educational inequities, or a misguided reform grounded in market reasoning that privileges efficiency and profit over educational concerns. Or, progressives are encouraged to support limited aspects of choice as a vehicle of pedagogical and curricular innovation, a facilitator of educational equity, and a tool of self-governance. Pulled in both directions, progressives are asked to see school choice as either a false hope or as somewhat of a panacea for students of color and low-income students. Yet both of these positions miss the complexity of the roots, politics, and implications of school choice.

Old-guard Leftists and their political and intellectual descendants in the field of educational research are locked in a 1960s vision of social change that continues to see school desegregation as the primary necessary remedy for educational and social inequality and that fails to incorporate the wide range of transformative possibilities from past generations. The Left seems mired in a deep hopelessness and despair and seems much more eager to identify challenges and enumerate profound problems in public education than to craft solutions. To many young, energized, reform-minded activists, the Left seems rigid, ossified, and mindlessly resistant to creative new thinking about school reform. The Left feels out of touch with the contemporary realities facing the institution of schooling in America. Their ideas are outdated; their vision is clouded; their agenda is bankrupt.

In response, this book puts forward a new voice on the Left, the beginning of a pioneering progressive response to school choice from a new generation of educators, primarily young and early-career researchers, policymakers, and school leaders. We use the term *progressive* rather than *liberal* because we wholeheartedly believe that there must be a fundamental revisioning of American institutions and cultures if we are to become a nation that truly achieves equity, justice, and participatory democracy. We believe that rather than tinkering with the current organization of schooling in America, a radical rethinking and daring restructuring of public education is called for. In place of perennial reforms, we seek to transform the institutions of our culture so that they serve as engines to redistribute power and resources and engage in a reinvigorated and searching examination of the politics of race, class, gender, and sexuality. We believe public schooling is central to this radical transformation.

We aim to open a conversation among progressives of various generations, perspectives, and social locations about one specific reform initiative—charter schools—in order to begin to open up a wider discussion of a new, progressive vision for public education. We hope the discussion generated from the essays in this book will rock the very foundations of progressive thinking about public education. We are well aware that the analyses and philosophies represented in this volume might be seen as a new generation of progressive thinkers taking their mentors to task. We hope this project will push the debate on school choice and contribute to and broaden the discussion of how public schooling can serve social equality. We want to break up a discussion that, to us, has seemed profoundly superficial and trapped in the values, understandings, and experiences of an earlier generation and an earlier sociopolitical context.

We offer this volume with respect for the rich and ambitious progressive tradition in politics and education. But we also offer this volume without apology. The authors represented in this collection have solid track records in a variety of social change movements and have been part of efforts to move progressive politics out of the 1960s and into the new millennium. While we expect we may be derided by some established leaders within the academic Left, we firmly believe that the conversation we intend to open with this book will result in a resurrection of progressive educational activism and a bold new vision for public education.

Hence we aim for this collection to move the political Left's position on school choice forward, to offer a nuanced discussion of current school choice reforms and their meanings in a variety of communities. We have brought together here a number of scholars and educators who both study and participate in school choice reform. Acknowledging the ways in which we ourselves have grappled with our simultaneous support for and skepticism of many school choice efforts, we have urged our authors to be bold in their questioning and assertive in their own ambivalence about this complicated school policy. In so doing, we hope this book will push progressives' thinking on school choice, particularly on issues that are underexamined in the literature, such as the impact of school choice on race and class politics and inequalities. For school choice has never been race- or class-neutral, and we cannot have a truly progressive position on choice that does not focus on race and class analyses.

This book comes out unabashedly, yet not uncritically, in favor of the charter school reform initiative. We believe that unlike vouchers, the first decade of charter school reform illustrates that charters are playing a powerful role in reviving democratic participation in public education, expanding opportunities for progressive methods in public school classrooms, and providing new energy to community-based, community-controlled school initiatives for communities of color. In this collection, John B. King, Jr.'s chapter on Roxbury Preparatory Charter School, Nina K. Buchanan and Robert A. Fox's work on three Native Hawai'ian charter schools, Patty Yancey's chapter on African American charter schools and their connection to African American independent school movements, and Mary Jiron Belgarde's chapter on Native American charter schooling and school politics demonstrate the range of ways in which educators, parents, and students of color have embraced the charter reform as a means to educational excellence and community control.

This book also takes as a starting assumption that the complexity of school choice discourse must be recognized and examined if we truly are to build liberatory school choice plans. In this volume, Stacy Smith and Alex Medler offer tools to begin this process through their reading and critique of the discourses of charter schooling. We take seriously, as well, the importance of recognizing and grappling openly with the ways in which our support of charter schools seemingly clashes with our progressive politics—or seems to pit us against long-standing political allies. Melissa Steel King's chapter introduces us to a group of charter school educators, all of whom identify as political progressives, who wrestle with this reconciliation of their politics and their charter school enthusiasm and commitment.

This broad, multidisciplinary, and progressive look at school choice is important for a few primary reasons. For one, school choice reforms raise two questions that are of the utmost urgency. First, how viable are some public schools in general today? Second, and quite relatedly, can public schools as an entity adequately address and redress American race and class inequalities? This kind of exploration of school choice is also sociologically interesting because it raises the question of the capacity and limitation of the state to meet the needs and interests of its citizens. It also confronts the issue of what it means to resist existing institutions and perhaps, through this resistance, to unwittingly participate in reproducing existing inequalities. Eric Rofes's chapter grapples with this question by bringing the work of the late sociologist Pierre Bourdieu to bear on charter schools. Finally, this approach to the study of school choice points to the importance of learning from history. As Lisa M. Stulberg's chapter argues, an attention to history leads us to some of the most fruitful questions about school choice. It can then teach us volumes about what is necessary to build progressive analyses of choice and to construct equitable and just school choice reforms that truly serve all students.

We have noted a long-standing practice among the educational Left of faulting bureaucratic organization of public education for the reproduction of social inequities, while simultaneously opposing innovative efforts to transform the organization of public education and the governance of schooling. Ultimately, as two progressive scholars early in our academic careers, we intend for this volume to serve as a challenge to many of our more senior colleagues who fail to distinguish between various choice mechanisms, mistake the radical potential of charters to revive participatory democracy in education as an undercutting of long-established bureaucratic forms of schooling, and repeatedly patronize the enthusiasm of communities of color for charter schools as "false consciousness." We hope all people who think of themselves as educational and political progressives and reform activists will join in this groundbreaking, nuanced, and, we believe, ultimately hopeful discussion of school choice.

CHAPTER 1

What History Offers Progressive Choice Scholarship

LISA M. STULBERG

We must devise new structures, new institutions to replace those forms or to make them responsive. There is nothing sacred or inevitable about old institutions . . .

—Stokely Carmichael and Charles V. Hamilton,
Black Power: The Politics of Liberation

Introduction

Thurgood Marshall did not dream this school in May 1954 when he stood before the Supreme Court and heard the news that he had won. Martin Luther King, Jr., did not dream this school in October 1958, when he marched in Washington, D.C. for integrated schooling. Stokely Carmichael certainly did not dream this school in 1967, when he called for African Americans to control their own community institutions. Yet, here it stood, one of the few educational opportunities for African American adolescents in the birthplace of the Black Panther Party, West Oakland, California.

This district middle school served a neighborhood deemed the poorest in the city according to the 1990 census, with more than 75% of the neighborhood living below the poverty line (Noguera, 1996, p. 6; Oakland Citizens Committee for Urban Renewal, 1998; Urban Strategies Council, 1996, p.18). It serves a student body with almost 50% more African American students than the district as a whole. The school is failing these students, letting them graduate with reading and math skills well below the national average, with correspondingly low grades (Oakland Coalition of Congregations, 1999, pp. 2, 23). The school often fails quite publicly, but it languishes quietly. When students graduate, they go on, for the most part, to the only high school in the neighborhood, where fewer than 20% of entering freshman eventually graduate and those who do are almost assured of receiving an education that will leave them unprepared to enter college (Oakland Coalition of Congregations, 1999, p. 25; Ruenzel, 1998, p. 34). To the civil rights and Black Power movements, which envisioned that successful and thriving schools for Black students could be tools for racial equality and justice, this school stands as an affront. Yet it is the school that serves many African American middle schoolers in West Oakland.

Housed in an old and active Lutheran church, the West Oakland Community School (WOCS) exists as an alternative to everything that its neighboring school is not: small, safe, academically rigorous, thriving, and embedded in the rich community that surrounds it. This charter school also works specifically to serve African American children in this segregated neighborhood. It reaches into history to find its inspiration in the Black Panthers and civil rights legends like Ella Baker, seeking to provide quality education that can equalize life chances for African Americans and revitalize African American communities.

Charter schools like WOCS have provided educational alternatives for just a little more than a decade. Born in Minnesota in 1991, these public schools of choice have proliferated quickly. From the two schools founded during the 1992–93 school year, the number of charter schools founded grew to 100 by 1994–95, to 432 by 1996–97 and to 1122 by 1998–99 (RPP International, 2000, p.11). There are now, as of the summer of 2003, charter laws on the books in forty states plus the District of Columbia. Partisan data, compiled by the procharter Center for Education Reform (2003), put the number of charter schools in operation in the fall of 2002 at approximately 2,700 and the number of students served by charters at 684,000.

Public and private school choice of the last decade has provoked prolific and vigorous public debate and policy attention, yet school choice is not a new reform. For years, school choice has produced improbable bedfellows of politically progressive and conservative academics, policymakers, educators, and communities. In the early days of school choice policy and politics, scholars from Milton Friedman on the Right to Christopher Jencks on the Left asked the fundamental questions of schooling. Albeit from widely different political perspectives, they examined the purpose of schooling, the viability of public education, and the ability of public schooling to adequately serve the educational and political needs of traditionally marginalized Americans. While school choice scholars and experts today draw on the legacy of the 1960s debates, their hindsight lacks depth and breadth. They narrow the scope of the debate on school choice, constricting the conversation about the pros and cons of charter schools, vouchers, and other public school choice plans. They fail to ask the broad and complicated questions about the ways in which public and private school choice fits into a vision of American schooling.

In contrast and in response to the current scholarship on school choice reforms, we must introduce and examine this rich, varied, and eminently relevant school choice history to ask the questions that are of the utmost importance for the new millennium. First, how viable are public schools in general today? How can public schools become fully viable? Second, and quite relatedly, can public schools adequately mitigate American race and class inequalities? These are the questions that can frame a truly progressive politics of school choice. History delivers these questions to us and provides us with complicated answers to them. Through a reading of history, we can come to see the ways in which a reform like charter schooling stands at a complex intersection of the politics of race and schooling. History, viewed broadly, also allows us to critically assess the current academic and public debates on school choice and it provides us with tools to measure the political and academic successes and failures of current school choice initiatives.

School Choice History and Its Scholarship

This relevant history could begin almost anywhere. It is tempting to start with the Founding Fathers and the ways in which they conceived of American public education as a nation-building endeavor designed to instill distinctly American values and loyalties.[1] This would not be an analytical stretch in the story of the school choice reform. But for modern school reform debates, the landmark 1954 Supreme Court school desegregation decision of *Brown v. Board of Education of Topeka* provides the most apt starting point.

First, the *Brown* decision is an important beginning for school choice scholarship because it is a substantial historical touchstone that weds race and school politics from 1954 onward. It reminds us that we cannot assess American educational achievement or school policies in the post-*Brown* age without taking racial inequality as a central problematic. Second, *Brown* assigns to schools a broad responsibility for mitigating American racial inequality. Schools thus take a central place in the American struggle for

racial equality and justice. Third, after *Brown*, the goal of racially desegregated schools became a way to measure school reform efforts and successes.
As I will discuss below, this has certainly been the case in recent debates on
school choice. Both supporters and opponents wield the legacy of *Brown*
in their assessment of school choice reforms. In this, they assign meaning
and intention to the National Association for the Advancement of Colored
People's (NAACP) legal battle and the Court's charge in the *Brown* decision. *Brown* and school desegregation are still active symbols that play a discursive role in current school choice discussions. Thus it is important to
turn to the decision itself and to understand the extent to which the
NAACP and its supporters believed desegregated schooling to be part of a
broad struggle for excellence and equality in education.

The *Brown* decision was a watershed of the twentieth century for a
number of reasons. It was not the beginning of attention to or advocacy
of school desegregation. But it was the culmination of two decades of
legal challenges to unequal, segregated public higher education by the
NAACP. It represented, as well, an extension of the way in which the
federal government had come to see its charge in remedying racial inequality, representing another instance of the "entry of the federal government as the guarantor of black rights" (Katznelson and Weir, 1985, p.
205). Finally, it represented an expansion of the definition of educational equality, a ruling from the Court that equal opportunity must be
predicated on desegregation.

Brown was also a significant new beginning. First, it heralded a new
social movement (Kluger, 1975). This movement relied heavily on access
and desegregation as a strategy for racial equality. Some of the most significant and most public confrontations of the civil rights movement were
school desegregation struggles, from the desegregation of Central High
School in Little Rock, Arkansas, in 1957 to James Meredith's integration
of the University of Mississippi in 1962. Second, the *Brown* decision and
the NAACP's arguments before the Court brought an unprecedented
joining of racial concerns and politics with public schooling. Ira Katznelson and Margaret Weir (1985) argue that *Brown* touched off a "reopening
of fundamental questions of race and schooling" (p. 182). Schools became
a central focus when civil rights activists called into question African
Americans' lack of access to American institutions and the American
Dream (also see Henig, Hula, Orr, & Pedescleaux, 1999; Kirp, 1982).
David L. Kirp (1982) contends that it was *Brown* that cemented the connection between racial justice and equal educational opportunity and that
intertwined the previously distinct national concerns about race and pub-

lic education (see also Newby and Tyack, 1971; Tyack and Hansot, 1982). After *Brown*, and through the 1960s, debates about the nature of racial equality and the means to racial justice took place primarily in the reinvigorated and robust fight over schooling. For civil rights activists, educators, policymakers, and social scientists, public schools became a "staging ground in the quest for racial justice" (Tyack, 1974, p. 279). This has left its mark on all African American school activism—desegregation-related or not—for generations to come (Katznelson and Weir, 1985; Kirp, 1982; Newby and Tyack, 1971). In the decades following *Brown*, public schooling was also a site for racial justice struggles for Latino and Asian American parents and communities. Latino parents, for instance, challenged segregated schooling and school funding inequity in *Keyes v. Denver School District No. 1* (1973) and *San Antonio Independent School District v. Rodriguez* (1973) (see Kluger 1975; Orfield, Eaton, & Harvard Project on School Desegregation, 1996), and Chinese American parents in San Francisco successfully challenged the lack of bilingual public education in the *Lau v. Nichols* unanimous Supreme Court ruling of 1974 (Wang, 1995).

In the set of cases that were jointly ruled upon in the *Brown* decision of 1954, the NAACP's lawyers and expert witnesses testified before the Supreme Court that the public schools could play a key part in alleviating racial inequality. The Court responded by handing public schools this new responsibility. This charge was founded on two new assumptions. The first was that equality could not be achieved as long as "unequal educational opportunities" in the form of legal segregation persisted. Second, the Court assumed that it had a role to play in both perpetuating racial discrimination and redressing it. This represented a radical departure from the standing precedent, the 1896 *Plessy v. Ferguson* decision, which retained the constitutionality of separate public facilities. In this early case, the Court had ruled that racial prejudices and "instincts" would not be abolished through law and should not be the charge of the courts (e.g., Kirp, 1982; Kluger, 1975).

When the NAACP turned to the issue of desegregated schooling, it did so as part of a broad strategy to gain civil rights for African Americans. The NAACP launched the first of its five initial direct challenges to *Plessy* with a case against the Clarendon County, South Carolina segregated public schools.[2] In December 1952, NAACP lawyers argued before the Supreme Court that school segregation itself was a violation of the equal protection clause of the Fourteenth Amendment. As Robert Carter argued for the NAACP in the Topeka *Brown* case, "the act of separation and the act of segregation in and of itself denies . . . equal educational opportunities which the Fourteenth Amendment secures." Buttressed by a significant amount of sociological and psychological research entered in the case and by a finding by the lower Kansas court in *Brown* that school segregation had harmful effects on African American children, NAACP lawyers asked the Court to remove the legal barriers to integrated schooling (Carter, quoted in Kluger, 1975, p. 564; also see p. 525).

The Court, though slow to rule, delivered a decision on May 17, 1954. Designed to achieve a unanimous, and thus unequivocal, ruling, the order was balanced in its approach and tone. Chief Justice Warren wrote:

> We conclude that in the field of public education the doctrine of "separate but equal" has no place. Separate educational facilities are inherently unequal. Therefore, we hold that the plaintiffs and others similarly situated for whom the actions have been brought are, by reason of the segregation complained of, deprived of the equal protection of the laws guaranteed by the Fourteenth Amendment. (quoted in Kluger, 1975, pp. 781–82)

In the four state cases that made up the *Brown* ruling, the court found that segregation per se denied "equal educational opportunities" and therefore denied equal protection. Quoting the lower court in the Kansas case, Warren noted that the social and psychological "impact [of segregation] is greater when it has the sanction of the law; for the policy of separating the races is usually interpreted as denoting the inferiority of the negro group" (quoted in Kluger, 1975, p. 782). As with the NAACP's focus, then, the Court directed its decision to state actions that explicitly sorted students by race, which concentrated attention on the South and the border states (Kluger, 1975; Orfield, 1981). Despite this ruling, the Court took its time and allowed school districts to move slowly on the question of implementation. In *Brown II*, the Warren Court ruled in May 1955 that districts were simply to act "with all deliberate speed" in establishing desegregation plans (see Kluger, 1975).

Through the *Brown* ruling, the NAACP hoped to achieve a broad goal in African American schooling. The organization's attorneys urged an end to segregated public schooling as a strategy for quality schooling for African American children. In the 1950s, desegregation was conceived of as an equalization tool, given the existing unequal distribution of public school resources by race, including disparities in district spending, teacher training, curriculum, facilities, and intangibles like school prestige.[3] The NAACP of the 1950s argued that these inequities could no longer be corrected through segregated institutions. Furthermore, the NAACP used social scientific evidence to demonstrate that racial segregation produced deleterious social and psychological effects for both Black and White children. School desegregation was not, then, only an end in itself. It was, rather, primarily a means to quality schooling and quality of life in the context of an unequal distribution of educational resources by race and class. As educational historian David Tyack (1974) writes of the movement as it progressed through the 1960s to the North, "The demand for desegregation in northern cities was for most blacks a quest for equality and quality in schooling more than some vague aspiration for mixing of ethnic groups; the white power structure could be trusted to teach Negro children adequately only if there were white children there as well" (p. 280; also see Dentler, 1991; Willie, 1989).

While the *Brown* decision is an important part of school choice history, the concept of school choice itself played a role in *Brown* only as it stood for a conservative response to the ruling. As some current school choice researchers argue, school choice became associated with southern evasion of the Court ruling through "freedom of choice" plans that rested school desegregation on simply giving individual students the ostensible choice of school attendance. Though the Court of the late 1960s and early 1970s struck down these plans, choice became a symbol of resistance to desegregation following the Court's 1954 decision.

Some choice scholars, most notably Amy Stuart Wells and Jeffrey R. Henig, also argue that the meaning of school choice shifted with the introduction of a kind of public school of choice, magnet schools, in the early 1970s. Through magnet schooling, choice was redefined as a tool to facilitate (voluntary) school desegregation, deemed legitimate by the courts beginning in the early 1970s and supported by the Republican presidents who opposed a heavy state hand in desegregation.[4] During the 1970s and early 1980s, many northern cities, backed by additional federal funding, established magnet schools as a "vehicle for managing integration" (Henig, 1994, p. 106), to curb White flight from cities and public schools, stave off court desegregation orders, or achieve desegregation under a court order (Blank, Levine, & Steel, 1996; Henig, 1994; Kozol, 1982; 1991; Raywid, 1994; Wells, 1991a; 1993; Young, 1990).[5] In the 1980s, under Presidents Reagan and George H. W. Bush, these schools became increasingly decoupled from desegregation goals. Bush even proposed federal funding for magnets regardless of their impact on desegregation.[6]

The school choice researchers who focus on the historical roots of current choice initiatives, particularly Wells and Henig, also locate the development of school choice through magnet schooling in the proliferation of public and private alternative schools in the 1960s and 1970s. These schools were generally created by small groups of parents or community activists who wanted the freedom to implement their own philosophies and pedagogical perspectives on childhood and schooling.

Independent alternative schools began not as market-driven solutions to the monopoly of public education, but as outgrowths of 1960s social movements. Founded mainly in the late 1960s and early 1970s, often by members of the White Left and counterculture, these were also known as "free" or "community" schools. The schools in this growing movement were ideologically diverse. But many took their ideological and pedagogical cues from some key writings of the time, from A.S. Neill's *Summerhill*, to Ivan Illich's *Deschooling Society*, to a number of author-educators criticizing public education from the Left, like John Holt, Jonathan Kozol, and Herbert Kohl. School founders focused on achieving freedom from the traditional authoritarian nature of public schooling. They embedded a philosophy of education in the understanding that children are naturally curious and driven to learn and the belief that schools should be a place to nurture children's independence rather than stifle it. Most of these schools were small and predominantly White and charged tuition on a sliding scale, supplemented with some foundation support.[7]

These private schools inspired a wide range of public alternatives. As alternative schooling became an acceptable and possible response by many communities to their criticisms of traditional public schools, the number of public alternatives leapt from just 464 in 1973 to an estimated 5,000 by the fall of 1975. These generally small, often urban schools varied in academic focus and ideology.[8] In the early 1970s these public schools were often initiated and supported by community groups and parents and backed by Left cultural movements. But the schools of the early to mid-1970s, as with much of the politics of the time, rather quickly yielded to increasing conservatism. Rather than boasting variety and grassroots initiation, the alternative schools of the 1980s tended toward quantifiable and standardized basic skill building (Cuban, 1993; Raywid, 1983; 1994; Wells, 1993; Young, 1990).

School choice scholarship recognizes another reform in its story of the roots of current school choice politics: school vouchers. Those who do draw on the past to understand the present moment in school choice reform look to the voucher debates of the 1960s and early 1970s. These scholars primarily cite conservative economist Milton Friedman and the school voucher plan that he introduced in a 1955 essay and developed in a chapter of his 1962 book, *Capitalism and Freedom*. Friedman's plan was driven by free-market assumptions that competition and choice would produce a higher quality educational product. Friedman recommended that parents be given a choice to spend in private schools the equivalent of the funds spent on their child in their local district. The state's role would be minimal. It would disburse funds and ensure simply "minimum standards."[9]

Friedman's plan drew unlikely attention from the Left. In a 1966 article titled "Is the Public School Obsolete?" sociologist Christopher Jencks condemned the organization of city schools, arguing that many urban public schools were dull, oppressive, and uninspired and were undeserving of additional financial support. The fact of centralized public governance itself, coupled with a shortage of resources, fostered stagnation in public schools (pp. 21–23, 27). In this early piece, Jencks began to articulate an argument for tuition vouchers for low-income urban students, asserting that failing public schools survived only because they had a monopoly on education for those who could not afford private schools. Given a choice, families would take their business elsewhere, joining or creating schools that would have to be responsive to their needs in order to retain a clientele. Jencks also contended that these private alternatives might be more racially and economically integrated than their public counterparts, since they would not be neighborhood based (pp. 23–25).

Motivated by a concern for educational equality rather than free-market deregulation of schooling, Jencks proposed, in 1970, a heavily regulated voucher plan aimed at low-income students and designed to equalize schooling by making it possible for students to opt out of public schools that were underserving them. Under the Nixon administration's Office of Economic Opportunity, Jencks devised a small, regulated voucher experiment designed primarily to equalize schooling for low-income students and students of color and render schools more responsive to their needs and their participation. When implemented in 1972 in Alum Rock, California, the OEO program was not much more than a public school choice plan that brought additional resources to participating schools. Teachers' unions, civil rights groups, and others who were worried about achieving school desegregation and retaining public school constituencies opposed the inclusion and support of private schools in Jencks's plan.[10]

A Broader Look at History

We do learn a substantial amount from the history of school choice as it has been told thus far. For instance, we learn that public and private school choice is not a product of the 1980s and 1990s, as much of the ahistorical current public debate might have us believe.[11] We learn that public and private school choice has historically drawn support and opposition from both the Left and the Right, serving as the site for some very complicated coalitions. We learn, as well, that some of the same groups that now vocally defend or criticize school choice are the same groups that participated in school choice debates a generation ago. For example, unions and civil rights groups faced off against voucher supporters in the Alum Rock case thirty years ago, just as they do now in voucher battles in Milwaukee or Cleveland. We also learn that movements for school choice have sometimes sprung from non-school-based social movements. Progressive alternative schools, for instance, grew from the White Left in the late 1960s and early 1970s. Finally, we learn that the politics of school choice have always been bound to the politics of race, particularly as school choice reforms raised concerns about the future of racially desegregated schooling. School choice scholars who have been particularly useful in bringing this history to light include Wells (1993; 2000a; 2000b; 2000c), Henig (1994), and Bulman and Kirp (1999).

Yet there is also a lot we do not learn from this scholarship. First, the scholarship falls significantly short of fully examining the race politics of school choice history. In neglecting this history, the literature does not present us with adequate analytical tools to make sense of the current politics of race with respect to school choice debates and reforms. When scholars examine the history and sociology of race and schooling, they rightly focus on the *Brown v. Board of Education* ruling as a watershed. Yet they often interpret *Brown* and its legacy solely through a desegregation lens. They tend to assume that it is through desegregation struggles that the politics of race have driven school politics, and they mark the history of race and schooling of the past fifty years by the ebb and flow of desegregation politics and policies.[12] This is true, as well, for school choice scholarship. Those who address the politics of race at all do so primarily to locate the story of school choice reforms in the history and politics of desegregation. This focus on school choice and the politics of desegregation is important, but it is not enough. As I will discuss in more detail below, school choice movements have their ideological, political, and educational roots in a number of movements and initiatives for racial justice, equality, and identity that are *not* integration focused.

Apart from the historical story, the school choice debates on race primarily center on the extent to which charter schools and school vouchers exacerbate racial segregation in schooling. In large part, these discussions draw on *Brown* as a symbolic reference point. Scholars situate their investigation of the politics of charter schooling in a debate about the extent to which charters schooling can be understood as a legacy of the *Brown* decision. Charter schools, for instance, receive praise from academics and practitioners, like Minnesota charter activist Joe Nathan, the recently resigned President and CEO of the National Urban League Hugh Price, and civil rights activist Rosa Parks (Nathan, 2002; Price, 1999). Many of these and other supporters hail charter schools as the current legacy of the *Brown* decision and the civil rights movement, providing equal educational opportunities where the 1954 decision left off.

Nathan, for instance, often likens the charter movement to the civil rights movement, the movement for workers' rights led by Cesar Chávez, and women's suffrage movements. He writes, for instance, "For many advocates, the charter public school movement is an expansion of opportunity, similar to that proposed by people like Susan B. Anthony, Dr. Martin Luther King, Jr., and Cesar Chávez" (1996b, p. 18; also see 1996a, p. xiii). Other supporters argue that schools of choice provide a kind of quality education that desegregation advocates seek. They thus paint school choice as a more authentic, genuine response to educational inequality. For example, the conservative voucher and charter school proponent, the Center for Education Reform, frames vouchers as a modern and immediate response to racial inequality in schooling. Under a story marking the anniversary of *Brown* and noting its unfulfilled promise, the organization's May 1999 newsletter included a piece entitled "Nero Fiddles while Rome Burns." The story, oddly, mentioned only African American, Jewish, and labor leaders who oppose vouchers, accusing, "[T]hey'd rather fiddle, than help pull the children from the flames of mediocrity and failure" (p. 1).

By contrast, researchers like Wells, Bruce Fuller, and Gary Orfield are skeptical of school choice reforms. They argue that charter schools have the capacity to deflect attention from or further entrench racial and economic inequalities in schooling (see, for example, Elmore and Fuller, 1996; Fuller, Elmore, and Orfield, 1996; Orfield, 1998; UCLA Charter School Study, 1998; Wells, 2000a; 2000b; 2000c). These critics tend to see charter schools that focus on students of color as well meaning yet misguided in their attempt to equalize educational opportunities. Some see these schools as a kind of affront to the legacy of *Brown* in that they will likely preserve and even exacerbate racial segregation in schooling.

Orfield must be acknowledged and praised for his long history of commitment to racial justice and his research on desegregation and resegregation. This work has been invaluable to my own thinking and to that of many scholars concerned with equal educational opportunity. Wells, too, has been one of the only school choice scholars who has taken seriously the questions that charter schools raise for race and class inequalities. She has taken a broad, creative, and useful approach to American public school history and applied it to a reflective critique of charter schooling. She also, unusually within the highly polarized academic and public charter school conversation, has been willing to recognize how complicated charter schooling is as a solution to the failings of American public education. Both Wells and Orfield, along with others, like Fuller (Elmore and Fuller, 1996; Fuller, 2000a and 2000b; Fuller et al., 1996), approach charter schools with a strong and abiding commitment to an educational equality that they believe is achievable largely through school integration. They study charter schooling within a broader research agenda that questions how school reform efforts impact school de- and resegregation by race and income (see, for instance, Wells and Crain, 1997).

But this analytical and political context does not allow for a broader reading of the *Brown* decision and its legacy in the current school choice movement or a broad assessment of the way in which charter schools are serving or failing to serve students and communities of color. More than this, perhaps, it focuses on the problem of charter schools—that they contribute to racial and economic segregation—without offering solutions to the problem of racial and economic inequality that might work in the new millennium.

Recent scholarship documents the extent to which school choice plans contribute to racial segregation in schooling and a stratification of school options that privileges White and middle-class families. Some studies allay the fear that charter schools will tend to serve White and middle-class students with their finding that charters generally match the racial and socioeconomic demographics of their districts (American Federation of Teachers, 1996; Little Hoover Commission, 1996; RPP International and the University of Minnesota, 1997; RPP International, 1998; 1999; 2000). The 1998 national charter school study found that 60% of charter schools tended to broadly reflect—within 20%—the demographics of their districts, while approximately 35% tended to serve a higher proportion (by more than 20%) of students of color than their host districts (RPP International, 1998, pp. 47–57). Two years later, the 2000 national report found that 69% of charter schools tended to mirror their district's racial/ethnic demographics, while approximately 17% served a higher proportion of students of color than their districts (RPP International, 2000, pp. 30–31). This varies significantly by state. In California, for instance, White students are overrepresented in charter schools. African American students are also slightly overrepresented, making up 8.4% of total public school students and 10.8% of charter school students in the state in 1997–98 (RPP International, 2000, pp. 32–33; also see 1998, pp. 49–57). The 1998 study reported that just 32 charter schools in the country served a student body that was at least two-thirds African American (RPP International, 1998, p. 63).

Others studies, by contrast, find that charter schools tend to disproportionately serve one racial or ethnic group and have the capacity to exacerbate racial segregation. Wells has parsed the national data to argue that the broad finding that charter schools reflect district demographics masks significant race and class segregation. She notes in 2000 that "[c]areful analysis suggests that individual charter schools are serving more students at the extreme ends of the ethnicity and socio-economic continuums." She concludes that "charter school reform may have simply added another layer to an already stratified system" (2000c, np). Wells's high-profile 1998 UCLA Charter School Study of 17 charter schools in 10 California districts found of the majority of the schools in its study that "at least one racial or ethnic group was over- or under-represented by 15 percent or more in comparison to their districts' racial make up" (UCLA Charter School Study, 1998, p. 47). Wells and her colleagues concluded:

> Perhaps the most obvious issue is the lack of attention being paid to whether or not California charter schools reflect the racial make-up of their school districts. Despite the fact that this is a clearly stated requirement in the legislation, we found that most charter schools were not in compliance. (p. 62)

They acknowledged the extent to which all public schools exhibit racial segregation, and they also recognized the potential value in schools that do serve particular groups of color. But they urged the state to provide means through which charter schools could serve racial integration, rather than act as a barrier to it (UCLA Charter School Study, 1998; see also Wells in "Saving Public Education," 1997; Wells, Lopez, Scott, & Holme, 1999).

Proponents and critics of charter schools disagree on the meaning and legacy of *Brown*. When it addresses the race politics of the charter reform at all, the current debate centers on whether charters will mitigate or exacerbate racial segregation in schooling or whether this focus on desegregated schooling should give way to school choice as the most current and viable strategy of equal schooling. Those who support charter schools tend, at least rhetorically, to take a broader view of the *Brown* decision, arguing that the goal of equal educational opportunity that was so central to the *Brown* case can be achieved through strategies in schooling that may not focus on racial and economic desegregation. Those who are skeptical of or oppose charter schools, like Wells and Orfield, tend to read *Brown* for the strategy of equal schooling that it and subsequent related court decisions provided (desegregated schooling), and they tend to hold onto this strategy as the primary means by which educational equality will be achieved. Most anticharter literature that focuses on racial inequality at all, like the literature on race and schooling in general, continues to assess *Brown*'s success by a narrow measure of the extent to which public schools have achieved racial (and sometimes, in the literature, economic) desegregation.

Yet neither proponents nor critics, as they stake their ground in this highly polarized area of study, adequately treat the race and school politics of school choice. In part, this is due to the fact that the current scholarship of race and school choice does not do justice to the legacy of *Brown*, despite the fact that the *Brown* decision and the strategy of desegregation provide symbolic and political touchstones for charter school advocates and opponents. Scholars and practitioners on both sides do not take the opportunity of the charter school reform that *Brown* affords us. The *Brown* ruling connected school and race politics in new and important ways. The landmark Supreme Court decision established desegregation as a national strategy to combat racial inequality in schooling. But beyond a fairly narrow legal ruling that was even more narrowly (and slowly) implemented, the *Brown* decision opened up the political, social scientific, and educational discussion about the meaning and purpose of schooling, the ability of schools to address and redress broad social inequalities, and the meaning of racial justice.[13]

This first shortcoming in the literature is related to the second way in which the current scholarship of school choice fails to provide an adequate account of history. Current school choice scholarship and debate miss the large questions of the purpose and purview of schooling, as raised by some early school choice supporters. The school choice scholarship draws on the voucher debates on the 1960s and early 1970s as ideological, political, and policy predecessors to the current voucher and public school choice politics. Yet this literature generally does not address the extent to which some of the first and most active supporters of vouchers, from the Left and the Right, asked and answered broad questions about the meaning and potential of public schooling. As an example, I focus here on Christopher Jencks, who, beginning in the mid-1960s, became a central theorist and practitioner of school choice policies. In the school choice history as it has been told, Jencks primarily plays the role of a liberal academic who bridged a political gap as he devised a Nixon-administration-sponsored small voucher initiative in California, a voucher supporter on the opposite end of the political spectrum from Friedman. But Jencks is also a sociologist who participated in a critical sociological and political conversation, spurred by the *Brown* ruling, on the connection between schooling and social equality and the viability of public schooling in general.

As race and school politics and reform came together in new ways through *Brown* and subsequent court rulings on school desegregation, many of the country's most prominent social scientists took on the sociological and policy questions of race and schooling. These scholars—prominent among them Kenneth Clark, Daniel Patrick Moynihan, James S. Coleman, and Jencks—made careers of documenting, understanding, and shaping the relationship between racial inequality and schooling.[14] Social scientists debated three key issues. First, in the years following *Brown*, they considered the definition of educational equality and the relationship between quality schooling, equal educational opportunity, and racial integration in schooling. Second, they grappled with the relationship between school politics and race politics and whether and how unequal or separate schooling contributed to a broader racial inequality. Third, they debated whether public schools were more capable than private schools of providing school excellence and equality to all students. Through these debates, social scientists wrestled with the fundamental relationship between public schooling and social inequality.

For his part, Jencks went against some of the prevailing wisdom of the time on the question of the efficacy of school desegregation. His landmark 1972 study, *Inequality*, was published after the civil rights movement had given way to Black nationalist movements and after school desegregation had made its way north in the form of busing plans. In this massive statistical report, a team of researchers based their findings, in part, on a reanalysis of the rich data of the 1966 Coleman Report. Jencks recognized the extent of American educational inequality and racial segregation, but he denied that remedying either would significantly narrow academic achievement gaps or equalize life chances (On the significance of the Jencks study, also see Karabel and Halsey, 1977). Instead, for schooling, Jencks and his coauthors advocated expanding school choice, finding, "The effects of segregation on test scores are certainly not large enough to justify overriding the preferences of parents and students" (p. 106; also see pp. 40–41). Jencks reached a similar conclusion about the impact of segregation more than twenty-five years later (Jencks and Phillips, 1998).

On the question of the extent of the relationship between public schooling and American social inequalities, for much of his career Jencks did not believe that public schools could significantly impact life chances or mitigate racial and economic inequalities.[15] Jencks's position was founded on a broader critique of American capitalism and his belief that inequality of economic opportunity and income, and its accompanying inequities in schooling, were deeply ingrained in and sustained by American values and institutions. He asserted pessimistically in a 1966 piece that Americans would not be willing to accomplish the radical changes in schooling (or other social institutions) that would be necessary to begin to seriously combat social inequalities. Despite abundant claims to the contrary, he wrote, "[a]lmost nobody really wants to make America an egalitarian society." (p. 20; also see Jencks et al. 1972).

Jencks's 1972 study, initially begun as a book project entitled *The Limits of Schooling*, intended to argue that the Johnson administration's social policies that relied on schooling as a means to broad social equality were misguided (Jencks et al., 1972; Karabel and Halsey, 1977). In *Inequality*, Jencks and his colleagues argued that school reform could not meaningfully diminish academic disparities, let alone economic, social and political inequalities. They wrote:

> None of the evidence we reviewed suggests that school reform can be expected to bring about significant social changes outside the schools. More specifically, the evidence suggests that equalizing educational opportunity would do very little to make adults more equal. (p. 255)

While they advocated a focus on equalizing public school resources and spending for its immediate benefits for children, Jencks and his coauthors rejected the analytic leap that translated these benefits to adults. Schools, they argued, were an important public good, but no more so necessarily than parks and sanitation (pp. 16-17). Schools were "marginal institutions" with respect to income redistribution and political equality. Only a "direct approach" aimed at gaining "political control over the economic institutions that shape our society" could achieve this sea change (pp. 263, 265).

As social scientists grappled with the relationship between public schooling and social inequalities, they also debated the power and potential of public schooling itself. Driven by a limited belief in the power of public schooling, Jencks wrote an article in 1968 for the *New York Times Magazine* in which he endorsed an African American private school system in New York City. He did so not because he felt that private schools could do a better job of educating Black children, or because he believed that academic achievement within these schools would help African Americans to achieve economic, social, and political parity. Rather, Jencks supported these private initiatives as a political solution, as a way to meet the demands of African American leaders. Here, he condemned the way in which the current public school system underserved urban students of color and acknowledged the limits of both public and private schooling in mitigating racial and economic inequality. But he recognized that schools represented a significant political site and played an important part in African American social movements of the day. He also argued that the development of an alternative school system controlled by African Americans might take schooling off the African American political agenda and focus attention to "more critical arenas" (pp. 137–138). As Jencks acknowledged the limits of all schooling to affect significant social change, he endorsed private alternatives as those that would be more academically and politically responsive to Black communities.

Jencks, along with his colleagues during the time following the *Brown* decision, dedicated his career to asking and answering some of the most fundamental questions in the sociology and politics of race and schooling. These broad questions provide important tools with which to examine charter schools and measure their educational and political success. Yet most of the school choice scholarship does not raise these broad questions, even in reference to Jencks's work. While some literature details the central role of early school choice scholars and practitioners like Jencks, it does not recognize that Jencks and others devised school choice plans within very broad concerns for American schooling and its ability to impact social inequalities. Furthermore, the literature does not adequately acknowledge the extent to which Jencks centered race and class in his early advocacy of public and private school choice. Grounding some of his earliest plans for publicly funded private schools in his support for African American independent schooling, Jencks recognized school choice particularly as a political solution. Finally, Jencks offered both a critique of current schooling as an educational and political solution and a solution first in the form of independent Black schools and, then, in the form of vouchers geared toward low-income families and families of color. In removing Jencks's support of school choice from most of his broader questions and concerns about American public schooling, current school choice scholarship again fails to fully acknowledge, understand, and make use of school choice history.

Third and finally, current school choice scholarship does not do justice to history in the narrow way in which it identifies predecessors to current

school choice movements and initiatives. When it looks at all, the literature
looks to desegregation struggles and to social movements like the White
Left of the late 1960s and early 1970s to find the roots of current school
choice in magnet schooling, free or alternative schools, and early voucher
plans. Yet from the 1960s on, a much broader historical trajectory has
brought us to the current school choice politics and policies. Particularly,
here, the literature does not adequately treat the historical connections between current school choice reforms and alternative schools built and controlled by communities of color. There were a number of such progressive,
community-centered alternative school-building movements from the 1960s
through the 1980s that organizationally, politically, and ideologically informed
the charter school movement.

   For example, the movement for public school community control,
which drew national attention in the late 1960s in New York's Harlem and
Ocean Hill-Brownsville, serves as an important predecessor to the charter
school movement.[16] The New York community control effort was one of
the earliest and most high profile post-*Brown* challenges to the goal of desegregated schooling by northern African American activists and parents.
Beginning in 1966 African American and Latino parents' frustration with
the city's inaction on desegregation prompted the shift in demand for access to a demand for control of public schooling. Groups of parents, local
activists, and community and church leaders in Harlem and Brooklyn demanded control over school personnel, budget, and curriculum in small
clusters of five schools in Harlem and eight schools in Ocean Hill-
Brownsville, Brooklyn. The communities served by these projects were
both predominantly African American and low income.[17] Both communities, too, were severely underserved by their district schools.[18] The New
York movement drew the most attention because it involved a highly public struggle between the community groups and the New York City teachers' union, which resulted in three city-wide school strikes during the
1968–69 school year. But, the New York movement was not an isolated
case. A number of public school community control struggles, particularly
in large urban districts, followed the New York example (Fantini, Gittell,
& Magat, 1970; Parsons, 1969).[19]

   The New York movement also has another important historical connection to the charter school concept. The head of the New York City
teachers' union during this time and one of the most vocal and visible opponents to community control in Brooklyn and Harlem, Albert Shanker,
was an important player in the birth of charter schools in Minnesota in
the early 1990s. In a speech at the National Press Club in March of 1988,

Shanker sketched a proposal that would make him one of the founding visionaries of the charter school movement. As then-president of the American Federation of Teachers, Shanker proposed a plan for a "movement" that the AFT would champion: new teacher-built "schools of choice," approved by and created in partnership with school districts. He presented the proposal to a conference of Minnesota educators, acknowledging a debt to a recent book by Ray Budde, *Education by Charter: Restructuring School Districts*.[20] Later, Shanker and the union he headed distanced themselves from the charter reform and became quite critical of charter laws as they were implemented in the years following Shanker's proposal (American Federation of Teachers, 1996; Nathan, 1996a). But Shanker, a central figure in opposition to community control in New York City in the 1960s, was instrumental in the early conception of charter schooling.

The New York community control movement also set the stage for public schools of choice in the city and the nation. In this model, community control provided a broad vision of community schooling on which many alternative school movements since have drawn. For instance, District 4, which was created in East Harlem as a result of New York State's 1969 decentralization law, became a model of public school choice and alternative schooling in the decades that followed (see Carnegie Foundation, 1992; Cookson, 1994; Henig, 1994; Kirp, 1992; Meier, 1995; Wells, 1993). Also, the New York movement for control of public schooling contributed directly to the development of movements for community-controlled African American, Chicano/Latino, and Native American independent schools (Fantini et al., 1970; Gittell, 1970). These independent schools were often connected to political movements, as was the case with the Black Panther schools, like the Oakland Community School, and with free schools that served urban communities of color that were affiliated with the White political Left, like the Children's Community School in Ann Arbor, Michigan, where both Bill Ayers and Diana Oughton of the Weather Underground taught (Ayers, 2001; Van Deburg, 1992).

These independent schools are another important predecessor of charter schooling that are rarely recognized as such in the existing literature. Urban community-controlled independent schools often grew directly from public school community control efforts (Parsons, 1970). This progression can be seen in the example of the career of Leslie Campbell. Once a leader of the public school community control movement in New York and a teacher at one of the community schools in Ocean Hill-Brownsville, Campbell opted out of the public system after the end of community control. In early 1970, Campbell, who was then known as

Jitu Weusi, founded the independent school Uhuru Sasa Shule in Ocean Hill (Shujaa and Afrik, 1996). Campbell (1970) wrote that his experience with Ocean Hill-Brownsville's experiment in public community control convinced him that financial and institutional independence—from both public and White-run private sources—was necessary to build and sustain quality schooling that served African American liberation. The number of urban independent schools, supported with various public and private funds, grew in the late 1960s and early 1970s (Gittell, 1970; Hechinger, 1968; Parsons, 1970; Van Deburg, 1992). Many were tuition free and served primarily preschool and elementary school students in urban areas from West Philadelphia to Milwaukee. Independent school initiatives included the Urban League's Street Academies, Harlem Prep, New York's West Side Community School, and Boston's Roxbury Community School (Berube, 1969; Fantini et al., 1970; Gittell, 1970; "Pennsylvania Aids Non-Public Schools," 1969).

Significant among the independent school initiatives of this period was the Council of Independent Black Institutions (CIBI), an organization that grew directly out of Black nationalist activism and the New York movement for control of public schooling and that became a core organization of the 1970s movement for African American independent schooling.[21] According to its website, CIBI "is an umbrella organization for independent Afrikan-centered schools and individuals who are advocates for Afrikan-centered education." The organization defines "Afrikan-centered education" as "the means by which Afrikan culture—including the knowledge, attitudes, values and skills needed to maintain and perpetuate it throughout the nation building process—is developed and advanced through practice. . . ." (Council of Independent Black Institutions, "CIBI's Definition of . . ."). Still in existence, CIBI provides technical assistance, teacher training, newsletters, and curricular support to its member schools. Most of its schools are small elementary schools, serving fewer than 200 students each. By 1992, the Council of Independent Black Institutions had 38 schools, in cities including Trenton, Buffalo, Washington, Columbus, Detroit, and East Palo Alto (Lomotey, 1992. A recent check of the organization's "CIBI Institutional Members" list on its website, however, indicates that currently 12 schools are included as "institutional members").

Urban independent schooling, including the African American independent school movement, was an important, and often overlooked, precursor to the current school choice movements. These independent schools have also been, in some cases, direct precursors to and participants in current public and private school choice plans. For instance, CIBI now allows charter schools, provided that they meet the other requirements for membership, and a number of its member schools have become public charter schools ("Eight Important Questions Related to CIBI's New Membership Policy," CIBI website).

These school movements of the last generation are also important to school choice history in that they were linked to movements for social justice that are not often recognized as historical precursors to current movements for public and private school choice. The public school community control movement in the mid- to late 1960s mirrored and was bolstered by concurrent changes in the civil rights movement, gaining national prominence in the context of an emerging Black Power movement. One of the foundational texts of this new phase of the movement for African American racial justice, *Black Power* by Stokely Carmichael and Charles V. Hamilton, called for "community control" of a wide range of social, political, and economic institutions.[22] In this 1967 work, as part of a larger critique of the integrationist goals and gains of the civil rights movement, Carmichael and Hamilton wrote that school integration was a drain on the power of Black communities and a threat to the very existence of these communities (pp. 54–55). They proposed, instead, that African American communities control their own "parallel community institutions," including schools (p. 43).

Many independent Black schools grew from this social movement context as well. They traced their roots to the cultural nationalism, the Black Arts movement, and Pan Africanism that had succeeded the more pluralist Black Power philosophy of Carmichael and Hamilton by the early 1970s (Carmichael and Hamilton, 1967; Lee, 1992; Lomotey, 1992).[23] Mwalimu Shujaa (1994a), a professor of education and cofounder of an IBI in Trenton, New Jersey, wrote that the term "independent Black institution" was first used by Amiri Baraka's organization, the Congress of African People, and was then adopted by the Council of Independent Black Institutions (p. 362). The Congress of African People grounded its political activism in the cultural nationalism of Baraka and Maulana Karenga (Smith, 1996). Shujaa and others also grounded their turn to schooling in a significant critique of existing public schools. Shujaa, for instance, argues that African American children have received "too much schooling, too little education." Schooling, Shujaa (1994b) argues, is a "process *intended* to perpetuate and maintain the society's existing power relations and the institutional structures that support those arrangements," while education is a positive and liberating "process of transmitting from one generation to the next knowledge of the values, aesthetics, spiritual beliefs, and all things that give a particular cultural orientation its uniqueness" (p. 15, emphasis in original). Cultural nationalism and other African American social movements of the 1960s and 1970s, and their focus on alternative schooling, certainly are not the only social justice movements by communities of color that impacted school choice politics and reforms. But they are important examples, and they are virtually ignored as such by those who look to history to find the roots of current school choice initiatives.

The broad institutional and political history from which we must learn in building a progressive politics of school choice is not then yet featured in the existing literature. The history that we must construct and draw lessons from first centers race and class in a way that the current literature does not. A broad attention to race and class means a focus on the politics of desegregation and the politics of educational self-determination for a variety of underserved communities.[24] Second, we must learn from a history that takes schools and school choice politics seriously as sites for a wide range of social justice struggles, and, informed by this history, we must see school choice as both a political and educational movement. Third, we must draw on the social science of school choice in a way that the current literature fails to do. In this, we learn to look to social scientists like Jencks and his colleagues, to ask the broad questions that should frame any school debate—on the purpose and viability of public schooling in general and the ability of public schools to mitigate inequality. This history and the questions it raises teach us not to either dismiss charter schools out of hand or to accept them uncritically as the solution to systemic educational inequality.

Reading School Choice Today

Progressives need every tool of history they can acquire to understand the current moment in the politics of school choice. Charter school politics are complicated and messy, bringing together unlikely allies and confusing many pundits and academics who generally know quite quickly where and with whom they stand. When Oakland Mayor and former California Governor Jerry Brown and President George W. Bush both support charter schools, the politics of charter schools are confusing. When conservative critic and 2000 Republican presidential candidate Alan Keyes, and the liberal academic who served as President Bill Clinton's Labor Secretary and was a recent Massachusetts gubernatorial candidate, Robert Reich (2000), both support some form of school voucher, the politics of private school choice are complicated. Many political progressives are ambivalent about charter schools and other forms of public and private school choice. This ambivalence is important to acknowledge and take seriously as a starting point for inquiry. As noted radical activist and educator Ayers asked of charters in 1998, "The question is, are they part of an attempt to reform the schools or are they part of an attempt to undermine public education? . . . I'm willing to say let's try charter schools, but I'm also skeptical" (quoted in Hendrie, 1998a, p. 18).

The politics of school choice are particularly complicated with respect to race politics. The renewed focus on public and private school choice in the past decade takes place in a time of significant flux and reconfiguration of national race politics. Changes in the economy, the political landscape, and urban demographics have come with changes in the way Americans see race relations and racial inequalities. A growing income and wealth gap, increasing racial segregation, Republican control of the White House through the 1980s and Congress since 1994 (Chávez, 1998; Sleeper, 1997; Wicker, 1996) and the decline of mass social movements have all set the stage for a national rethinking of many of the premises, aims, and tactics of the civil rights movement.[25] This is most dramatically evidenced in the recent national assault on affirmative action and retreat from school desegregation. Legislative action reflects shifts in public attitudes and discourse. Courts, too, are increasingly willing to overturn school desegregation orders and constrict or repeal affirmative action programs.

As Douglas S. Massey and Nancy A. Denton (1993) argue—and 2000 census data later supported (see Schmitt, 2001)—the current level of residential "hypersegregation" by race remains high in American cities. Fifty years after *Brown*, most schools in America, like most residential spaces, are still highly racially segregated (Orfield, 1996a). Current research even indicates that gains in desegregation made between the *Brown* decision and the late 1980s have begun to be lost. Frankenberg and Lee (2002) of Harvard's Civil Rights Project found "a steady unraveling of almost 25 years worth of increased integration" (p. 4). Yet we are now at a "historic turning point," when courts, communities of color, legislatures, and city leaders are beginning to question the efficacy of school desegregation as a tool for equalizing educational opportunity (Orfield, 1996b; 1996c; Orfield quoted in Applebome, 1997). It is almost difficult to keep up with the number of school districts that, in the past few years, have either returned to a version of neighborhood schooling or that have considered it to replace their desegregation programs. Courts have been increasingly willing to end long-standing desegregation orders, as cities from Boston to San Francisco have begun to develop alternative school assignment plans that may not take race into account. These plans, often devised to keep students closer to home, are likely to exacerbate already increasing racial segregation (Applebome, 1997; Frankenberg and Lee, 2002; Hendrie, 1998b; Loury, 1997).

Since the mid-1990s, another staple of civil rights legislation and implementation has fallen under attack. Led primarily by challenges in higher education, the nation has begun to reconsider affirmative action as a tool of racial equality and equal opportunity. On the heels of the passage of the anti-immigrant Proposition 187 in 1994 (Schrag, 1998),[26] California led the national retreat from affirmative action. In the summer of 1995 the regents of the University of California voted to end race- and gender-based affirmative action in hiring and admissions (Holland, 1995). This decision was followed by the November 1996 passage of Proposition 209, which ostensibly ended "preferential treatment" on the basis of race and gender and in reality virtually annulled affirmative action in the state of California. This measure, which passed with 54% of California votes, withstood legal challenge and took effect in the fall of 1997, earning the top story in the *New York Times* on the day it did (Chávez 1998; Golden, 1997; Purdum, 1997; Schrag, 1998). A 1998 report found that thirteen state legislatures considered and rejected anti-affirmative action bills during 1996 and 1997 (Holmes, 1998).

While anti–affirmative action ballot measures and legislative initiatives have met with mixed results, a number of major public universities have also reviewed or revoked their affirmative action plans. Schools that have annulled their admissions plans include the University of Washington, after a statewide ballot initiative; the University of Texas, after a 1996 federal court decision; the University of Georgia, after a 2001 federal appellate court decision; and the Florida state schools under the leadership of Governor Jeb Bush (Bragg, 1999; Bronner, 1999; Bush, 2000; Hebel, 2001; Holmes, 1998; Selingo, 1999, 2000; Zeller, 1999).

Most recently, affirmative action has garnered national attention, as the Supreme Court took up and ruled on the question of its constitutionality. Two University of Michigan cases, on undergraduate and law school admissions, were heard by the Sixth Circuit Court of Appeals in December 2001. In May 2002, the appellate court upheld the law school's affirmative action admission plan, and it has yet to rule on the undergraduate admissions case (Wilgoren, 2002). The Supreme Court heard the cases in the spring of 2003, and, on June 23, 2003, the Court delivered a mixed

6–3 and 5–4 decision in the undergraduate and law school cases, respectively. The rulings did not go so far as to overturn the 1978 landmark affirmative action *Bakke* ruling, or to bar the use of race as a factor in admissions, but they did narrowly define the ways in which consideration of applicants' race can be used to achieve a "diverse" student body (see, for example, Greenhouse, 2003; Steinberg, 2003). Some speculated that these rulings "may prompt return of race-conscious admissions at some colleges" (Selingo, 2003). Affirmative action opponents also have vowed new action in response to the Court's decisions, calling for a Proposition 209-like ballot measure for Michigan voters to consider (Arenson, 2003).

Given these current politics of race, it is not surprising that school choice politics have become a significant site on which to do battle over the meaning of and means to racial justice. Yet, there is little in the existing school choice literature on the way in which these current race politics impact school choice politics and reform. There is little attention to the way in which the politics of race and schooling have created discursive and political openings for school choice reforms, and there is little acknowledgement that schools of choice play a significant role in the refashioning of post–Civil Rights-era race politics at the turn of the new millennium. We need not only to examine the way in which school choice reforms emerge within this rethinking of the strategies and legacies of civil rights reforms. As part of our analysis, we need to look more closely and critically at the race politics of school choice initiatives themselves.

In some ways here, the work on school vouchers has been more extensive than the work on charter schools. This may be because the coalitions that have developed around voucher schooling are in such obvious need of explanation. It may not be surprising that African American conservative Alan Keyes, during a discussion of the Supreme Court's hearing on Cleveland's voucher program, praised school vouchers as a legacy of the *Brown* decision on his television show "Alan Keyes is Making Sense" on MSNBC on February 20, 2002. Keyes has been joined by other conservatives from the Secretary of Education Rod Paige to the Institute for Justice attorney Clint Bolick in drawing a connection between the *Brown* decision and the Supreme Court's June 2002 voucher ruling, in *Zelman v. Simmons-Harris*, that upheld the constitutionality of Cleveland's program (Greenhouse, 2002; Institute for Justice, 2002; Nagourney, 2002; Paige, 2002). But vouchers were not simply born from multiracial alliances of like-minded people. Vouchers in their latest incarnation were born in Milwaukee in the late 1980s, out of a coalition that included the state's Republican governor at the time, Tommy G. Thompson, and some of the city's most progressive African American lawmakers, parents, community activists, and academics, including State Representative Annette "Polly" Williams and education professor Howard Fuller. With the passage in May 1990 of the Wisconsin Parental Choice Plan, Milwaukee became the first city in the country with a publicly funded school voucher program.[27]

As if winning over African American support confers legitimacy on the voucher movement, many White voucher leaders tout their alliances with African American parents and community groups. A huge portion of articles on vouchers with accompanying photos feature African American voucher supporters or private school students who have benefited from voucher programs. Some African American academics and activists have organized for and spoken publicly in support of this private school option (see, for example, Owens, 2002). Howard Fuller, of Milwaukee, for example, is the Chair of the Board of Black Alliance for Educational Options (BAEO), a procharter and provoucher organization that was founded in 2000. BAEO supports vouchers as a means to educational quality and equality, parental choice, and parental control:

> BAEO believes we must develop new systems of learning opportunities to complement and expand existing systems. We need systems that truly empower parents, that allow dollars to follow students, that hold adults as well as students accountable for academic achievement, and that alter the power arrangements that are the foundation for existing systems. (Black Alliance for Educational Options, "BAEO Manifesto")

BAEO has been highly active and visible, particularly following the *Zelman* voucher decision in the summer of 2002, and, according to its website, the organization currently has chapters in 20 states and the District of Columbia (Black Alliance for Educational Options, "BAEO Receives . . .").

At the same time, research shows that African American response to vouchers is decidedly mixed. Many African American leaders have recognized the irony of the voucher supporters who suddenly espouse a concern for students of color and the public school system that underserves them. For instance, the NAACP's chairman of the board, Julian Bond, spoke out against vouchers in his address to the organization's 1998 annual convention: "And the fools who offer fools gold run to us and to suggest, when they have never cared before about what's happening in our public schools, that a voucher now is going to make a difference because it will help a few children" (Bond, 1998; also see Hilliard, 1998). Some African American voucher supporters claim that there is a growing "chasm between traditional black leaders and the majority of African Americans on this issue of vouchers" (Gonsalves, 2002, n.p.). But even the African American leader who exemplifies voucher support and the unlikely alliances this support produces, Milwaukee's Williams, has recently questioned the extent to which African American and low-income families will benefit from the movement: "Affluent folks are going to take it all on as their own. . . . Yuppies who have choices are going to be the beneficiaries now" (quoted in White, 1999, p. 36; also see Bulman and Kirp, 1999).

More work is needed on the race politics of voucher support. Yet whatever attention has been paid to the roles and positions of African Americans in voucher politics, there is still far less work on charter schools. We need to undertake a broad and critical race and class analysis of charter schools and charter politics. But we need to move beyond a critique that simply rests on the claim that charter schools can and do sustain and contribute to race and class segregation in schooling. We can take our cues from the voucher literature here, in, for instance, its focus on coalitions that develop to support this private choice option.

As Bulman and Kirp (1999) wrote about the voucher movement, "To many market-oriented conservatives, equity-based choice is a politically expedient way to promote broader, market-based choice" (p. 50). These same politics play out in the charter movement. For instance, in North Carolina a conservative legal group planned to ask a court to block the desegregation component of the state's charter law (Schnaiberg, 1998). Recently, as well, the fact that courts have blocked the approval and opening of charter schools deemed to jeopardize existing desegregation court orders has prompted parents and charter supporters in twenty states to seek the end of these orders (McQueen, 1999). These legal challenges create unlikely bedfellows. As has been the case in North Carolina, conservative legal groups team with schools and families of color to bring these lawsuits. These legal groups bring suits to end desegregation orders in the name of equal access to school choice. Yet these are the same legal groups that have challenged affirmative action policies in their states. Bolick, who provides legal supports to many school choice programs through his Institute for Justice, provides one such example. This former member of Reagan's Justice Department defends vouchers and charter schools, fights desegregation orders that ostensibly stand in their way, and actively opposes affirmative action (Dent, 1998; Walsh, 1998; also see Levin, 1999; Schmidt, 2003)

Relatedly, we need to study the political and educational impact of those partnerships that have developed around charter school funding. The UCLA Charter School Study (1998) found that most charter schools in California cannot remain financially solvent on public money alone. Most charter schools must rely on private money to supplement their insufficient public support. Given public school funding structures, this is particularly true for charter schools in low-income communities (pp. 35–39; also see Wells, Lopez, Scott, & Holme, 1999, p. 187). Wells and her colleagues found that access to funding depends on cultural and political capital and the ability of charter school leaders to make connections with those who could supply funding or information about it. Charter schools with leaders who are able to tap political and financial connections tend to be those that remain financially healthy (UCLA Charter School Study, 1998, pp. 36–41). This means that there is a market for private donations and, thus, the involvement of large foundations that choose to support charter schools. This finding regarding the inequity in charter school political and economic capital is absolutely critical to the charter school debate, particularly as it relates to the capacity for self-determination for charter schools in low-income neighborhoods.

Given this, we need to ask what it means that avowedly conservative groups, like those backed by the Walton family (of Wal-Mart fame), are some of the most significant private funders of the charter movement. The Walton family supports charter schools in part through the School Futures Research Foundation. As a source of funding and technical assistance and management, School Futures is a San Diego-based nonprofit organization backed by philanthropist John Walton that began to seek out partnerships with California charter schools in the late 1990s.[28] The Walton family supports charter schools as part of a broader embrace of public and private school choice. John Walton, who continues to be a strong voucher supporter, provided financial support to the voucher initiative on the November 1993 ballot in California, Proposition 174 (Bonsteel, 1997; "John Walton . . . ," 2000). Walton also cofunded the largest private voucher program in the country, the Children's Scholarship Fund.[29] Bulman and Kirp (1999) note this tactic as a broader trend in the current politics of choice, writing that "voucher advocates support charters as a foot in the door of the public school monopoly" (p. 61). Other conservative groups that also support school vouchers, like the Center for Education Reform, are visible and active charter proponents and often provide the public face of the charter school movement. These coalitions of people who found, lobby for, support, and fund charter schools raise a number of political questions that are certainly not race- or class-neutral. These questions must be part of building a progressive study and analysis of charter schooling.

These political questions also come in connection with significant educational questions on charter school performance. Despite the definitive tones of proponents and opponents, there are still not sufficient data on the impact of charter schooling on academic achievement, in part because the reform is relatively new (Gill, Timpane, Ross, & Brewer, 2001). Existing data seem to indicate that charter schools, like other public schools, vary significantly on measures of student achievement. Just as with district schools, there are some truly outstanding charter schools, and there are some charter schools that are doing an utter disservice to their students. A recent review found that existing research reports "mixed results" in many states with charter schools. The review concluded, "No conclusive data indicate that charter schools overall are failing their students, and some charters are showing positive achievement results. Additional research on student achievement is needed . . ." (Bulkley and Fisler, 2002, p. 8). A Rand study that reviewed the research on school choice also found that "evidence on the academic effectiveness of charter schools is mixed" (Gill, Timpane, Ross, & Brewer, 2001, p. 95). In particular, the study raised the important question of the "long-term academic effects of charter schools":

> [I]t is not yet known whether newly created nonreligious charter schools can succeed in becoming "focus schools" that are effective not only at raising test scores, but also at promoting long-term academic outcomes such as high school graduation and college attendance. (p. 97)

As charter schools progress through their second decade, it remains important to take an honest look at charter school academic successes and failures.

The data are also quite mixed on the impact of charter schools on their districts. While charter schools may have some impact on district practices, it is not clear that they have generally spurred significant or systemic change in their districts' public schools, as proponents have argued they would. A review of existing data suggests, "Any real long-term and sustained influences on the broader system are likely to emerge very slowly. Some districts are making important adaptations, but these have not reached core district operations" (Bulkley and Fisler, 2002, p. 9; also see Gill, Timpane, Ross, & Brewer, 2001, pp. 110–111). The impact of charter schools on districts has been particularly weak in urban districts (Rofes, 1998).

Conclusion: Toward Progressive Choice Scholarship and Politics

A broader turn to the historical roots of the current school choice debates helps us to build the nuanced, complicated, and progressive analysis of school choice that the debate so desperately needs. As I have argued here, this turn to history can help us ask and answer three sets of questions that have been truly underexamined in the charter school literature. First, we can gain a more complete sense of the race politics of school choice as they have developed through the decades since *Brown*. It is important to understand the way in which school choice politics developed out of the 1954 decision and desegregation plans. But, it is also critical to acknowledge that the politics of self-determination and community control have always been central to school choice reforms. Understanding the interplay of desegregation politics and the politics of educational self-determination for communities of color is critical to our examination of the current politics of choice, especially at this particular moment of flux in the politics of race in this country. Second, we can learn from history that the politics of choice have, in previous generations, been attached to some of the broadest questions on the purpose and potential of public schools. We must ask these questions again when we evaluate school choice reforms and politics. We must recognize the questions that scholars like Jencks asked, and we must understand why their answers led them to support a range of school choice reforms. These questions get to the very meaning of American public schooling and its ability to impact a broad American equality. Finally, history teaches us that school choice politics have always been bound to a range of educational and political movements. This is important in part because it widens our understanding of ways in which politics of race and class impact school politics. It is important, as well, because it encourages us to see the educational and the political as truly linked. It also teaches us to widen our analytical lens, to look at schools and school reform efforts as rich sites for the politics of the day—those that seem to speak directly to schooling and those that do not.

These questions lead us to a much more dynamic analysis of charter schooling and other school choice reforms. How we view school choice, though, is not simply academic. It is situated in a context of a persistent achievement gap, failing school systems, and a public that seems increasingly apathetic or resigned to the fact of permanent segregation and race and class inequality. It is situated in continued assaults on affirmative action and other remedies designed to combat these inequalities. It is situated in the context of a school like the district school that opened this chapter—not by any means alone in the way in which it neglects to provide its students with a safe environment, a rigorous curriculum, and a hopeful vision for their futures.

Notes

1. For just a few examples of the extensive literature on pre-twentieth century American schooling, see Cremin, 1980, 1988; Katz, 1987; Katznelson and Weir, 1985; Perkinson, 1995; Tyack, 1974; Tyack and Cuban, 1995; and Tyack et al., 1984.

2. The story of this case, *Briggs v. Elliot*, and its four counterparts from Virginia, Kansas, Delaware, and the District of Columbia, which came to make up the 1954 *Brown* ruling, is told in fascinating detail by Kluger (1975).

3. This is a measure of school quality that the Court had added to its ruling in the 1950 *Sweatt v. Painter* case (Kluger, 1975).

4. On this political shift from "freedom of choice" plans to magnet schools, see Fuller et al., 1996; Henig, 1994, chapters 4–5; Peterson, 1995; Wells, 1993, chapter 3. On court support of magnet schooling for desegregation, also see Rossell, 1990; Smrekar and Goldring, 1999; Young, 1990; Wells, 1991b.

5. During the 1980s, for example, magnet schools and programs almost doubled. Most of these schools (86% during the 1991–92 school year) were found in large urban districts (Smrekar and Goldring, 1999, p. 7).

6. Henig (1994) points to the progression in the politics of magnet schools as a sign of the shift in school concerns. He argues that school choice in the 1950s and 1960s was associated with antidesegregation efforts. Magnet schools were considered less a choice reform than a desegregation tool. But Reagan reframed magnet schooling as a choice program, praising the desegregation reform in an attempt to push for more market-driven choice plans, while absolving choice of its negative connotations vis-à-vis desegregation and inequality (78–84). On this point, also see Henig, 1996 and Wells, 1991b.

7. On independent free schools see Graubard, 1972; Miller, 1997; Ravitch, 1983; Swidler, 1979; Tyack and Cuban, 1995; Wells, 1993, chapter 2; Young, 1990. Of the 346 schools in his survey, Graubard (1972) found free schools had student bodies that were 77 percent White and 16 percent Black (of approximately 11,500–13,000 students total) (p. 357).

8. On public alternative schools see Deal and Nolan, 1978; Kozol, 1982; Ravitch, 1983; Young, 1990; Wells, 1993; Henig, 1994; Raywid, 1994; Peterson, 1995.

9. On Friedman's and Jencks's plans discussed in the following paragraphs, see Friedman, 1962, chapter 6; Jencks, 1970; Areen and Jencks, 1972; Wells, 1993; Henig, 1994; Bulman and Kirp, 1999.

10. The Office of Economic Opportunity, established by President Johnson and still steeped in War on Poverty support for community organization, backed the Harvard sociologist through his Center for the Study of Public Policy. Alum Rock, a district of 15,000 near San Jose serving primarily African American and Latino students, received OEO support for five years. It drew funds to

establish public "minischools" of choice within existing schools. These schools
had more freedom than their district counterparts to devise and fund their own
curriculum and programming (Jencks, 1970; Areen and Jencks, 1972; Wells,
1993; Henig, 1994; Ascher, Fruchter, & Berne, 1996; Fuller et al., 1996; Bulman
and Kirp, 1999).

11. See Tyack (1999), who argues, "The current debate about school choice
has raised the most basic questions about the structure of education since the
nineteenth century. But the debate has been relentlessly ahistorical, as if amnesia
were a virtue."

12. See, for example, Ravitch 1980, 1981, 1983; Coleman 1981; Willie
1981, 1989; Hochschild 1984; Henig 1994; Orfield's work, particularly recently
the pieces in his 1996 coauthored collection, *Dismantling Desegregation: The Quiet
Reversal of* Brown v. Board of Education.

13. See Kirp (1982), who argues that three distinct visions of racial justice,
which he calls *integration, redistribution*, and *Black power*, can trace their roots to
Brown (chapter 2).

14. For the work of Clark, Coleman, and Moynihan, see Clark, 1965,
1968, 1969, 1973; Kluger, 1975; Coleman et al., 1966; Coleman et al., 1982;
Coleman, 1981, 1994a, 1994b; Moynihan, 1967a, 1967b.

15. Jencks later revised this position in research copublished in 1998 with
Meredith Phillips. This 1998 work represents Jencks's fundamental rethinking of
the relationship between schooling and adult life chances. Based on this new research on the test score gap between White and African American students,
Jencks and his coauthor concluded that schooling mattered in ways that it had not
a generation earlier, such that school achievement was now a significant determi-
nant of adult earnings. A focus on schooling, therefore, was imperative to a concern for racial equality and justice. Documenting the positive relationship
between test scores and earnings, they argued, "But if racial equality is America's
goal, reducing the black-white test score gap would probably do more to promote
this goal than any other strategy that could command broad political support. Reducing the test score gap is probably both necessary and sufficient for substantially reducing racial inequality in educational attainment and earnings" (p. 45).
Jencks and Phillips acknowledged that this conclusion directly contradicted
Jencks's argument in his earlier work. They asserted both that there had been a
significant change in the relationship between schooling and the economy and
that research of the past decade had successfully documented that despite family
background differences and economic inequalities, schools could play an important part in boosting student achievement (p. 48).

16. The literature on Ocean Hill-Brownsville is extensive. But along with
the citations below, see Diane Ravitch's (1974) account, as well as two useful
dissertations by Daniel Perlstein (1994) and Jerald E. Podair (1997).

17. By the 1960 census count, the Ocean Hill-Brownsville population of
120,000 was 73% African American and 24% Puerto Rican (Ford Foundation,

1969, p. 172). Ocean Hill-Brownsville's median household income was about half of the $10,000 designated by the Bureau of Labor Statistics as the minimum a family of four needed to live in New York (Urofsky, 1970, p. 12). The Harlem complex drew a student population that was approximately 83% African American and 16% Puerto Rican, The median annual family income for this complex was $3700 (Wilson, 1968, p. 403; Gittell, 1971, p. 8).

18. In Ocean Hill-Brownsville, for instance, the dropout rate was more than 70%, and less than 1% of those high school graduates received academic diplomas. Before 1967, most students were at least two years below grade level in reading, with almost 60% of students behind three or more years (Parsons, 1970, p. 31; Urofsky, 1970, p. 12). Also see Podair (1997, pp. 31–37) for background on the neighborhood of Ocean Hill-Brownsville and its schools.

19. For examples of public and independent community-controlled schools during this early period, see Hechinger, 1968; Levine, 1969; Parsons, 1969, 1970; Fantini et al., 1970; Gittell, 1970. Some of these initiatives were linked to other movements for self-determination, such as the Rough Rock Demonstration School, founded by a Native American group on a Navajo reservation in Arizona (Parsons, 1969, p. 2).

20. On the Minnesota charter school legislation and on Shanker's early involvement, see Wells, 1993; Cookson, 1994; American Federation of Teachers, 1996; Nathan, 1996a, 1996b; Bulman and Kirp, 1999.

21. On the founding of CIBI, see Morrison, 1972; "Black Teachers," 1972; Doughty, 1973; Shujaa and Afrik, 1996.

22. Van Deburg (1992) writes that the term *Black Power* included both pluralists and nationalists. Pluralists, he argues, focused on "community control" for the purpose of eventual participation and leadership in mainstream American institutions and political processes, while nationalists did not hold out for this eventual participation (pp. 112–113). Karenga (1982), quoting himself, defines Black nationalism as "a social theory and practice organized around the concept and conviction that Blacks are a distinct and historical personality and that they should therefore 'unite in order to gain the structural capacity to define, defend, and develop their interests. . . .'" He writes that one way in which Black nationalism manifested itself was in the "thrust to build alternative structures, which check the deprivation and deformation of European institutions and house and advance Black aspirations and interests" (pp. 247–248).

23. Cultural nationalism was grounded in celebrating Black beauty and culture, and focused on African American liberation through the adherence to a set of ostensibly African values, the seven principles of Kawida, developed by Maulana Karenga (Smith, 1996). Cultural nationalism, particularly through the Black Arts movement it spurred, was also devoted to advancing Black art and literary forms as a means for transforming Black consciousness (Van Deburg, 1992). Karenga (1982) defines Pan-Africanism as it was manifest in the United States primarily as "thought and practice directed toward the liberation, unity and mutual

support of African people throughout the world," a strand of which is directed toward return of African diaspora to Africa (p. 248).

24. For those school choice analyses that center race through a desegregation lens, see Wells, 1993, chapters 2 and 3; Henig, 1994, chapters 4 and 5.

25. For further discussion of the growing socioeconomic gap among and between Whites and African Americans, see Wilson, 1978; 1987; Hacker, 1992, especially chapters 6 and 7; Wicker, 1996; Patterson, 1997, chapter 1; Conley, 1999.

26. Chávez (1998) argues that Proposition 187 ushered in a Republican control of the state, which set the stage for the anti-affirmative action politics in the years following the passage of the 1994 ballot initiative (p. 82).

27. For the story of Milwaukee's voucher politics and policies, see particularly Bell, 1989; Farrell and Mathews, 1990; George and Farrell, 1990; Carnegie, 1992; Carl, 1996; McGroarty, 1996; Bonsteel and Bonilla, 1997; Bulman and Kirp, 1999; White, 1999; Holt, 2000.

28. On the Walton family's involvement in charter schooling, and the politics of this involvement, see Schorr, 1999; 2002.

29. The Children's Scholarship Fund was established in 1998 by John Walton and Theodore J. Forstmann. The two businessmen, who had collaborated on a similar project in Washington, D.C., contributed $50 million each and raised approximately an additional $70 million to provide vouchers to low-income students. The Children's Scholarship Fund has provided "scholarships," of an average of $1,049, to 40,000 students (Archer, 1998; Moe, 1999; Coeyman, 2001; Mollison, 2001).

References

American Federation of Teachers. (1996). *Charter school laws: Do they measure up?* Washington, DC: American Federation of Teachers Educational Issues Department.

Applebome, P. (1997, April 8). Schools see re-emergence of "separate but equal." *New York Times*, A8.

Archer, J. (1998, June 10). Millionaires to back national voucher project. *Education Week, 17*(39), 3.

Areen, J., & Jencks, C. (1972). Educational vouchers: A proposal for diversity and choice. In R. C. Rist (Ed.), *Restructuring American education: Innovations and alternatives* (pp. 68–82). New Brunswick, NJ: Transaction Books.

Arenson, K. W. (2003, July 10). Ballot measure seen in wake of court ruling. *New York Times*, A17.

Ascher, C., Fruchter, N., & Berne, R. (1996). *Hard lessons: Public schools and privatization.* New York: Twentieth Century Fund Press.

Ayers, B. (2001). *Fugitive days: A memoir.* Boston: Beacon Press.

Bell, D. (1989). The case for a separate Black school system. In W. D. Smith & E. W. Chunn (Eds.), *Black education: A quest for equity and excellence* (pp. 136-145). New Brunswick, NJ: Transaction Publishers.

Berube, M. R. (1969, April 11). Black Power and the learning process. *Commonweal*, 98-101.

Black Alliance for Educational Options. BAEO manifesto. Retrieved November 1, 2002 from http://www.baeo.org

Black Alliance for Educational Options. BAEO receives $600,000 grant from education department: Group plans campaign to alert parents to No Child Left Behind. Retrieved November 1, 2002, from http://www.baeo.org

Black teachers hold 3-day meeting here. (1972, April 22). *Amsterdam News*.

Blank, R. K., Levine, R. E., & Steel, L. (1996). After 15 years: Magnet schools in urban education. In B. Fuller & and R. F. Elmore with G. Orfield (Eds.), *Who chooses? Who loses?: Culture, institutions, and the unequal effects of school choice* (pp. 154-172). New York: Teachers College Press.

Bond, J. (1998, July 7). The NAACP—Yesterday, today, and tomorrow. *NAACP Convention Address*. Retrieved July 13, 2002, from http://www.naacp.org

Bonilla, C. A. (1997). ZIP code segregation in the public schools. In A. Bonsteel & and C. A. Bonilla, *A choice for our children: Curing the crisis in America's schools* (pp. 79-83). San Francisco: ICS Press.

Bonsteel, A., & Bonilla, C. A. (1997). The Polly Williams story. In A. Bonsteel & and C. A. Bonilla, *A choice for our children: Curing the crisis in America's schools* (pp. 7-13). San Francisco: ICS Press.

Bragg, R. (1999, November 11). Florida plan would change admissions based on race. *New York Times*, A1.

Bronner, E. (1999, January 26). Conservatives open drive against affirmative action. *New York Times*, A10.

Budde, R. (1988). *Education by charter: Restructuring school districts*. Andover, MA: Regional Laboratory for Educational Improvement of the Northeast and Islands.

Bulkley, K., & Fisler, J. (2002, April). A decade of charter schools: From theory to practice. *CPRE Policy Briefs*. Philadelphia: Graduate School of Education, University of Pennsylvania.

Bulman, R. C., & Kirp, D. L. (1999). The shifting politics of school choice. In S. D. Sugarman & F. R. Kemerer (Eds.), *School choice and social controversy: Politics, policy, and law* (pp. 36-67). Washington, DC: Brookings Institution Press.

Bush, J. (2000, September 15). Better than affirmative. *New York Times*, A31.

Campbell, L. (1970). The devil can never educate us. In N. Wright, Jr. (Ed.), *What Black educators are saying* (pp. 27-30). New York: Hawthorn Books.

Carl, J. (1996, Winter). Unusual allies: Elite and grass-roots origins of parental choice in Milwaukee. *Teachers College Record*, 98(2), 266-285.

Carmichael, S., & Hamilton, C. V. (1992). *Black Power: The politics of liberation.* New York: Vintage Books.

Carnegie Foundation for the Advancement of Teaching. (1992). *School choice.* Princeton, NJ.

Center for Education Reform. (1999, May). Newsletter. Washington, DC.

Center for Education Reform. Charter school highlights and statistics. Retrieved July 16, 2003 from http://edreform.com/pubs/chglance.htm

Chávez, L. (1998). *The color bind: California's battle to end affirmative action.* Berkeley: University of California Press.

Clark, K. B. (1965). *Dark ghetto: Dilemmas of social power.* 2nd ed. Hanover, NH: Wesleyan University Press.

Clark, K. B. (1968). Thoughts on Black Power. *Dissent,* 98+.

Clark, K. B. (1969). The social scientists, the Brown decision, and contemporary confusion. In L. Friedman (Ed.), *Argument: The oral argument before the Supreme Court in Brown v. Board of Education of Topeka, 1952-55* (pp. xxxi-l). New York: Chelsea House Publishers.

Clark, K. B. (1973). Issues in urban education. In J. Haskins (Ed.), *Black manifesto for education* (pp. 74-94). New York: William Morrow.

Coeyman, M. (2001, September 11). Vouchers stay visible. *Christian Science Monitor,* 17.

Coleman, J. S. (1981). The role of incentives in school desegregation. In A. Yarmolinsky, L. Liebman, & C. S. Schelling (Eds.), *Race and schooling in the city* (pp. 182-193). Cambridge: Harvard University Press.

Coleman, J. S. (1994a). The concept of equality of educational opportunity. In J. Kretovics & E. J. Nussel (Eds.), *Transforming urban education* (pp. 18-31). Boston: Allyn and Bacon.

Coleman, J. S. (1994b). Quality and equality in American education: Public and Catholic schools. In J. Kretovics & E. J. Nussel (Eds.), *Transforming urban education* (pp. 228-238). Boston: Allyn and Bacon.

Coleman, J. S., Campbell, E. Q., Hobson, C. J., McPartland, J., Mood, A. M., Weinfeld, F. D., & York, R. L. (1966). *Equality of educational opportunity.* Washington, DC: U.S. Government Printing Office.

Coleman, J. S., Hoffer, T., & Kilgore, S. (1982). *High school achievement: Public, Catholic, and private schools compared.* New York: Basic Books.

Conley, D. (1999). *Being Black, living in the red: Race, wealth, and social policy in America.* Berkeley: University of California Press.

Cookson, P. W., Jr. (1994). *School choice: The struggle for the soul of American education.* New Haven, CT: Yale University Press.

Council of Independent Black Institutions. CIBI institutional members. Retrieved July 16, 2003 from http://www.cibi.org/schools.html

Council of Independent Black Institutions. CIBI's definition of Afrikan Centered Education: A position statement (adopted November 11, 1994). Retrieved July 16, 2003 from http://www.cibi.org/about.htm

Cremin, L. A. (1980). *American education: The national experience, 1783–1876.* New York: Harper & Row.

Cremin, L. A. (1988). *American education: The metropolitan experience, 1876–1980.* New York: Harper & Row.

Cuban, L. (1993). *How teachers taught: Constancy and change in American class-rooms, 1890–1990* (2nd ed.). New York: Teachers College Press.

Deal, T. E., & Nolan, R. R. (1978). An overview of alternative schools. In T. E. Deal & R. R. Nolan (Eds.), *Alternative schools: Ideologies, realities, guide-lines* (pp. 1–17). Chicago: Nelson-Hall.

Dent, D. J. (1998, December 23). Diversity rules threaten North Carolina charter schools that aid Blacks. *New York Times,* A22.

Dentler, R. A. (1991). School desegregation since Gunnar Myrdal's *American Dilemma.* In C. V. Willie, A. M. Garibaldi, & W. L. Reed (Eds.), *The Ed-ucation of African-Americans* (pp. 27–50). New York: Auburn House.

Doughty, J. J. (1973). *A historical analysis of Black education—Focusing on the con-temporary Independent Black School Movement.* Ph.D. dissertation, Ohio State University.

Elmore, R. F., & Fuller, B. (1996). Empirical research on educational choice: What are the implications for policy-makers? In B. Fuller & and R. F. Elmore with G. Orfield (Eds.), *Who chooses? Who loses?: Culture, institutions, and the un-equal effects of school choice* (pp. 187–201). New York: Teachers College Press.

Fantini, M., Gittell, M., & Magat, R. (1970). *Community control and the urban school.* New York: Praeger Publishers.

Farrell, W. C., Jr., & Mathews, J. E. (1990). School choice and the educational op-portunities of African American children. *Journal of Negro Education, 59*(4), 526–537.

Ford Foundation. (1969, May). And then, there were the children. . . : An assess-ment of efforts to test decentralization in New York City's public school system. Report #002149, Ford Foundation Archives.

Frankenberg, E., & Lee, C. (2002, August). Race in American public schools: Rapidly resegregating school districts. Cambridge: Harvard University, The Civil Rights Project.

Friedman, M. (1962). *Capitalism and freedom.* Chicago: University of Chicago Press.

Fuller, B. (2000a). Introduction: Growing charter schools, decentering the state. In B. Fuller (Ed.), *Inside charter schools: The paradox of radical decentraliza-tion* (pp. 1–11). Cambridge: Harvard University Press.

Fuller, B. (2000b). The public square, big or small? Charter schools in political context. In B. Fuller (Ed.), *Inside charter schools: The paradox of radical decentralization* (pp. 12–65). Cambridge: Harvard University Press.

Fuller, B., Elmore, R. F., & Orfield, G. (1996). Policy-making in the dark: Illumi-nating the school choice debate. In B. Fuller & R. F. Elmore with G. Or-field (Eds.), *Who chooses? Who loses?: Culture, institutions, and the unequal effects of school choice* (pp. 1–21). New York: Teachers College Press.

George, G. R., & Farrell, W. C., Jr. (1990). School choice and African American students: A legislative view. *Journal of Negro Education, 59*(4), 521–525.

Gill, B. P., Timpane, M., Ross, K. E., & Brewer, D. J. (2001). *Rhetoric versus reality: What we know and what we need to know about vouchers and charter schools.* Santa Monica, CA: Rand Corporation.

Gittell, M. (1970, February). The community school in the nation. *Community Issues, 2*(1).

Gittell, M. (1971). *Demonstration for social change: An experiment in local control.* New York: Institute for Community Studies, Queens College of the City University of New York.

Golden, T. (1997, August 29). California adapts as 1996 initiative ends preferences. *New York Times,* A1+.

Gonsalves, S. (2002, July 9). Vouchers good for Black students. *Seattle Post-Intelligencer.* Retrieved July 11, 2002 from http://seattlepi.com/opinion/77699_sean9.shtml

Graubard, A. (1972, August). The free school movement. *Harvard Educational Review, 42*(3), 351–373.

Greenhouse, L. (2002, June 28). Ruling in Ohio case. *New York Times,* A1+.

Greenhouse, L. (2003, June 24). Justices back affirmative action by 5 to 4, but wider vote bans a racial point system. *New York Times,* A1+.

Hacker, A. (1992). *Two nations: Black and White, separate, hostile, unequal.* New York: Ballantine Books.

Hebel, S. (2001, December 14). U. of Georgia eliminates use of race in admissions decisions. *Chronicle of Higher Education,* A26.

Hechinger, F. M. (1968, September 22). A conflict with no easy solution. *New York Times,* E2.

Hendrie, C. (1998a, May 6). For small schools, an identity crisis. *Education Week, 17*(34), 1+.

Hendrie, C. (1998b, June 17). Pressure for community schools grows as court oversight wanes. *Education Week, 17*(40), 23.

Henig, J. R. (1994). *Rethinking school choice: Limits of the market metaphor.* Princeton, NJ: Princeton University Press.

Henig, J. R. (1996). The local dynamics of choice: Ethnic preferences and institutional responses. In B. Fuller & and R. F. Elmore with G. Orfield (Eds.), *Who chooses? Who loses?: Culture, institutions, and the unequal effects of school choice* (pp. 95–117). New York: Teachers College Press.

Henig, J. R., Hula, R. C., Orr, M., & Pedescleaux, D. S. (1999). *The color of school reform: Race, politics, and the challenge of urban education.* Princeton, NJ: Princeton University Press.

Hilliard, A. G., III. (1998, Summer). The standards movement: Quality control or decoy? *Rethinking Schools,* 4–5.

Hochschild, J. L. (1984). *The new American dilemma: Liberal democracy and school desegregation.* New Haven, CT: Yale University Press.

Holland, G. (1995, July 20). Calif. to vote on race-based college entry. *USA Today*, 3A.

Holmes, S. A. (1998, May 4). Washington state is stage for fight over preferences. *New York Times*, A1+.

Holt, M. (2000). *Not yet "free at last." The unfinished business of the Civil Rights Movement: Our battle for school choice*. Oakland: ICS Press.

Illich, I. (1971). *Deschooling society*. New York: Harper & Row.

Institute for Justice. (2002, June 27). Victory for school choice. Press Release. Retrieved July 11, 2002, from http://www.ij.org/media/school_choice/ohio/6-27-02pr.shtml

Jencks, C. (1966, Winter). Is the public school obsolete? *The Public Interest*, 2, 18–27.

Jencks, C. (1968, November 3). Private schools for Black children. *New York Times Magazine*, 30+.

Jencks, C. (1970, July 4). Giving parents money to pay for schooling: Education vouchers. *The New Republic*, 163(1), 19–21.

Jencks, C., Smith, M., Acland, H., Bane, M. J., Cohen, D., Gintis, H., Heyns, B., & Michelson, S. (1972). *Inequality: A reassessment of the effect of family and schooling in America*. New York: Basic Books.

Jencks, C., & Phillips, M. (1998, September-October). America's next achievement test: Closing the Black-White test score gap. *The American Prospect*, 44–53.

John Walton: Making a world-class education available to every child. (2000, February 7). *Businessweek Online*. Retrieved October 31, 2002 from http://www.businessweek.com.

Karabel, J., & Halsey, A. H. (1977). Educational research: A review and an interpretation. In J. Karabel & A. H. Halsey (Eds.), *Power and Ideology in Education* (pp. 1–85). New York: Oxford University Press.

Karenga, M. (1982). *Introduction to Black studies*. Los Angeles: University of Sankore Press.

Katz, M. B. (1987). *Reconstructing American education*. Cambridge: Harvard University Press.

Katznelson, I., & Weir, M. (1985). *Schooling for all: Class, race, and the decline of the democratic ideal*. New York: Basic Books.

Kirp, D. L. (1982). *Just schools: The idea of racial equality in American education*. Berkeley: University of California Press.

Kirp, D. L. (1992, November). What school choice really means. *Atlantic Monthly*, 119–132.

Kluger, R. (1975). *Simple justice: The history of Brown v. Board of Education and Black America's struggle for equality*. New York: Vintage Books.

Kozol, J. (1982). *Alternative schools: A guide for educators*. New York: Continuum.

Kozol, J. (1991). *Savage inequalities: Children in America's schools*. New York, Harper-Perennial.

Lee, C. D. (1992, Spring). Profile of an Independent Black Institution: African-centered education at work. *Journal of Negro Education, 61*(2), 160–177.

Levin, B. (1999). Race and school choice. In S. D. Sugarman & F. R. Kemerer (Eds.), *School choice and social controversy: Politics, policy, and law* (pp. 266–299). Washington, DC: Brookings Institution Press.

Levine, D. U. (1969, February). Black Power: Implications for the urban educator. *Education and Urban Society, 1*(2), 139–159.

Little Hoover Commission. (1996, March). *The charter movement: Education reform school by school.* Sacramento, CA: Author.

Lomotey, K. (1992, Fall). Independent Black Institutions: African-centered education models. *Journal of Negro Education, 61,* 455–462.

Loury, G. C. (1997, April 23). Integration has had its day. *New York Times,* A21.

Massey, D. S., & Denton, N. A. (1993). *American apartheid: Segregation and the making of the underclass.* Cambridge: Harvard University Press.

McGroarty, D. (1996). *Break these chains: The battle for school choice.* Rocklin, CA: Forum.

McQueen, A. (1999, October 15). Charter backers fight school desegregation. *Atlanta Journal and Constitution,* 18A.

Meier, D. (1995). *The power of their ideas: Lessons for America from a small school in Harlem.* Boston: Beacon Press.

Miller, R. (1997). *What are schools for?: Holistic education in American culture.* 3rd rev. ed. Brandon, VT: Holistic Education Press.

Moe, T. M. (1999, May 9). A look at school vouchers: The public revolution private money might bring. *Washington Post,* B3.

Mollison, A. (2001, April 4). Philanthropist seeks to break up public education "monopoly"; Private school "competition" seen. *Atlanta Journal and Constitution,* 11A.

Morrison, D. (1972, May 12). NYC Black teachers hold convention. *The Militant,* 14.

Moynihan, D. P. (1967a, Fall). Education of the urban poor. *Harvard Graduate School of Education Association Bulletin, 12*(2), 2–13.

Moynihan, D. P. (1967b). The Negro family: The case for national action. In L. Rainwater & W. L. Yancey, *The Moynihan Report and the politics of controversy.* Cambridge: M.I.T. Press.

Nagourney, A. (2000, June 28). The battleground shifts. *New York Times,* A1+.

Nathan, J. (1996a). *Charter schools: Creating hope and opportunity for American education.* San Francisco: Jossey-Bass Publishers.

Nathan, J. (1996b). Possibilities, problems, and progress: Early lessons from the charter movement. *Phi Delta Kappan, 78*(1), 18–23.

Nathan, J. (2002, May 29). A charter school decade. *Education Week, 21*(38), 32+.

Neill, A. S. (1960). *Summerhill: A radical approach to child rearing.* New York: Hart Publishing.

Newby, R. G. (1979, September-October). Desegregation: Its inequities and paradoxes. *The Black Scholar, 11*(1), 17–28+.

Newby, R. G., & Tyack, D. B. (1971, Summer). Victims without "crimes": Some historical perspectives on Black education. *Journal of Negro Education, 40*(3), 192–206.

Noguera, P. A. (1994). More democracy not less: Confronting the challenge of privatization in public education. *Journal of Negro Education, 63*, 237–250.

Noguera, P. A. (1996). Confronting the urban in urban school reform. *The Urban Review, 28*, 1–19.

Oakland Citizens Committee for Urban Renewal. (1998). Neighborhood profiles: West Oakland. Oakland, CA: Author.

Oakland Coalition of Congregations, in partnership with the Oakland Unified School District, the Oakland Education Association and the Post Newspapers. (1999). 1999 annual report to the community: Oakland Public Schools. *Oakland Tribune* supplement.

Orfield, G. (1981). Why it worked in Dixie: Southern school desegregation and its implications for the North. In A. Yarmolinsky, L. Liebman & C. S. Schelling (Eds.), *Race and schooling in the city* (pp. 24–44). Cambridge: Harvard University Press.

Orfield, G. (1996a). The growth of segregation: African Americans, Latinos, and unequal education. In G. Orfield, S. E. Eaton, & the Harvard Project on School Desegregation, *Dismantling desegregation: The quiet reversal of* Brown v. Board of Education (pp. 53–71). New York: New Press.

Orfield, G. (1996b). *Plessy* parallels: Back to traditional assumptions. In G. Orfield, S. E. Eaton, & the Harvard Project on School Desegregation, *Dismantling desegregation: The quiet reversal of* Brown v. Board of Education (pp. 23–51). New York: New Press.

Orfield, G. (1996c). Turning back to segregation. In G. Orfield, S. E. Eaton & the Harvard Project on School Desegregation, *Dismantling desegregation: The quiet reversal of* Brown v. Board of Education (pp. 1–22). New York: New Press.

Orfield, G. (1998, January 2). Charter schools won't save education. *New York Times*, A15.

Orfield, G., Eaton, S. E., & the Harvard Project on School Desegregation, (1996). *Dismantling desegregation: The quiet reversal of* Brown v. Board of Education. New York: New Press.

Owens, M. L. (2002, February 26). Why Blacks support vouchers. *New York Times*, A27.

Paige, R. (2002, June 28). A win for America's children. *Washington Post*, A29.

Parsons, T. (1969, February). Community control across the nation. *Community, 1*(3), 1–2.

Parsons, T. (1970, December). The community school movement. *Community Issues, 2*(6).

Patterson, O. (1997). *The ordeal of integration: Progress and resentment in America's "racial" crisis.* Washington, DC: Civitas/Counterpoint.

Pennsylvania aids non-public schools. (March–April 1969). *Community, 1*(4), 6.

Perkinson, H. J. (1995). *The imperfect panacea: American faith in education* (4th ed.). New York: McGraw-Hill.

Perlstein, D. (1994). *The 1968 New York City school crisis: Teacher politics, racial politics and the decline of liberalism.* Ph.D. dissertation, Stanford University.

Peterson, P. E. (1995). The new politics of choice. In D. Ravitch & M. A. Vinovskis (Eds.), *Learning from the past: What history teaches us about school reform* (pp. 217–240). Baltimore: Johns Hopkins University Press.

Podair, J. E. (1997). *Like strangers: Blacks, Whites, and New York City's Ocean Hill-Brownsville crisis, 1945–1980.* Ph.D. dissertation, Princeton University.

Price, H. (1999, December 8). Urban education: A radical plan. *Education Week, 19*(15), 44+.

Purdum, T. S. (1997, November 4). Supreme Court declines to hear challenge to California's ban on affirmative action. *New York Times,* A13.

Ravitch, D. (1974). *The great school wars: New York City, 1805–1973. A history of the public schools as battlefield of social change.* New York: Basic Books.

Ravitch, D. (1980). Desegregation: Varieties of meaning. In D. Bell (Ed.), *Shades of Brown: New perspectives on school desegregation* (pp. 31–47). New York: Teachers College Press.

Ravitch, D. (1981). The evolution of school desegregation policy, 1964–1979. In A. Yarmolinsky, L. Liebman, & C. S. Schelling (Eds.), *Race and schooling in the city* (pp. 9–23). Cambridge: Harvard University Press.

Ravitch, D. (1983). *The troubled crusade: American education, 1945–1980.* New York: Basic Books.

Raywid, M. A. (1983, June). Schools of choice: Their current nature and prospects. *Phi Delta Kappan, 64*(10), 684–688.

Raywid, M. A. (1994). Synthesis of research on schools of choice. In J. Kretovics & E. J. Nussel (Eds.), *Transforming urban education* (pp. 214–227). Boston: Allyn and Bacon.

Reich, R. B. (2000, November 6). The liverwurst solution. *The American Prospect, 11*(23).

Rofes, E. (1998, April). *How are school districts responding to charter laws and charter schools?* Berkeley: Policy Analysis for California Education.

Rossell, C. H. (1990). *The carrot or the stick for school desegregation policy: Magnet schools or forced busing.* Philadelphia: Temple University Press.

RPP International. (1998, July). *A national study of charter schools: Second year report, 1998.* Washington, DC: Office of Educational Research and Improvement, U.S. Department of Education.

RPP International. (1999, June). *The state of charter schools 1999: Third-year report.* Washington, DC: Office of Educational Research and Improvement, U.S. Department of Education.

RPP International. (2000, January). *The state of charter schools 2000: Fourth-year report.* Washington, DC: Office of Educational Research and Improvement, U.S. Department of Education.

RPP International and the University of Minnesota. (1997, May). *A study of charter schools: First year report, 1997.* Washington, DC: Office of Educational Research and Improvement, U.S. Department of Education.

Ruenzel, D. (1998, September 16). War of attrition. *Education Week*, 32–37.

Saving public education: Progressive educators explain what it will take to get beyond the gimmicks. (1997, February 17). *Nation, 264*(6), 16–25.

Schmidt, P. (2003, April 4). Behind the fight over race-conscious admissions: Advocacy groups—working together—helped shape the legal and political debate. *Chronicle of Higher Education, 49*(30), A22–A25.

Schmitt, E. (2001, April 4). Analysis of census finds segregation along with diversity. *New York Times*, A15.

Schnaiberg, L. (1998, August 5). Predominantly Black charters focus of debate in N.C. *Education Week, 17*(43), 22.

Schorr, J. (1999, February 9). A chart to Oakland's charters. *Oakland Tribune*, news—1+.

Schorr, J. (2002). *Hard lessons: The promise of an inner city charter school.* New York: Ballantine Books.

Schrag, P. (1998). *Paradise lost: California's experience, America's future.* Berkeley: University of California Press.

Selingo, J. (1999, December 3). A quiet end to the use of race in college admissions in Florida. *Chronicle of Higher Education*, A31.

Selingo, J. (2000, January 28). Lawmakers' sit-in spurs delay in Fla. affirmative-action vote. *Chronicle of Higher Education*, A37.

Selingo, J. (2003, June 24). Decisions may prompt return of race-conscious admissions at some colleges. *Chronicle of Higher Education* on-line daily news. Retrieved July 8, 2003 from http://chronicle.com/daily/2003/06/2003062402n.htm

Shujaa, M. J. (1994a). Afrocentric transformation and parental choice in African-American independent schools. In M. J. Shujaa (Ed.), *Too much schooling, too little education: A paradox of Black life in White societies* (pp. 361–376). Trenton, NJ: Africa World Press.

Shujaa, M. J. (1994b). Education and schooling: You can have one without the other. In M. J. Shujaa (Ed.), *Too much schooling, too little education: A paradox of Black life in White societies* (pp. 13–36). Trenton, NJ: Africa World Press.

Shujaa, M. J., & Afrik, H. T. (1996). School desegregation, the politics of culture, and the Council of Independent Black Institutions. In M. J. Shujaa (Ed.), *Beyond desegregation: The politics of quality in African American schooling* (pp. 253–268). Thousand Oaks, CA: Corwin Press.

Sleeper, J. (1997). *Liberal racism.* New York: Penguin Books.

Smith, R. C. (1996). *We have no leaders: African Americans in the post–Civil Rights era.* Albany: State University of New York Press.

Smrekar, C., & Goldring, E. (1999). *School choice in urban America: Magnet schools and the pursuit of equity.* New York: Teachers College Press.

Steinberg, J. (2003, June 24). An admissions guide. *New York Times,* A1+.

Swidler, A. (1979). *Organization without authority: Dilemmas of social control in free schools.* Cambridge: Harvard University Press.

Tyack, D. B. (1974). *The one best system: A history of American urban education.* Cambridge: Harvard University Press.

Tyack, D. (1999, January–February). Choice options: School choice, yes—But what kind? *The American Prospect,* 42.

Tyack, D., & Cuban, L. (1995). *Tinkering toward utopia: A century of public school reform.* Cambridge: Harvard University Press.

Tyack, D., & Hansot, E. (1982). *Managers of virtue: Public school leadership in America, 1820–1980.* New York: Basic Books.

Tyack, D., Lowe, R., & Hansot E. (1984). *Public schools in hard times: The Great Depression and recent years.* Cambridge: Harvard University Press.

UCLA Charter School Study. (1998). *Beyond the rhetoric of charter school reform: A study of ten California school districts.* Los Angeles: Author.

Urban Strategies Council with the Youth Development Initiative Working Group. (1996). *Call to action: An Oakland blueprint for youth development.* Oakland: Urban Strategies Council.

Urofsky, M. I. (1970). Reflections on Ocean Hill. In M. I. Urofsky (Ed.), *Why teachers strike: Teachers' rights and community control.* Garden City, NY: Anchor Books.

Van Deburg, W. L. (1992). *New day in Babylon: The Black Power movement and American culture, 1965–1975.* Chicago: University of Chicago Press.

Walsh, M. (1998, April 1). Bolick v. Chanin. *Education Week,* 40–45.

Wang, L. L. (1995). *Lau v. Nichols:* History of a struggle for equal and quality education. In D. T. Nakanishi & T. Y. Nishida (Eds.), *The Asian American educational experience: A source book for teachers and students* (pp. 58–91). New York: Routledge.

Wells, A. S. (1991a, Fall). Choice in education: Examining the evidence on equity. *Teachers College Record,* 93(1), 137–155.

Wells, A. S. (1991b, January 9). Once a desegregation tool, magnet schools become schools of choice. *New York Times,* B6.

Wells, A. S. (1993). *Time to choose: America at the crossroads of school choice policy.* New York: Hill and Wang.

Wells, A. S. (2000a, November 2). In search of uncommon schools: Charter school reform in historical perspective (Part 1): Revisiting the ideology of the common school. *Teachers College Record.* Retrieved March 28, 2003 from http://www.tcrecord.org

Wells, A. S. (2000b, November 2). In search of uncommon schools: Charter school reform in historical perspective (Part 2): Resisting common association. *Teachers College Record.* Retrieved March 28, 2003 from http://www.tcrecord.org

Wells, A. S. (2000c, November 2). In search of uncommon schools: Charter school reform in historical perspective (Part 3): Charter schools as uncommon schools. *Teachers College Record*. Retrieved March 28, 2003 from http://www.tcrecord.org

Wells, A. S., & Crain, R. L. (1997). *Stepping over the color line: African-American students in White suburban schools*. New Haven, CT: Yale University Press.

Wells, A. S., Lopez, A., Scott, J., & Holme, J. J. (1999, Summer). Charter schools as postmodern paradox: Rethinking social stratification in an age of deregulated school choice. *Harvard Educational Review, 69*(2), 172–204.

White, K. A. (1999, January 13). Ahead of the curve. *Education Week*, 32–36.

Wicker, T. (1996). *Tragic failure: Racial integration in America*. New York: William Morrow.

Wilgoren, J. (2002, October 1). Justices asked to rule early on university admissions. *New York Times*, A28.

Willie, C. V. (1981). The demographic basis of urban educational reform. In A. Yarmolinsky, L. Liebman, & C. S. Schelling (Eds.), *Race and schooling in the city* (pp. 126–135). Cambridge: Harvard University Press.

Willie, C. V. (1989). The intended and unintended benefits of school desegregation. In W. D. Smith & E. W. Chunn (Eds.), *Black education: A quest for equity and excellence* (pp. 127–135). New Brunswick, NJ: Transaction Publishers.

Wilson, C. E. (1968, Fall). Lessons of the 201 complex in Harlem. *Freedomways, 8*(4), 399–406.

Wilson, W. J. (1978). *The declining significance of race: Blacks and changing American institutions*. Chicago: University of Chicago Press.

Wilson, W. J. (1987). *The truly disadvantaged: The inner city, the underclass, and public policy*. Chicago: University of Chicago Press.

Young, T. W. (1990). *Public alternative education: Options and choice for today's schools*. New York: Teachers College Press.

Zeller, T. R. (1999, January 20). Affirmative action ruling ripples throughout Texas. *New York Times*, C22.

Part I

PROGRESSIVE
CHARTER SCHOOLING
IN PRACTICE

CHAPTER 2

Fulfilling the Hope of *Brown v. Board of Education* through Charter Schools

JOHN B. KING, JR.

Introduction

In 1954, when the Supreme Court declared segregation in public schools unconstitutional in *Brown v. Board of Education*, the Court's decision was viewed not only as a major victory in the struggle against legally mandated segregation, but as a critical step toward equal educational opportunity. Yet fifty years later most political and educational leaders acknowledge that equal educational opportunity for African Americans has not been realized. Despite significant progress made during the 1970s and 1980s, a dramatic gap in academic achievement between Black students and White students persists (Haycock, 2001). Jencks and Phillips (1998) gloomily report, "African-Americans currently score lower than European Americans on vocabulary, reading, and mathematics tests, as well as on tests that claim to measure scholastic aptitude and intelligence. . . . [T]he typical American Black still scores below 75 percent of American Whites on most standardized tests" (p. 1). This academic achievement gap contributes to similar racial gaps in educational attainment, employment, and family income, and its persistence has led to calls for increasingly radical educational experiments. One such experiment is the charter schools movement.

Sarason (1998) describes charter schools as "the most radical education reform effort in the post World War II era in that states encourage and permit these schools to be created exempt from burdensome, stifling, innovation-killing features of the culture of existing systems" (p. vii). Charter schools constitute a dramatic departure from traditional educational practices because, in exchange for greater accountability, they are granted substantially more freedom than traditional district schools. Essentially, charters function as contracts between charter schools and the charter-granting agency, typically the state department of education or local district. In their charter proposals, the schools define the academic goals they hope to achieve and outline the policies and procedures they plan to implement to accomplish those goals. Charter-granting agencies review each proposal and select the most promising ones for implementation. Periodically—usually every three to seven years—the charter-granting agency reviews how successfully each charter school is meeting the terms of its charter. Failing schools may be discontinued through revocation of their charters, while those that are succeeding have their charters renewed. Although required to operate within the constraints imposed by state standards, state assessment systems, and federal laws regarding Title I, special education, and civil rights, charter schools enjoy considerable autonomy in four key areas: (1) designing and implementing the school's curriculum and instructional practices; (2) hiring, managing, evaluating, and, when necessary, firing school personnel; (3) developing the school budget; and (4) establishing and maintaining the school culture.

Today, there are almost 2,700 charter schools in thirty-six states and the District of Columbia, enrolling over 684,000 students (Center for Education Reform). Despite enthusiasm among politicians, parents, and educators for expanding the charter school movement, there is limited available research on effective urban charter school practice. Most research to date on charter schools has focused on determining whether these schools as a whole are living up to the promises made by their advocates and whether they are outperforming district schools (American Federation of Teachers, 2002; Finn, Manno, & Vanourek, 2000; Gill, Timpane, Ross, & Brewer, 2001; Miron and Nelson, 2001; SRI International, 1997; UCLA, 1998). While proponents point to promising early indications of success, critics focus on studies that show charter schools do not consistently outperform their district counterparts. Despite this debate within the education research community, the political reality is that the charter school movement has substantial momentum, particularly among urban families of color, and will likely involve increasing numbers of urban students (Reid, 2001). Therefore, there is a critical need for research on the internal workings of urban charter schools to explore the relationship between charter status and student outcomes. In particular, given the national concern about the Black-White achievement gap and the underrepresentation of African

Americans in higher education, education researchers must focus on what is being done differently in those charter schools that are succeeding in bridging the gap for low-income African American students. Thus, this chapter seeks to (1) offer a rationale for research on effective charter school practices, and (2) use an examination of Roxbury Preparatory Charter School, a Boston charter school cofounded by this author that is succeeding in bridging the achievement gap, to illustrate what can be learned from this potential new direction in charter school research.

Relevant Literature and Critical Assumptions

Effective Schools, School Culture, and Achievement Gap Research

Although charter schools are relatively new to the education research landscape, concern about the achievement gap is not. In fact, an entire body of literature, published primarily during the 1970s and 1980s, focused on identifying and describing schools effective in raising the achievement of urban students of color. This literature, known as effective schools research, began in response to two major studies in the mid-1960s, the Coleman Report (1966) and a subsequent study entitled *Inequality: A Reassessment of the Effect of Family and Schooling in America* (Jencks et al., 1972), both of which suggest that family background has a significantly greater effect on academic achievement than do schools. Effective schools researchers (such as Brookover, Beady, Flood, Scweitzer, & Wisenbaker, 1979; Coleman et al., 1981; Edmonds, 1979, 1986; Phi Delta Kappan, 1980; Rutter, Maughan, Mortimore, Ouston, & Smith, 1979; Weber, 1971) used outlier studies, case studies, program evaluations, and surveys to explore the practices of schools whose performance on standardized tests was significantly higher than would be predicted by student demographics. Whatever its methodological flaws, this research established that individual schools have the capacity to be effective in bridging the achievement gap between African American students and White students.

Although their observations and conclusions differed in some areas, a consensus emerged among effective schools researchers about the practices of effective schools. Frequently occurring items on the list of effective practices were a focus on core literacy and math skills, strong principal leadership, a disciplined school environment, and high expectations for students throughout the school community (Brookover, Beady, Flood, Scweitzer, & Wisenbaker, 1979; Edmonds, 1979, 1986; Phi Delta Kappa,

1980; Weber, 1971). Many resulting effective schools initiatives, including federal, state, and district programs as well as individual school change efforts, embraced these lists as formulas for effective school reform.

This approach was challenged by a critique of the effective schools movement that emerged in the 1980s and 1990s, questioning whether lists of effective characteristics adequately address issues of school organization and culture. For example, Purkey and Smith (1983) challenge the effective schools literature as "weak in many respects, most notably in its tendency to present narrow, often simplistic recipes for school improvement" (p. 427). This skepticism led to a shift away from descriptions of school characteristics toward a more thorough exploration of school culture in effective schools, what Purkey and Smith called the "structure, process, and climate of values and norms that emphasize successful teaching and learning" (p. 442). As a result, Purkey and Smith (1983), Deal and Kennedy (1983), Rosenholtz (1985), and subsequent researchers interested in issues of school culture began to focus not only on what effective schools do, but also on how they do it.

More recent research that has focused on identifying how particular schools are effective in raising student achievement, particularly the achievement of students in urban schools, has identified a variety of practices in the areas of budgets, staffing, curriculum and instruction, and school culture associated with improved educational outcomes. In analyzing the relationship between school budgets and student achievements, researchers identify smaller schools and smaller classes, reduced teacher loads that provide time for data analysis and reflection, professional development carefully coordinated with curricular and instructional reforms, and programs that increase student learning time and expanded student access to academic tutoring as crucial investments (Darling-Hammond, 1997; Elmore, 2002; Finn and Achilles, 1999; Heath and McLaughlin, 1994; Miles, 2001; Newmann, Smith, Allensworth, & Bryk, 2001). Current scholarship emphasizes the role of staffing in school success and advocates measures such as hiring teachers who have high expectations for students, a thorough understanding of instructional methods, and content expertise; creating dynamic roles and consistent learning opportunities for teachers that ensure their continued professional growth and encourage their persistence in the field; removing or "counseling out" teachers who fail to advance student achievement; and hiring and developing school leaders who prioritize instructional leadership and the creation of collaborative staff cultures (Darling-Hammond and Falk, 1997; Dreeben and Gamoran, 1986; Elmore, 1995; Ferguson, 1998; Fullan, 2002; Sebring and Bryk, 2000).

In terms of curriculum and instruction, recent research links several critical features to improved academic results: structures that support teaching for understanding and differentiated instruction, instructional coherence, continuous use of student performance data to drive instructional improvements, internal assessment systems designed to yield rich data on student knowledge and skills, and culturally responsive curricula (Elmore, 1995; 2002; Newmann, Smith, Allensworth, & Bryk, 2001; Ogbu and Simons, 1998; Shepard, 2000; Steele, 1992; Steele and Aronson, 1998). School culture is an area of particular interest for researchers focused on the achievement gap and they offer several strategies for developing cultures that facilitate the bridging of the achievement gap including structures that support the development of trusting relationships between students and school staff; academic and social interventions that directly address the tension between the cultural experience of institutional oppression and discrimination and the goal of success within educational institutions; cultivation of safe, academically rigorous, and respectful environments; and trust-building home-school communication (Bryk and Schneider, 2002; Darling-Hammond and Falk, 1997; Hill, Foster, & Gendler, 1990; Ogbu and Simons, 1998; Steele, 1992). Without question, the blueprint offered by recent scholarship in education for the creation of schools effective in bridging the achievement gap requires changes in educational practice significantly more complex and organic than those proposed by the early effective schools researchers.

Charter School Research

Neither the prescriptions of effective schools researchers nor the reform proposals of subsequent researchers that focused on educational practices effective in bridging the achievement gap have yielded the desired transformation in educational outcomes. Many educators and policymakers have attributed the failure of these reform initiatives to intractable structural challenges (such as inefficient school district bureaucracies, teachers and administrators immune as a result of union contracts from accountability for results, and so forth). As a result, a shift in the national debate on education occurred in the 1990s toward an examination of structural obstacles to school improvement. School-based management, schools-within-schools, and school vouchers were all a part of this new conversation in education reform. In this context, education policymakers began to explore the idea of creating new schools—charter schools—that would be free from many (although certainly not all) of the constraints of existing school systems, but accountable for producing the achievement gains long sought by the effective schools movement. Nathan (1999), Finn, Manno, and Vanourek (2000), and other charter school advocates reference the effective schools literature in making the case for charter schools' capacity to overcome structural obstacles to school reform. For example, Finn, Manno, and Vanourek (2000) argue, "Effective schools, it turned out, have certain predictable (and commonsensical) features. . . . [M]ost have also wrested a measure of autonomy from the system and have carved out a zone within which they can shape their own destinies" (p. 63). Thus, charter school proponents offer the autonomy of charter schools—school-level freedom with school-level accountability—as a path to widespread adoption of effective practices that have been difficult for traditional public schools to implement within the confines of the existing system.

Evidence on whether the claims of charter school enthusiasts have been borne out over the past ten years is mixed. National and state studies, with large sample sizes across diverse regions, have tended to suggest that charter schools are not yet meeting the promise of outperforming district schools (American Federation of Teachers, 2002; Gill, Timpane, Ross, & Brewer, 2001; Miron and Nelson, 2001; SRI International, 1997; UCLA, 1998). For example, Miron and Nelson (2001), in a meta-analysis of statewide studies of charter schools conducted since passage of the first charter school law in 1991, found that "the existing body of research on charter schools' impact on student achievement reveals a mixed picture, with studies from some states suggesting positive impacts, studies from other states suggesting negative impacts, and some providing evidence of both positive and negative impacts" (p. 30). More in-depth studies of life within charter schools have tended to profile pitfalls and missteps that have led individual schools to fail in their pursuit of higher student achievement (Fuller, 2000; Good and Braden, 2000; Sarason, 1998). However, even charter school critics acknowledge the existence of individual charter schools with phenomenal academic results. Thus, what is missing from the existing literature is careful exploration of what successful charter schools, particularly those serving low-income students of color, are doing right.

Because charter schools offer the powerful opportunity to examine what is possible when schools are granted autonomy to implement effective practices, there is perhaps no more urgent research needed than a better understanding of the behavior of charter schools that are succeeding in bridging the achievement gap. Explaining this new direction for charter school research, education researcher Paul Hill told *Education Week,* "We're moving away from the Black-box questions to questions about what kind of instruction goes on in charter schools. . . . Is it coherent? Does it increase opportunities for kids, and, then, under what circumstances do these things happen?" (Viadero, 2001, p. 6). Examining life within successful charter schools will allow education researchers to explore if, and how, these schools are putting into practice the ideas advanced by the effective schools literature and the achievement gap literature. Descriptions of the behavior of these schools will help educators and policymakers to determine the extent to which the autonomy—freedom and accountability—celebrated by charter school proponents is helping these schools to bridge the achievement gap. In addition, traditional district schools may be able to learn from such research ways they might grant greater flexibility in certain areas to promote best practices. Finally, the stories of successful charter schools can offer not a recipe, but rather a resource for charter school founders, leaders, teachers, and parents as they seek to provide better educational opportunities for urban students of color. Roxbury Preparatory Charter School in Boston presents one such story.

An Illustrative Example:
Roxbury Preparatory Charter School

Unique Results

Roxbury Preparatory Charter School, a 6th through 8th grade Boston public charter school serving 170 African American (80%) and Latino (20%) students, prepares students to enter, succeed in, and graduate from college. Roxbury Prep was founded in 1999 on the philosophy that all students are entitled to and can succeed in college preparatory programs when (1) the curriculum is rigorous, engaging, and well planned; (2) the school emphasizes student character, community responsibility, and exposure to life's possibilities; and (3) a community network supports student academic, social, and physical well-being. Roxbury Prep helps its 8th grade students gain admission to outstanding public and private college preparatory high schools. The school's focus on college preparation responds directly to the student body and its needs. Of the school's 170 students in the 2002-2003 academic year,

- 65% qualify for free or reduced price lunch;

- 59% come from single parent households;

- 33% score, upon entering Roxbury Prep, two or more grade levels behind on the Stanford 9 (a national test of basic skills) in math, reading, and English grammar and usage; and

- 83% come from the neighborhoods of Roxbury, Dorchester, Mattapan, and Hyde Park.

These statistics indicate that the majority of students have characteristics that research has shown, without Roxbury Prep's intervention, would decrease and endanger their likelihood of attending college.

Although Roxbury Prep's student demographics and college prep aspirations are not unique, its results are. During the two years in which Roxbury Prep students have participated in the Massachusetts Comprehensive Assessment System (MCAS) exams, they have dramatically outperformed the Boston Public Schools and have essentially bridged the achievement gap with White students statewide (see figs. 2.1 and 2.2). The MCAS tests are mandatory statewide assessments designed to measure students' progress toward the Massachusetts Curriculum Standards in math, English, science, and history and are a national model for standards-based assessment consistent with the provisions of the No Child Left Behind Act. It is important to note that these tests are far more elaborate assessments of academic performance than the multiple-choice tests relied upon by early effective schools researchers to identify successful schools. While each test has a multiple-choice section, the MCAS tests are designed to assess a wider range of skills. For

Fig. 2.1
2002 MCAS: Average Score Comparison

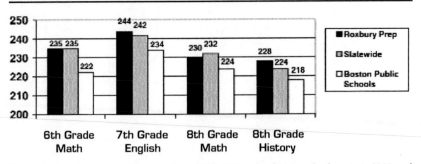

Source: Roxbury Preparatory Charter School, 2002–2003 Annual Report. Roxbury MA, 2003; and Massachusetts Department of Education website <www.doe.mass.edu/mcas/results.html?yr=02>.

FIG. 2.2
2002 MCAS: Percentage of Students Passing by Race
Overcoming the Achievement Gap for Black Students

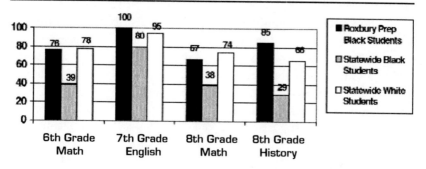

Source: Roxbury Preparatory Charter School, 2002–2003 Annual Report. Roxbury MA, 2003; and Massachusetts Department of Education website <www.doe.mass.edu/mcas/results.html?yr=02>.

example, the 6th and 8th grade math tests ask students both to show their work and to describe their strategies in answering complex, multistep problems. The 7th grade English test includes open response questions requiring students to use evidence from a given text, and a composition section in which students must write a coherent and thoughtful essay in response to a prompt. The 8th grade history test includes open response questions that require students to write persuasively using relevant evidence from their knowledge of history. Moreover, given that 10th grade students must pass the MCAS tests in order to earn a high school diploma in the state, performance on these tests constitutes the pivotal measure of "academic success" as defined by the Commonwealth of Massachusetts.

For two years in a row on the 6th grade math MCAS, Roxbury Prep had the highest average score of any predominantly Black school in Massachusetts. For 2002, Roxbury Prep's average score was fourth highest of thirty-four public schools in Boston. On the 7th grade English language arts MCAS, Roxbury Prep improved in 2002 from having the second highest average score in 2001 to having the *highest* average score of any predominantly Black school in Massachusetts. This 2002 score was second highest of thirty-one nonexam public schools in Boston. On the school's first administration of the 8th grade math and history MCAS exams, Roxbury Prep students in 2002 had the second highest average scores of any predominantly Black school in Massachusetts. These 2002 scores were fifth highest and third highest, respectively, of thirty-one nonexam public schools in Boston. In addition, Roxbury Prep's impressive MCAS results are confirmed by impressive student gains on the Stanford 9, a multiple-choice test of basic skills more similar to the tests relied upon by effective schools researchers. Moreover, Roxbury Prep students' success in high school placement further confirms the school's positive impact on students' academic lives: 100% of graduates have matriculated to college prep high schools, with over one-third earning scholarships to attend private and parochial schools with highly competitive admissions processes.

Understanding how Roxbury Prep is achieving its results requires an understanding of how the school is using its autonomy in curriculum and instruction, staffing, budgets, and school culture. It must be noted, however, that no attempt is being made here to attribute Roxbury Prep's results solely to the behavior of the school. Indeed, selection bias (as a result of requiring parental applications) must be acknowledged as a factor in Roxbury Prep's impressive results. At the same time, admission by lottery, required under Massachusetts law, mitigates against selection bias, as does an influx of parents, attracted by positive publicity, whose children have consistently struggled in traditional district schools. Moreover, as Hill, Foster, and Gendler (1990) point out in their study of successful alternative schools, "granting the validity of the concept of selection bias does not require education or public officials to reject the possibility that students now in zoned schools would do better in schools with the central features of focus schools" (p. 60). Thus, important lessons can be learned from Roxbury Prep's experience even if one assumes that some portion of the school's success can be traced to student inputs.

Curriculum

One of the central dilemmas of charter school reform is the seemingly paradoxical decision by state education policymakers to create schools free from district-level curricular restraints while simultaneously introducing uniform statewide curriculum standards and assessments. While some charter school leaders accuse the state of policy schizophrenia and bemoan standards-based reform, Roxbury Prep has instead embraced both state curriculum standards and assessments and the freedom to innovate in curriculum and instruction. Roxbury Prep's philosophy of "Massachusetts standards plus" is at the foundation of the school's academic program.

Using success on the MCAS as a nonnegotiable outcome, Roxbury Prep teachers work for three weeks each summer to develop and revise rigorous internal academic standards and curricula aligned with the Massachusetts curriculum frameworks that ensure that students have the skills and knowledge they will need to succeed in college prep high schools and in college. Teachers also use the summer to design and revise comprehensive end-of-year assessments, final exams, and projects for each course that students must pass in order to be promoted. This approach allows teachers to integrate content knowledge and skills that they believe to be important, but that is deemphasized or even ignored in the Massachusetts standards and on the MCAS. For example, while the history of West African civilizations is given limited attention in the Massachusetts history standards, Roxbury Prep teachers believe it is imperative that students, particularly students of color, be exposed to the history of Africa before the trans-Atlantic slave trade. Similarly, while the 8th grade science MCAS, piloted in 2002 for implementation in 2003, requires students to respond in writing to questions that ask them to analyze and construct scientific experiments, Roxbury Prep teachers also require students to demonstrate their understanding of the scientific method and the content of each year's curriculum by designing and implementing a science experiment or project as a final comprehensive assessment. When students fail to meet Roxbury Prep's more rigorous standards, as expressed in the school's comprehensive assessments, they must either attend and pass summer school or, if they have failed to meet the standards in three or more classes, repeat the grade.

Perhaps the best illustrations of Roxbury Prep's "Massachusetts standards plus" approach to curriculum and instruction are found in the design of the school's mathematics and literacy programs. Rather than choose sides in the math wars, between constructivists who favor instruction based on problem solving and traditionalists who favor an intense focus on basic computational skills, Roxbury Prep has chosen a "double math" approach. In each grade level, students at Roxbury Prep take two year-long math courses, one in math procedures and the other in math problem solving. This means, for example, that a Roxbury Prep 6th grader may spend fifty minutes in the morning doing drills on decimal operations, and then spend fifty minutes in the afternoon using decimals to construct graphs on average rainfall in different U.S. states. While traditional districts lurch between constructivist and traditionalist approaches, Roxbury Prep is able, thanks to the freedom provided by its charter status, to choose a third way. Roxbury Prep's daily schedule, staffing, professional development, and budget all reflect the school's "double math" philosophy.

Similarly, Roxbury Prep's literacy program reflects a philosophical choice not to be drawn into false dichotomies. The school has chosen a "double English" approach, in which students have two periods of English instruction a day—one focused on the writing process and grammar, one focused on reading comprehension and literature. Using Lisa Delpit's (1988) "The Silenced Dialogue: Power and Pedagogy in Educating Other People's

Children" as a guide, Roxbury Prep's English teachers have set aside long-standing debates in education between grammar traditionalists and those who advocate a focus on the writing process. Instead, English teachers at Roxbury Prep assume students need instruction in both grammar and the writing process and they use one of the fifty-minute English periods to provide both. The other English period, focused exclusively on reading skills, reflects the school's commitment to literacy as the foundation for learning in all disciplines. This commitment is also reflected in the school's daily silent schoolwide reading period which occurs during the first twenty-five minutes of the day, a time during which everyone at the school—students, teachers, and even administrators—silently read books of their own choosing. Although these approaches may not be entirely unique to Roxbury Prep, they do reflect the school's ability as a charter school to make critical curriculum decisions at the school level and then to organize the school's resources (for example, daily schedule, staffing, professional development, and budget) to implement those decisions.

Staffing

One Boston charter school leader, with experience in both district and charter schools, is fond of asking charter school critics the rhetorical question, "What CEO would take over a company knowing he does not have the power to hire or fire any of his subordinates?" He asks that question, of course, because one of the signature elements of charter school legislation is the freedom to hire, evaluate, and, if necessary, fire staff members free from the constraints of traditional district-union contracts. Indeed, the freedom to make staffing decisions has been critical to Roxbury Prep's success.

Collins (2001), in a study of elite companies with sustained outstanding performance entitled *Good to Great*, offers an apt metaphor in arguing that a key to organizational greatness is getting "the right people on the bus" (p. 13). Roxbury Prep lives this philosophy through the components of its rigorous hiring process: (1) cast a wide net by contacting high caliber graduate schools of education, networks of urban educators, and private school placement services; (2) emphasize staff diversity (which results in a 2002–03 staff comprised of 56% people of color); (3) review dozens of resumes for each position and interview selected candidates on the phone or in person; (4) invite the most promising candidates to the school to teach a sample lesson and to meet with their prospective colleagues in their subject teams and/or grade-level teams; (5) contact references and review transcripts and writing samples; (6) put off hiring decisions until the right fit is identified; and (7) hire only those candidates who possess excellent content knowledge, urban teaching experience, and a deep commitment to the school's mission and philosophy. While traditional district schools may be assigned teachers from the central office or must limit their candidate pool to those who have jumped through elaborate teacher certification hoops, Roxbury Prep is able to seek out the best possible fit for every position.

An excellent illustration of Roxbury Prep's successful use of staffing autonomy is our 6th grade Math Procedures teacher. She is a Latina woman who grew up in East Los Angeles, attended an elite California independent school through the A Better Chance (ABC) scholarship program, graduated with a degree in mathematics from Wellesley College, and taught for a year in an East Los Angeles parochial school. She is a fabulous teacher—she knows math inside and out, she sets high standards for her students and herself, she connects well with students, and she will tutor before school, at lunch, after school, on Saturdays, and whenever else she can to ensure her students' success. Her efficacy in the classroom is reflected in her students' performance on the 6th grade math MCAS, internal assessments of students' math skills, and the praise of parents amazed by how much progress their children make in her class. However, a traditional district school would have had difficulty hiring her because she is not Massachusetts certified. It is only because of Roxbury Prep's ability to hire noncertified teachers that the school's 6th graders have the benefit of this teacher's talents.

In addition to getting the right people on the bus, Roxbury Prep is able to use its staffing autonomy to accomplish two other Collins (2001) recommendations for organizational greatness: "getting the right people in the right seats and getting the wrong people off the bus" (p. 13). While district schools are often burdened with positions and staffing structures mandated by the central office, charter schools have the freedom to design positions that maximize the efficacy of their personnel. For example, Roxbury Prep designed a four-fifths position in order to persuade a senior administrator and veteran teacher to choose Roxbury Prep over retirement. The school also created a special schedule for four teachers in which they arrive at school two hours later than their colleagues and then remain after school to run a homework center from 4:15 PM to 6:00 PM for students who struggle with homework completion. Similarly, Roxbury Prep has a nontraditional administrative structure with two codirectors instead of the traditional principal and assistant principal. Having a codirector for curriculum and instruction and a codirector for operations and finance ensures that the school's instructional leader is not constantly distracted from the work of supporting teachers by operations issues, but also ensures that the instructional leader is able to share in all major operations decisions. While flexibility in staffing patterns has allowed Roxbury Prep to be creative in tapping staff members' strengths, the school has also used its autonomy to address situations where staff members' weaknesses perpetually overwhelm their strengths. When teachers have consistently resisted feedback from their colleagues and the codirectors, or refused to adapt their curricula and instructional strategies to maximize student achievement, Roxbury Prep has not renewed those teachers' contracts or has even asked that they leave the school mid-year. While these decisions are difficult, Roxbury Prep's philosophy is that the stakes for students are too high to tolerate continually ineffective instruction or a poisonous presence in the staff culture. Too often, district principals cannot pursue a similar course because they are hampered by teacher tenure policies that protect the interests of adults over those of students.

Culture

Visitors to Roxbury Prep are often stuck by how dramatically the culture of the school differs from so many of the traditional urban district schools they have visited. The visitors are surprised by the focused and orderly classes, the number of hands raised high to answer questions, silent hallway transitions, neat student uniforms (beige or navy blue khakis, light blue collared dress shirts, dress shoes, ties for the boys), and outstanding student work decorating the hallways. "How," they ask, "has such a strong culture been developed and maintained?" The answer is surprisingly uncomplicated: Roxbury Prep's culture reflects the expectations that the school's administrators and teachers consistently communicate and reinforce to each other, to students, and to students' families.

Roxbury Prep has used its autonomy in school culture to establish a dress code, a strict code of conduct, and an achievement-focused environment. The school's founders believe that student uniforms contribute to a serious academic tone and eliminate distractions like inappropriately revealing clothing or arguments over whose clothes are more expensive. From the very first information session that prospective Roxbury Prep parents attend, they learn that the uniform is a central component of the school's culture and nonnegotiable. Similarly, in the information sessions, a June orientation, and an August orientation, parents of incoming 6th graders learn that Roxbury Prep operates on the conviction that a disciplined environment is a prerequisite for academic achievement. Students are encouraged to understand the code of conduct not as arbitrary edicts from a distant central office, but rather as standards for behavior based on the community's shared values as expressed in the school creed: scholarship, integrity, dignity, responsibility, perseverance, community, leadership, peace, social justice, and investment. This creed is further reinforced through a weekly character development class called "advisory" in which students explore the elements of the creed through readings, writing assignments, role plays, and class discussions. For example, as part of the advisory unit on dignity, teachers have asked students in single-sex groups to view contemporary music videos from BET and MTV with the sound turned down, and have then used the question, "What would an alien arriving on Earth and seeing these videos think about men and women of color in the United States?" to engage students in a dialogue, both written and oral, about the messages the images communicate. Such discussions are not meant to be preachy, but rather to engage students in thinking critically about the values expressed in the Roxbury Prep creed.

In class, in the halls, and in advisory, Roxbury Prep seeks to cultivate a community of scholars. Students are provided with frequent opportunities to demonstrate academic excellence, including 6th grade "coffee houses" at which every 6th grader reads an original piece of writing, the posting of outstanding work in every classroom and throughout the hallways, weekly community meetings at which students deliver academic presentations, and an 8th grade "Invention Convention" where 8th grade science projects are judged by attorneys from an area patent firm and then shared with students' families and other community members. Each year, every Roxbury Prep student participates in full-day visits to colleges like Williams College, Northeastern University, Boston College, and MIT to learn about life on campus and the academic offerings at each school. The honor roll at Roxbury Prep is a highly sought-after achievement and is recognized with the opportunity to participate in special trips, including a winter ski trip and a summer beach outing.

The school has also created a culture where students' families are routinely engaged as partners in students' academic success. Progress reports are sent home to students' families every four weeks listing every assignment in every class, how many points each assignment was worth, and how many points the student earned for each assignment. Advisors call students' families every other week to report on academic performance and behavior and to address parent questions. Assignments are regularly given that involve parents or other family members as historians, as audiences for student writing, and as mathematics problem solvers. Nightly homework assignments are even available via voice mail so students' families can call, hear the assignments, and then check that their children have completed their homework.

While each of the above initiatives may exist in district schools, what makes their implementation at Roxbury Prep unique is the deliberate saturation of students with the message, you can achieve academically and therefore, you will enter, succeed in, and graduate from college. Charter schools have the freedom to establish a unique mission and to bring that mission alive in every aspect of the school culture; this is precisely what Roxbury Prep has done.

Not only is student scholarship cultivated through school culture, but so too is teacher scholarship. Roxbury Prep has used its freedom to design a weekly schedule in which students attend class from 7:45 AM to 4:15 PM Monday through Thursday, and 7:45 AM to 1:15 PM on Fridays. While this schedule provides students with significantly more instructional time than local district schools, it also affords time every Friday for teacher professional development and collaboration. On Fridays, Roxbury Prep teachers meet for one hour in inquiry groups: a literacy inquiry group for English, reading, and history teachers, and a numeracy inquiry group for math and science teachers. In inquiry group meetings, teachers develop action research questions through which they share their own work and analyze student work to consider teacher efficacy, evidence of student learning, and achievement of goals. Also on Fridays, teachers meet for one hour in grade-level teams to develop the advisory character development curriculum and to discuss strategies to raise the achievement of individual students. Teachers also meet weekly in departments, during common department planning time built into the school schedule, to discuss shared instructional challenges and progress toward department goals for student learning at each grade level. The commitment of at least three hours each week to collaborative learning is supplemented by grants available to all teachers to support individual or joint professional development opportunities. By dedicating so much time and such substantial resources to professional learning, Roxbury Prep has created a culture in which teachers are constantly reflecting on their practice. From analyzing student performance on the MCAS to assessing student work with a common rubric, teachers at Roxbury Prep embrace a culture in which they continuously work together to refine the school's curricula and instruction.

Budget

Some conservative charter school advocates, particularly those aligned with for-profit education management organizations (EMOs), argue that successful charter schools demonstrate that the resources available to urban public schools are adequate. They are wrong; urban schools, even the most successful urban charter schools, are underresourced and clearly could be doing more for students if a large public investment would be made in urban kids. That said, successful charter schools' effective use of fiscal autonomy demonstrates that urban schools could be doing a better job of spending the money they receive if they had greater autonomy. Roxbury Prep's budgetary decisions exemplify this fact.

All of the innovations described above have significant financial implications. Roxbury Prep has chosen to invest in summer curriculum development time for teachers, an extended day, summer school, two periods of math and two periods of English per day, an after-school homework center, and professional development for teachers because the school believes those expenditures to be consistent with the school's mission and philosophy. On the other hand, the school has made choices about what it cannot afford. Roxbury Prep does not have substitute teachers; instead, teachers cover for each other when someone is sick. The school does not have indoor athletic facilities or an elaborate athletic program; in fact, its winter basketball teams practice in coats, hats, and sometimes gloves in a nearby park. Roxbury Prep also commits substantial administrative time and a full-time staff position to development. Without private funds, Roxbury Prep could not have its extended day or provide summer school for students who do not pass their final comprehensive assessments. The school receives approximately $9,500 per student in state funds that matches per pupil spending in the Boston Public Schools, but spends roughly an additional $2,500 per student generated from Title I funds, other state grants, and donations from foundations, corporations, and individuals. While some charter school critics may argue that Roxbury Prep's private fundraising makes comparisons with district schools illegitimate, the fact is that traditional districts and district schools do a great deal of private fundraising. Moreover, unlike charter schools, district schools receive public money for capital expenses and typically do not pay rent. Ultimately, Roxbury Prep's autonomy does not mean that it has more to spend, but rather that it gets to choose how it invests its resources, both public and private.

Conclusion

Is Roxbury Prep perfect? No. In fact, the school is only in its fifth year and still has much to learn about how to maximize student academic gains over the three short years of middle school. The codirectors and the school's trustees often say that until Roxbury Prep outperforms suburban schools such as those in Wellesley, Wayland, and Westin (three of the most affluent communities in Massachusetts), there is a lot more work to be done on figuring out how to bridge the achievement gap. However, examining Roxbury Prep's success thus far demonstrates how much could be learned about what is working in charter school education through in-depth research on successful charter schools. As in this brief examination of Roxbury Prep, four central school-level research questions should drive future quantitative and qualitative research in charter schools that are bridging the achievement gap:

- Curriculum and Instruction: How do these schools develop, assess, and refine their curricula and instruction in support of their effort to bridge the achievement gap?

- Staffing: How do these schools recruit, support, evaluate, and retain school staff in support of their effort to bridge the achievement gap?

- School Culture: How does each of these schools cultivate and sustain a student, family, and staff culture that supports their effort to bridge the achievement gap?

- Budgets: How do these schools allocate their resources in support of their effort to bridge the achievement gap?

In a 1999 *Education Week* editorial, Hugh Price, executive director of the National Urban League, urges the nation to "'charterize' all urban schools." In support of this proposal, Price (1999) argues, "For the sake of public education and, above all, for the sake of the children, what's urgently needed is truly radical reform that structures public education so that its raison d'être is student success" (p. 44). Price sees hope for public education in the freedom and accountability promised by the charter school movement. Although Price's grand vision does not seem likely to be realized in the near future, the charter school movement is a phenomenon growing in both size and permanence. Recent comments by Boston superintendent and charter school opponent Thomas Payzant exemplify this trend. In August 2002, Payzant told a gathering of Boston administrators, "Some of you may not like charter schools, but they're not going away folks. . . . The competition is real—for the resources and for the kids" (Szaniszlo, 2002, p. 15). Further evidence for this trend can be found in the comments of recently appointed New York City schools chancellor Joel Klein, leader of the nation's largest school system, who announced that creating a friendlier and more fertile environment for charter schools, an environment in which they "can feel supported and can thrive," would be a hallmark of his administration (Goodnough, 2002, p. B3). As charter schools become a more permanent presence in urban education, it is essential to understand how successful charter schools are achieving significant gains in student achievement.

And what of those who argue that standardized test scores should not be used as evidence of the success of Roxbury Prep or other charter schools? Their arguments ignore the realities of contemporary American society in which (1) simplistic multiple choice tests have been replaced by many states (certainly in Massachusetts) with rigorous assessments that require students to demonstrate what they know in multiple ways; (2) as Sizemore (1985) argues, if only a few schools are able to equip low-income African American students with the basic skills to pass such tests, then we should at least seek to understand what those schools are doing; and (3) most importantly, success on standardized tests is a prerequisite for everything from high school graduation to acceptance to medical school and admission to the bar. Although there is no doubt that *Brown v. Board of Education* was a case about racial desegregation, it was also a case about affording students of color access to genuinely equal opportunity. Today, it would be hard to find a better equalizer of opportunity than a rigorous college prep secondary school education, access to the spoken and written language of power, a 1500 on the SATs, and a scholarship to a four-year college.

As Jencks and Phillips (1998) contend, "[I]f racial equality is America's goal, reducing the black-white test score gap would probably do more to promote this goal than any other strategy that commands broad political support. Reducing the test score gap is probably both necessary and sufficient for substantially reducing racial inequality in educational attainment and earnings. Changes in education and earnings would in turn help reduce racial differences in crime, health, and family structure. . . ." (p .3). If a more just society can be achieved through effective schooling, then understanding schools that work, specifically urban charter schools that are succeeding in bridging the achievement gap, is not only important, it is morally urgent.

References

American Federation of Teachers. (2002). *Do charter schools measure up? The charter school experiment after 10 years: The AFT charter school study.* Washington, DC: Author.

Brookover, W. B., Beady, C., Flood, P., Scweitzer, J., & Wisenbaker, J. (1979). *School social systems and student achievement: Schools can make a difference.* New York: Praeger.

Bryk, A. S., & Schneider, B. (2002). *Trust in schools: A core resource for improvement.* New York: Russell Sage Foundation.

Center for Education Reform. Charter schools. Retrieved February 5, 2004 from http://www.edreform.com

Coleman, J. S., Campbell, E. Q., Hobson, C. J., McPartland, J., Mead, A. M., Weinfeld, F. D., & York, R. L. (1966). *Equality of educational opportunity.* Washington, DC: U.S. Department of Health, Education, and Welfare.

Coleman, J., Hoffer, T., & Kilgore, S. (1981). *Public and private schools* (National Center for Education Statistics Report No. 300-78-0208). Washington, DC: National Center for Education Statistics.

Collins, J. (2001). *Good to great: Why some companies make the leap and others don't.* New York: Harper Business.

Darling-Hammond, L. (1997). *The right to learn: A blueprint for creating schools that work.* San Francisco: Jossey-Bass.

Darling-Hammond, L., & Falk, B. (1997). Using standards and assessments to support student learning. *Phi Delta Kappan, 79*(3), 190–199.

Deal, T. E., & Kennedy, A. A. (1983). Culture and school performance. *Educational Leadership, 40,* 14–15.

Delpit, L. (1988). The silenced dialogue: Power and pedagogy in educating other people's children. *Harvard Educational Review, 56*(4), 280–298.

Dreeben, R., & Gamoran, A. (1986). Race, instruction, and learning. *American Sociological Review, 51,* 660–669.

Edmonds, R. (1979). Effective schools for the urban poor. *Educational Leadership, 37,* 15–18, 20–24.

Edmonds, R. (1986). Characteristics of effective schools. In U. Neisser (Ed.), *The school achievement of minority children: New perspectives* (pp. 93–104). Hillsdale, NJ: Lawrence Erlbaum Associates.

Elmore, R. F. (1995). Teaching, learning, and school organization: Principles of practice and the regularities of schooling. *Educational Administration Quarterly, 31*(3), 355–374.

Elmore, R. F. (2002). Hard questions about practice. *Educational Leadership, 59*(8), 22–25.

Ferguson, R. F. (1998). Teachers' perceptions and expectations and the Black-White test score gap. In C. Jencks & M. Phillips (Eds.), *The Black-White test score gap* (pp. 273–317). Washington, DC: Brookings Institution Press.

Finn, C. E., Jr., Manno, B. V., & Vanourek, G. (2000). *Charter schools in action: Renewing public education.* Princeton, NJ: Princeton University Press.

Finn, J.D., & Achilles, C.M. (1999). Tennessee's class size study: Finding, implications, misconceptions. *Educational Evaluation and Policy Analysis, 21*(2), 97-109.

Fullan, M. (2002). The change leader. *Educational Leadership, 59*(8), 16-20.

Fuller, B. (Ed.). (2000). *Inside charter schools: The paradox of radical decentralization.* Cambridge: Harvard University Press.

Gill, B.P., Timpane, P.M., Ross, K.E., & Brewer, D.J. (2001). *Rhetoric versus reality: What we know and what we need to know about vouchers and charter schools.* Santa Monica, CA: RAND Corporation.

Good, T. L., & Braden, J. S. (2000). Charter schools: Another reform failure or a worthwhile investment? *Phi Delta Kappan, 81*(10), 745-750.

Goodnough, A. (2002, October 17). Chancellor speaks up for charter schools. *New York Times,* p. B3.

Haycock, K. (2001). New frontiers for a new century: A national overview. *Thinking K-16, 5*(2), 1-2.

Heath, S. B., & McLaughlin, M. W. (1994). The best of both worlds: Connecting schools and community youth organizations for all-day, all-year learning. *Educational Administration Quarterly, 30*(3), 278-300.

Hill, P. T., Foster, G. E., & Gendler, T. (1990). *High schools with character.* Santa Monica, CA: RAND Corporation.

Jencks, C., & Phillips, M. (1998). The Black-White test score gap: An introduction. In C. Jencks & M. Phillips (Eds.), *The Black-White test score gap* (pp. 1-51). Washington, DC: Brookings Institution Press.

Jencks, C., Smith, M., Bane, M.J., Cohen, D., Gintis, H., Heyns, B., & Michelson, S. (1972). *Inequality: A reassessment of the effect of family and schooling in America.* New York: Basic Books.

Miles, K. H. (2001). Putting money where it matters. *Educational Leadership, 59*(1), 53-57.

Miron, G., & Nelson, C. (2001). *Student academic achievement in charter schools: What we know and why we know so little.* New York: National Center for the Study of Privatization in Education, Teachers College, Columbia University.

Nathan, J. (1999). *Charter schools: Creating hope and opportunity for American education.* San Francisco: Jossey-Bass Publishers.

Newmann, F. M., Smith, B., Allensworth, E., & Bryk, A.S. (2001). Instructional program coherence: What it is and why it should guide school improvement policy. *Educational Evaluation and Policy Analysis, 23*(4), 297-321.

Ogbu, J. U., & Simons, H. D. (1998). Voluntary and involuntary minorities: A cultural-ecological theory of school performance with some implications for education. *Anthropology & Education Quarterly, 29*(2), 155-188.

Phi Delta Kappan. (1980). *Why do some urban schools succeed? The Phi Delta Kappan study of exceptional urban elementary schools.* Bloomington, IN: Author.

Price, H. (1999, December 8). Urban education: A radical plan. *Education Week*, *19*, 29, 44.

Purkey, S. C., & Smith, M. S. (1983). Effective schools: A review. *The Elementary School Journal, 83*(4), 427–452.

Reid, K. S. (2001, December 5). Minority parents quietly embrace school choice. *Education Week, 21*, 1, 20–21.

Richards, C. (1991). The meaning and measure of school effectiveness. In J. Bliss, W. Firestone, & C. Richards (Eds.), *Rethinking effective schools: Research and practice* (pp. 28–42). New Jersey: Prentice-Hall.

Rosenholtz, S. J. (1985). Effective schools: interpreting the evidence. *American Journal of Education, 93*(3), 352–388.

Rutter, M., Maughan, B., Mortimore, P., Ouston, J., & Smith, A. (1979). *Fifteen thousand hours: Secondary schools and their effects on children.* Cambridge: Harvard University Press.

Sarason, S. S. (1998). *Charter schools: another flawed educational reform?* New York: Teachers College Press.

Sebring, P. B., & Bryk, A. S. (2000). School leadership and the bottom line in Chicago. *Phi Delta Kappan, 81*(6), 440–443.

Shepard, L. A. (2000). The role of assessment in a learning culture. *Educational Researcher, 29*(7), 4–14.

Sizemore, B. (1985). Pitfalls and promises of effective schools research. *Journal of Negro Education, 54*(3), 269–288.

SRI International. (1997). *Evaluation of charter school effectiveness: Part I.* Retrieved April 27, 2002, from http://www.lao.ca.gov/sri_charter_schools_1297-part1.html

Steele, C. M. (1992, April). Race and the schooling of Black Americans. *The Atlantic Monthly*, 68–78.

Steele, C. M., & Aronson, J. (1998). Stereotype threat and the test performance of academically successful African Americans. In C. Jencks & M. Phillips (Eds.), *The Black-White test score gap* (pp. 401–427). Washington, DC: Brookings Institution Press.

Szaniszlo, M. (2002, August 15). Payzant says public schools must compete with charters. *Boston Herald*, p. 15.

UCLA Charter School Study. (1998). *Beyond the rhetoric of charter school reform: A study of ten California school districts.* Los Angeles: Author.

Viadero, D. (2001, November 21). Scholars turn to evaluating charter schools from the inside. *Education Week, 21*, 6.

Weber, G. (1971). *Inner-city children can be taught to read: Four successful schools.* Washington, DC: Council for Basic Education.

CHAPTER 3

Back to the Future:
Ethnocentric Charter Schools in Hawai'i

NINA K. BUCHANAN AND ROBERT A. FOX

One social issue that has the potential to have an impact on the viability of charter schools is the possibility of restratifying, resegregating and further balkanizing an already ethnically and socioeconomically divided population (Bolick, 1997; Cobb and Glass, 1999; Crockett, 1999; Education Commission of the States, 1999; Shokraii, 1996; Wells, 2000c; Wells, Lopez, Scott, & Holme, 1999). In this chapter, we define ethnocentric schools, discuss historical factors that have contributed to the creation of ethnocentric charter schools in Hawai'i, compare three ethnocentric Native Hawaiian charter schools with traditional public schools in the same geographic area, and suggest implications that the reemergence of ethnically separate education might have for Hawai'i charter schools and the charter school movement in general.

Considering the extent to which they avow common goals, the Native Hawaiian charter schools included in this study display dramatic dissimilarities. To be sure, they are alike in their use of Hawaiian values as a fundamental philosophical and operational core. The curricula are heavily laden with local history, a treasured Hawaiian emphasis on experientially and observationally based learning, and the inclusion of Hawaiian phrases and words wherever possible. But the curricular emphasis and pedagogy are different enough so that one must look carefully to identify common features. Characteristic of charter schools nationally, their physical plants reflect different compromises that they have had to make to exist at all.

77

Despite their differences, similarities between the schools can be seen upon careful examination. With only one or two years of operation, these schools have not yet demonstrated higher academic achievement (based on Western criteria, to be sure) than the neighboring traditional schools. Nevertheless, consistent with charter school research nationally, parents, students, and teachers who have selected these schools all express such intense satisfaction with and enthusiasm for the ethnocentric emphasis that this move back to educational separatism cannot be ignored.

Ethnocentric Schools

In the past, the common public schools focused on building democracy, assimilating ethnic minorities into a homogenized, uniquely American culture, preparing a literate, disciplined pool of workers, and teaching people from different backgrounds to live together peacefully (Hlebowitsh and Tellez, 1997; Tyack, 1974; Wells, 2000a). From the civil rights movement in the 1960s until the 1980s, a federal policy of desegregation gradually led to increased school integration. Today, however, the diversity that has characterized American society at least since the Civil War has, for some, increasingly become a strength to be celebrated rather than a blemish to be removed. Instead of accepting a policy of assimilation, local community groups have begun advocating the distinctiveness of their own cultures and the contributions they can make to a pluralistic American culture. Together, each group adds character to the "salad bowl," not "melting pot" of America (Ravitch, 1990). The charter school movement has become one channel whereby an increasingly diverse public school population can translate demography into curriculum.

Current ethnocentric schooling in the United States has roots in the Black Power movement of the 1960s as a reaction to a Eurocentric common school that reflected a value system based on Judeo-Christian teaching (Cervantes, 1984). Impetus came from the Council of Independent Black Institutions (CIBI) that began establishing Afrocentric schools in the 1970s (Harris, 1992; Lomotey, 1992) to teach "children from the standpoint of their centeredness rather than their marginality" (Asante, 2002, n.p.). The curriculum was designed to help African American students see the world with Africa as the center and emphasize three essential areas: family-style communities of African American students, parents and teachers; traditional African values; and "Revolutionary Pan-African Nationalism" (Lomotey, 1992, p. 458).

These Afrocentric schools were designed to overcome inequalities in educational opportunity and discrimination that have resulted in lower levels of academic achievement, higher absenteeism and dropout rates, and overrepresentation in special education and remedial programs (Cervantes, 1984; Harris 1992; Lomotey, 1992). African American students lost their "sense of identity, purpose, or direction" and were unable to see the relevance of in-school learning to out-of-school life (Lomotey, 1992, p. 457). Ethnocentric schools were based on the assumption that culturally relevant education would improve self-esteem and then improve academic performance (Harris 1992; Lomotey, 1992). While African Americans may have been the first group to respond by creating ethnocentric schools, Native Americans and Native Hawaiians consistently experienced low levels of academic achievement and high dropout rates and also began to call for more relevant culturally based schools (Coleman, 1996; Reyhner, 1992). Magnet schools became another vehicle for parents, frustrated by resistance of neighborhood schools to change, to choose schools based in more culturally relevant, ethnocentric education (Coffey, 2002).

In general, ethnocentric schools emphasize change in one or more of these areas: social environment, values, content, pedagogy, and language. The social environment that characterizes ethnocentric schools (charter or otherwise) embraces cultural traditions and adopts interpersonal relationship styles designed to improve student self-esteem and promote cultural identity. For example, students from the Columbus Afrocentric School, as in many other Afrocentric schools and schools affiliated with CIBI, strive to adhere to principles of "unity (Umoja), self-determination (Kujichagulia), collective works (Ujima), cooperative economics (Ujamaa), purpose (Nia), creativity (Kuumba), and faith (Imani)" (Coffey, 2002, p. 3). In Hawai'i ethnocentric charter schools, students and their *kumu* (teachers) employ daily opening ceremonies which incorporate Hawaiian traditions such as reciting an *Oli* or chant asking permission to enter the school in the morning and awaiting the acceptance reply that allows them to enter.

Ethnocentric schools may also change the content emphasis to reflect the contributions of their ethnic group. For Afrocentric schools that has meant teaching African history and relying on texts written about or by Black writers. For Native Americans, it has meant viewing history from an indigenous people's perspective. For Hawaiian schools, it has meant viewing America from a Hawaiian Island perspective. Teaching the "Hawaiian experience" must include reference to the armed intervention of the U.S. military which resulted in the assimilation of the Hawaiian monarchy as America's fiftieth state.

Ethnocentric schools may also adopt different pedagogies and teaching styles that they believe better match cultural teaching and learning. For example, the Native American schools may adopt a collectivistic, rather than individualistic, pedagogy that features collaboration and cooperative learning (Capozza, 1999; Reyhner, 1992). One of the most cherished characteristics of Hawai'an pedagogy is the emphasis on hands-on experience and observation over deductive reasoning. Thus, we find that science and mathematics in Hawaiian ethnocentric charter schools are almost universally project based.

In addition to these changes, ethnocentric schools may incorporate native languages. Some start from English instruction and incorporate native words. Others may immerse students in their native language and assume that these students will practice English outside of school. We refer here to schools in which all or a major part of instruction is conducted in a language other than English as immersion schools. This issue of language has become one of the central tenets of contemporary Hawaiian education. One reason is the realization that unless a concerted effort is undertaken, Hawaiian, a language with an exclusively oral tradition, is in danger of dying out. As a recognition of this, the 1978 Hawai'i Constitutional Convention declared Hawai'an to be one of the two official languages of the State of Hawai'i and specifically mandated its preservation and teaching.

In this chapter, we define ethnocentric charter schools as charter schools whose mission is the promotion and study of one ethnic group as a means of providing students with a link to their cultural heritage, sometimes including language. As a result of participation in such schools, students may feel increased pride and confidence in their membership in the group. Ethnocentric schools employ teaching strategies that are believed by their proponents to be congruent with the learning styles and preferred ways of processing and acting on information that reflect the cultural heritage of their target population. The stated goal of such schools is to use these as vehicles for generating improved performance from students underserved by traditional schools.

The definition of "native Hawaiian" varies depending upon the organization proffering the definition. For example, as a criterion for service eligibility, both the Kamehameha Schools (a multi-billion-dollar private academy funded by the estate of Bernice Pauahi Bishop for the "education of the children of Hawai'i") and the Office of Hawaiian Affairs (established by the State of Hawai'i to manage funds held in trust for native Hawaiians) define as native Hawaiian any person who can prove Hawaiian ancestry, while the Department of Hawaiian Homes (another agency which assists citizens of Hawaiian ancestry to take up residency on lands that were originally held by the Hawaiian monarchy) requires that a person have 50% blood quantum to be considered native Hawaiian. Throughout this chapter, we use "native Hawaiian" and "part Hawaiian" to encompass any person of Hawaiian ancestry.

Ethnocentric Schools and the National Charter School Movement

National and state charter school reports provide data about the racial and ethnic and "at-risk" distribution of students in state or chartering districts (Center of Urban and Public Affairs, 2000; Nelson et al., 2000; Public Sector Consultants Inc., 2001; UCLA Charter School Study, 1998). So, for example, a Michigan study reports that "the percentage of minorities in the study-area charter schools is higher than in both the state as a whole and the traditional public school districts in which the charter schools are located" (Public Sector Consultants Inc., 2001, n.p.). However, Crocket (1999), in her study of California charter schools, found that charter schools were 63% Whiter than their sponsoring districts. Other researchers note that aggregate data reported in such national and state studies may actually mask ethnic stratification (Berv, 1998; Cobb, Glass, & Crockett, 2000; Fusarelli, 2000). These reports focus on the issue of White flight and skimming the brightest students into elite schools (Wells, 2000a; 2000b; 2000c). However, they fail to explore the impetus for and dynamics demonstrated in the purposeful creation of ethnocentric schools of choice for indigenous students, students of color, and minority populations.

Some reports have asserted that racial distribution may not be an appropriate criterion for judging the success of choice programs (Schellenberg, Osorio, & Porter, 2002). Instead of focusing on desegregation, the focus should more appropriately be on student achievement (Noblit and Corbett, 2001; Schellenberg, Osorio, & Porter, 2002). Short-term achievement results have been mixed (Gill, Timpane, Ross, & Brewer, 2001). A recent North Carolina evaluation comparing charter schools to traditional schools found that students in traditional schools outperformed students in charter schools on End of Grade tests. Further, the gap between White and Black students in mathematics was greater for students attending charter schools (Noblet and Corbett, 2001). The history of the charter school movement, however, is too short to permit confidence in any conclusions about their rel-

ative efficacy. What is clear is that the emergence of the charter school movement has provided a vehicle whereby groups who wish to provide an ethnically separate educational experience can obtain public funds in order to do
so. What had begun as an unquestioned assumption by communities of
color that "separate is unequal" may have evolved into the belief that only
through schools that emphasize difference can true equity emerge.

Native Hawaiian Education and Charter Schools

Before Captain Cook arrived in Hawai'i in 1778, education in Hawaiian society has been described as "practical, skill-oriented, socially-useful, in tune
with reality, environmentally aware, conserver-cognizant" (Kelly, 1982, p.
13). Children of commoners after the age of seven (also referred to as the
age of responsibility) were apprenticed to an expert either within or outside
the family. However, children of *ali'i* (chiefs) and *kahuna* (priests) were
trained for specialized roles in society from early childhood. Education emphasis was on learning socially acceptable roles commensurate with status
in the community.

With the arrival of missionaries, schools for Native Hawaiians pro-
ceeded through three distinct periods of development designed to "supplement and implement the efforts of organized religious work to raise the
Hawaiians from their alleged savagery and degradation and to help them
pattern themselves as a people after their western teachers" (Stueber,
1982, p. 16). In phase one, from 1820 to 1830, the missionaries organized
a system of native schools taught by missionary-trained native teachers primarily to adults. The curriculum consisted of religious materials translated
into Hawaiian. In 1831 there were fifty thousand adults in over one thousand schools. From 1830 to 1840, instruction shifted from a focus on
adults to children. Approximately 90% of adult Hawaiians had achieved
basic literacy (Kape'ahiokalani, Benham, & Heck, 1998). Children attended either the common schools taught by native teachers or select
schools taught for the upper class by missionaries. Both types of schools
conducted lessons in the Hawaiian language. The curriculum was designed to teach Calvinistic values of industry and delayed gratification and
to help the natives accept the authority of Western thought and become re-
generated. According to Stueber (1982), in 1836, "the missionaries
prophetically argued that unless the Hawaiian became competent in meeting and competing with the *haole* [White] on *haole* grounds they would, in
time become exiles in their own land" (p. 21).

During the third period of the development of schools in Hawai'i, the government became sponsors. The missionary budgets were being cut because of the American depression of 1837, and Catholic influence was on the rise. Protestants wanted to safeguard normal schools against Catholic control and Hawai'i's political leaders were anxious to acculturate Native Hawaiians to Western values and language in order for the newly written Hawaiian Kingdom Constitution to succeed (Kape'ahiokalani, Benham, & Heck, 1998). The shift from missionary-controlled to government-controlled schools signaled the beginning of a transition from instruction in the Hawaiian language to the language of business, commerce, and politics: English (Kape'ahiokalani, Benham, & Heck, 1998; Stueber, 1982). Initially, students attended either common schools or English standard schools that resulted in de facto segregation by language. Kape'ahiokalani, Benham, and Heck (1998) present convincing evidence that this switch from the use of Hawaiian to English as the medium for instruction resulted in a decrease in achievement of Native Hawaiian students and a downward spiral that eventually made Native Hawaiian students the lowest achieving ethnic group in Hawai'i.

Outside language and cultural groups were brought to Hawai'i by the White oligarchy in order to work on plantations. The Chinese arrived in 1851, followed by the Japanese in 1886. Both created schools to assure that children learned their home language and culture. By 1919, there were approximately 160 Japanese language schools (JLSs) (Stueber, 1982). Japanese children attended public school during the day and Japanese school after school and at other times when their parents worked in the fields. According to Hanaoka (1927), these schools were to improve communication between the children and their parents and also prepare them to return home to Japan. Beginning in 1919, public attitude toward JLSs became increasingly negative and hostile until legislation was passed to bring these schools under the supervision of the Department of Public Instruction. Although Act 30 was declared unconstitutional by the Hawai'i State Supreme Court in 1925, many JLSs had closed and would not be revived (Dotts and Sikkema, 1994).

During the interregnum between the fall of the Hawaiian monarchy and the achievement of statehood, education in Hawai'i, like virtually every facet of society, was aimed at the preservation of the oligarchy. The Hawaiian language was marginalized and eventually forbidden as a medium of instruction (Buchanan, 1998). Education for most groups reflected the fact that most children could look forward to a life in the fields or in service. The so-called English Standard Schools were available for families which, while unable to gain admission to the exclusive, mostly church-run, private schools, might aspire to higher achievement.

With statehood in 1950, little changed.

Hawai'i is the only single-district state in the United States. An elected board of education (BOE) appoints the superintendent of schools, serves as a policy-making governing body, and establishes priorities for the allocation of state funds subject to the political realities within which it must operate. In 1994, pressure from school reform advocates resulted in legislation that allowed for twenty-five existing schools to convert to student-centered schools, specifically avoiding the term *charter school*. Student-centered schools were given some budgetary control and the opportunity to request waivers of some rules and regulations from the Department of Education (DOE). Only two schools out of 253 chose to convert.

Legislation enabling twenty-five New Century Public Charter Schools, including start-ups, school-within-school programs, and whole-school conversions, was passed in April of 1999. By September of 1999, over thirty groups had submitted letters of intent to become charter schools. The new law clearly attracted two distinct populations whose needs were not being met by the current system. The first group consisted of native Hawaiian communities (50% of the letters of intent from throughout the state). The second overlapping group consisted of programs and groups from the neighbor islands (60%). In Hawai'i the central administration of the DOE and most other government agencies are located on the island of Oahu, geographically small but with the largest population. The other inhabited islands are often referred to as the "neighbor islands." The reasons for starting charter schools in Hawai'i appear to be autonomy from a distant center of control and the desire to serve a neglected special population of native Hawaiian and part Hawaiian children.

Although some form of state governing board for education exists in all fifty states, the District of Columbia and Puerto Rico, the state of Hawai'i is the only single statewide school district led by a single state superintendent responsible for all public K–12 education accountable to a single board of education. This reflects the history of the state that, until as recently as 1955, was controlled by an elite, primarily White oligarchy of plantation owners. The vast majority of citizens were descended either from displaced native Hawaiians or from populations imported from Japan, China, Korea, Portugal, and other countries to work in the fields (Langlas, 1998).

Both the organization and the philosophy of the Hawai'i State Department of Education has tended to reflect its heritage, with highly centralized decision making, dependence on rules, regulations, and rubrics, and the pervasive view that the central administration knows best (Dotts and Sikkema, 1994). The Department of Education oversees 253 schools, 180,000 students and 16,000 employees (Office of the Superintendent, 2001b). This is complicated by recent dramatic increases in the number of at-risk students. Since the 1990–91 school year the total school enrollment has grown by 8.3% while the number of students who receive free or reduced lunches has grown by 66%; those who are identified as in need of special education services by 97%; and those with limited English proficiency by over 70%. Only 49.4% of the school population is considered not disadvantaged (Office of the Superintendent/Planning, Budget, and Resource Development Office, 2001b). This comes at a time when Hawai'i leads the nation in unemployment and 31% of Hawai'i's children live in families where no parent has full-time, year-round employment (PRB/KIDS COUNT, 2002). Hawai'i has also been cited as having one of the largest average school sizes in the nation and the lowest annual increase in spending for education of comparable states (Office of the Superintendent, 2001). It is not surprising that this has resulted in a school system that is given a grade of C or less by 73.9% of the people in the Hawai'i Opinion Poll on Public Education 2001 (Office of the Superintendent, 2001a).

Adding to the stresses placed on Hawai'i's school system has been a growing realization on the part of indigenous Hawaiians that society in general and the school system in particular were neither meeting their needs nor sensitive to their culture (Buchanan, 1998). Native Hawaiians make up 0.8% and part Hawaiians 17.5% of the population of Hawai'i (Schmitt, 1998). A variety of structures unique to the state of Hawai'i originated with the forcible overthrow of Hawaiian Queen Liliuokalani. Hawaiian as a medium of instruction in the public schools was banned in 1896. Beginning in the late 1960s a cultural renaissance began that resulted in the revival of dance, music, cultural practice, and language. In 1978 the Hawai'i Constitutional Convention declared Hawaiian to be one of the two official languages of the state and mandated the provision of educational programs in Hawaiian language and culture. By 1984, a determined group of Hawaiian speakers successfully launched the first Punana Leo and Kaiapuni Hawai'i program that created preschool language immersion programs (Kapono, 1998). Legislation in 1986 expanded the immersion program from kindergarten through grade 12 with the result that immersion programs became, for the first time, a responsibility for the already overburdened public education system.

Like many social movements, the demand for educational reform initiated by the National Commission on Excellence in Education's 1983 report, "A Nation at Risk," reached Hawai'i (in the middle of the Pacific, 2500 miles from its nearest neighbor) considerably later than on the mainland. Indeed, it was not until 1989 that the Hawai'i legislature directed Hawai'i's Department of Education to design a School Community Based Management (SCBM) approach to incorporating parents, community leaders, and teachers into educational decision making. The SCBM program, though relatively short lived in Hawai'i, was notable primarily for two features: the extreme limitations placed on genuine efforts at reform by the central administration and the incorporation of traditional Hawaiian values such as *lokahi* (harmony), *kokua* (helpfulness), and *laulima* (cooperativeness) by local groups seeking reform. The community-based decision making that was allowed required consensus and emphasized avoidance of embarrassment over substance (Hawai'i State Department of Education, 2002).

In 1995, the legislature, recognizing that the Board of Education was unable or unwilling to bring about genuine school reform, passed legislation empowering local groups (under strict limitations) to form "Student Centered Schools" which, while public in most ways, were allowed limited local autonomy under a local school advisory board. These were to become the precursors of the charter school movement in Hawai'i. Typical of Hawai'i, the two conversion schools which were established under this legislation were located in two of the most economically elite areas in the state. The population of students at these two schools identified as indigenous Hawaiians or part Hawaiian are only 20% and 13% respectively while the largest ethnic populations at these schools are 59% White and 42% Japanese (Hawai'i State Department of Education Planning, Budget, and Resource Development Office, 2001). Although nominally locally controlled, these schools operated with virtually the same faculty and school-level administration, followed almost all Department of Education curricular, financial, and personnel procedures, remained in the buildings which they had previously occupied, and, for many, were distinguishable from traditional public schools in only the most superficial ways.

In 1999, when the legislature, abandoning even more its efforts to bring about change within the recalcitrant state educational system, passed Hawai'i's first real charter school empowering legislation, the two Student Centered Schools became Hawai'i's first "New Century Charter Schools." Soon, with the encouragement of the Federal Charter School Program, more than thirty groups prepared to compete for the remaining twenty-three charters permitted under the law. The schools discussed in this chapter emerged as various planning groups developed Detailed Implementation Plans (DIPs) in pursuit of the much-sought-after charters and, thereby, some freedom from the central Department of Education.

Sixty percent of the founder groups were located on islands distant from the state capital (Honolulu) located on the island of Oahu. And, even more striking, 50% identified themselves as being ethnically Hawaiian. For some, this meant a focus on the language and, indeed, five charter schools, referred to in Hawai'i as "immersion" schools, are currently conducted all or in part in Hawaiian. For others, the focus was on Hawaiian culture as a nurturing environment (absent, the argument went, in traditional public schools) within which disadvantaged students of Hawaiian ancestry were more likely to learn. Still a third group sought to apply Hawaiian epistemology as a means of conveying both traditional and Hawaiian subject matter.

What began as a law to empower the creation of a limited number of charter schools became a strong force for ethnocentric education in the state. This chapter examines three Hawaiian ethnocentric charter schools on the island of Hawai'i, referred to universally as the "Big Island" to distinguish its name from that of the state. However different these schools may be from one another, they share common features which sharply distinguish them from the traditional system from which they have come. Hawaiian ethnocentric charter schools generate impressive levels of "customer satisfaction" in their parents, students, and staff. As an unanticipated by-product, the evident enthusiasm for the Hawaiian charter school movement appears to have brought out the worst from the administrators of the public school system from which they fled. No discussion of Hawai'i charter schools would be complete without mention of the history of broken promises, charges and countercharges, and litigation that define the relationship between Hawai'i charter schools and their sole chartering agency. This relationship has become so bad that at its last session the state legislature found it necessary to pass legislation specifically forbidding charter schools to sue the state.

Methodology

In this section, we discuss the selection of the charter and comparison schools in this study. Then we explain the sources of data and collection procedures used. This extension of a previous study (Buchanan and Fox, 2002) utilized lessons learned and provided additional data upon which to base conclusions.

Selection

We selected three self-defined ethnocentric charter schools operating on the Big Island. Although all three share certain common characteristics, they permitted us to examine three unique, culturally based approaches to education. We have used pseudonyms to indicate these schools and their traditional counterparts. In addition, we observed classes and interviewed the principal of the traditional K–6 school that shares facilities with Makai Charter School. Because one of us (Buchanan) has been engaged in designing innovative secondary school programs and spent a great deal of time on traditional secondary campuses, we did not select comparison schools for the K–12 or 7–12 charter schools described below.

The first selected school was a total immersion Hawaiian language charter school situated on the campus of an existing traditional Department of Education school that conducts its classes in English. While the charter school classes are conducted in the Hawaiian language, its curriculum and structure reflect traditional knowledge and skills. Having previously operated as a school-within-a-school on the same campus, it might appropriately be considered a conversion charter school in many ways. This school, called Makai Charter School (MCS) for this report, is located in a community with an extremely high percentage of native Hawaiian residents.

The second, located some sixty miles from MCS, came into existence as Koa Public Charter (KCS) school by combining three components: a 9th–12th grade school-within-a-school sited on a local traditional high school campus, a preexisting private primary (preschool–4th grade) total immersion Hawaiian language school and a newly created 5th–8th grade middle school. Classes are conducted in English, although the Hawaiian language is heard frequently from both students and teachers. At the time of its formation as a public charter school, the school moved out of its previous site on a high school campus and might appropriately be seen as a start-up charter school. The ethos of the school reflects the founders' belief that traditional Western education has both failed native Hawaiian children and eroded traditional Hawaiian value systems.

The Hilo Charter School (HCS), a start-up charter school underwritten by an existing foundation dedicated to the preservation of Hawaiian culture and values, lies somewhere between the other two in its educational philosophy. Instruction is conducted in English, although the Hawaiian language may be heard everywhere throughout the school. While heavily devoted to the "Hawaiian way of life," HCS is less negative about the perceived failure of traditional Western education. Of the three schools, HCS draws most heavily on its connection to the local community and to the Hawaiian elders (*kupuna*) associated with its sponsoring foundation. It is located on a fourteen-acre site provided by the foundation and looks forward to significant construction of classrooms and instructional facilities.

Procedures

For this study, we gathered data from the precharter Detailed Implementation Plans (DIPs), postcharter documents and brochures describing the schools and their programs, observations of classrooms and school activities, and interviews with school directors and principals, staff, and students. Additionally, as cofounders of the University of Hawai'i Charter School Resource Center, we have extensively documented the development of charter schools in Hawai'i from their inception.

In Hawai'i, as a condition of being granted a charter by the state Board of Education, each potential founding group was required to submit a DIP setting forth the philosophy, curriculum, pedagogy, fiscal management, governance, and organization of the proposed charter school. We began by studying the DIP from each of the three schools, with particular focus on statements about ethnic identity, values, and the use of the Hawaiian language.

During a previous study (Buchanan and Fox, 2002), we had prepared a list of specific questions to use in formal interviews. We discovered, however, that the respondents were obviously very proud of what they had created and "wanted to talk about what they wanted to talk about," firmly but persistently resisting our efforts to refocus on the questions we wanted answered. The formal question and answer approach was not consistent with the Hawaiian tradition of "talk story" (Dotts and Sikkema, 1994). Upon reflection, we realized that Native Hawaiians rely on verbal rather than written history (Langlas, 1998) and concluded that the best course of action was to approach the interviews with more open-ended categories and let the interviewees lead us to an understanding of their perspective.

In addition to interacting closely with these schools in the pre–start-up period and reviewing the DIPs, we visited each school from two to four times to observe students and teachers in classrooms and at play and conduct formal and informal interviews of directors and principals, staff, students, and volunteers. The interview process was nonlinear. Each site had a predetermined visitation plan so we attempted to fit into the school's schedule. The schools were exceedingly generous in providing access, and the schedules we followed varied widely among schools. At one school, we visited every class accompanied by the director or principal. At another, we wandered freely from classroom to classroom and interviewed teachers, students, and other staff as opportunities arose.

School visits were specifically designed to discover, first, the way in which the schools manifested their "Hawaiianness" and second, the extent to which they differed from traditional schools in the same service area. We examined the extent to which various aspects of the school organization reflected its ethnocentric identity and differed from similar nonethnocentric schools. These aspects included:

1. Curriculum

2. Pedagogy

3. Parental and community involvement

4. Physical organization of the classrooms

5. Inculcation of values and attitudes

6. Student-student and student-staff interactions and affect

Case 1: Makai Charter School
(and its traditional school counterpart)

Finding the office of Makai Charter School (MCS) is a challenge. No signs distinguish it from the other classrooms and offices that house both a K–6 regular DOE school and Makai charter school. According to the most recent School Status and Improvement Report (2001), 24.2% of the students at the DOE school are Hawaiian and another 66.3% part Hawaiian for a total of 90.5%. Hawaiian/part Hawaiian student enrollment at Makai CS is above 94%. This can be compared to the two nearest DOE elementary schools, whose student bodies are 46% and 33% Hawaiian/part Hawaiian respectively.

The old wooden structures appear to need refurbishing, and the passage that leads to the MCS office passes a storage area of broken desks and other miscellaneous furniture. The office is a semiunderground area with painted pipes and exposed wiring running along the ceiling in an area which appears to have originally been under the building's support piers.

Coincidentally, this office is located almost exactly under the traditional school office located within the building proper. Despite the less than ideal physical surrounding, the principal, secretary, and clerk are productively engaged at their computers and phones preparing for the 8:15 AM to 2:15 PM school day to begin. They interrupt their normal routine and, joined by a young counselor, all enthusiastically greet us and answer questions about their school with pride. The office of MCS is a single, large, unpartitioned room reflecting what the principal describes as the Hawaiian way of working as an *ohana* (family or group).

Originally, MCS was a Hawaiian Language Immersion school-within-a-school (SWIS) established as a continuation of a Punana Leo language immersion preschool, part of the Native Hawaiian cultural renaissance. As a school-within-a-school, there was tension between the regular DOE and SWIS staff. Recently, with a new principal in the traditional school and a year of experience, cooperation between the two has replaced tension. Although not required, the traditional school shares parking spaces, the services of a school health aide, and playground facilities with MCS. Both principals are extremely positive about the relationship. Becoming a charter school meant new autonomy and self-determination for MCS. It empowered the staff to make more decisions about how and what to teach as well as how to schedule their time. This is the second year of operation as a charter school. The 149 students are grouped into seven classrooms (grades K/1, 1/2, 3/4, 4, 5, 5/6, and 6). The multiage groups are designed to accommodate the number of students, not for pedagogical or curricular reasons. MCS has adopted a trimester calendar and extended school day that facilitate language learning by replacing summer vacation with fall, winter, and summer intersessions with the longest a one-month summer intersession. This is also designed to counteract Hawai'i's short school year, the shortest of any state.

The MCS vision is "Inspired by our past. Empowered by our identity. Prepared for the future." Its mission is to be a "culturally-based indigenous K–6 Hawaiian Language Immersion school" that "promotes Hawaiian ways of knowing to strengthen and revitalize a Hawaiian identity" in "experiential-based Hawaiian learning environments" (DIP). The school's goals for students are the development of literacy and communication skills, personal and social responsibility, and thinking and reasoning skills. The Experiential-Based Activity Model (EBAM) designed to help students explore interdisciplinary problems and practical applications of knowledge and information (Moersch, 1994) is one of the main strategies employed at MCS. The Hawai'i Content and Performance Standards

II (HCPSII) that are mandated for use by all DOE schools guide the curriculum at MCS along with a commitment to Hawaiian language immersion, culture, and values. Since the Hawai'i Assessment Program has no tests translated into the Hawaiian language, the school is considering whether to begin formal English instruction earlier and thus become more fully bilingual. There is a tension between helping native Hawaiian students be successful in the modern world and preserving a native language unique to Hawai'i.

The sense of community and intergenerational continuity that is an essential part of the Hawaiian culture is evident at MCS. Indeed, the immersion school movement has, from its very beginning within the DOE, provided for mandatory parental involvement. This continues to be one of the most striking characteristics of Hawaiian ethnocentric charter schools.

There are many similarities in the physical environment between MCS and its traditional counterpart. The MCS classrooms contain typical elementary school decorations with colorful posters and student work evident on the walls, hanging from the ceiling and stored on shelves around the room. The use of these decorations is no different from those in the classrooms of the traditional school except that that they are all in Hawaiian. Certainly, there is no obvious difference in the student bodies of the two schools. They are dressed alike and their general physical appearance reflects the fact that most of them come from the same local culture. Likewise, one would learn nothing from the general appearance of the faculties of the two schools.

However, differences in the social environment and cultural values are manifest from the moment the school day begins. Before MCS students enter the school for the day, they gather outside and chant in Hawaiian, asking permission from their *kumu* (teachers) to enter the school. The faculty's chant gives them permission to enter and reminds them of their responsibilities to learn and behave. This daily Hawaiian protocol is followed by a Hawaiian song. The children seem particularly committed to this activity. There is a notable lack of fidgeting, horseplay between the children, even those hidden in the middle of the group, looking around, or failing to sing. The focus of the opening at MCS is the school. In contrast, at the traditional school, the beginning of the school day is a classroom-based activity. Students come directly to the assigned classroom where they are met by the teacher (not the faculty as a group) and where opening activities focus attention on their specific class.

In one MCS class a sixth grader stands at the front and spells one of the weekly words and then reads his sentence to the class. In the traditional classroom a student stands at his desk and reads a simile that he has constructed in response to the day's lesson. In an MCS classroom, the teacher reads a story in Hawaiian while in a traditional classroom, the teacher reads a story in English. At times in both classes students work independently on math worksheets.

Case 2: Koa Charter School

Upcountry Hawai'i offers lush landscape, almost constant wind, and alternating sun and clouds and rain. Koa Charter School (KCS) is off the main road unannounced by signs and situated on six acres of agricultural land lent to the school by the Department of Hawaiian Homelands and another four oceanfront acres used in collaboration with the YMCA about ten miles away. A third campus is being developed in a wooded area about four miles from the main campus. Under this arrangement, three different ecosystems provide natural classrooms for the school's focus on the importance of the land (*aina* in Hawaiian). The first site has a house that has been converted into offices—the nerve center of the school. Approaching the office one passes a large warehouse and two large and one small white-tarped quonset huts. The warehouse serves as a computer and technology lab, library, lunch distribution site, and instructional space. The two quonset huts are divided into two classrooms, each with bookshelf dividers between the rooms. The huts have cement floors and slanting sides that have wire strung to hold brightly colored student work. Whiteboards are set along the walls and bright Hawaiian cloth is suspended from poles that support the hut. One side is usually open but can be closed by fastening tarps at both sides.

The KCS vision is to become a comprehensive education and service center for Hawaiians of all ages. The school evolved from two antecedents: one a 9th–12th grade interdisciplinary academy school-within-a-school, and the other a Hawaiian Immersion preschool–4th grade school. These combined and included the intermediate grades to form a K–12 bilingual charter school. Its founders believe that indigenous peoples have the right to design and control their own education and further that Hawaiian people can be successful in the twenty-first century without giving up their culture, language, and traditions. The founders believe that Hawaiian culture has deteriorated because of Western philosophy, religion, and laws that advocate that people subdue the earth for profit and personal gain rather than exist as stewards of the land. Another impetus for the school was a desire to slow the out migration of Hawaiians and develop an economy that would allow Hawaiian graduates to remain in the islands. The KCS vision is "strive to reach your highest potential" (DIP). Students and staff at KCS are expected to love one another, take care of their responsibilities, give and receive help, and be thankful for what they have.

The KCS curriculum is a balance of culturally driven and standards-based strategies that emphasize reading, writing, and communication in both Hawaiian and English; the ability to apply math and science; the ability to access, evaluate, and use a variety of technologies; the ability to apply critical thinking and problem solving; the mastery of academics, culture, and workplace skill; and the development of work ethics necessary for economic self-sufficiency.

Originally, the plan was to have two multiaged groups of students with approximately 25 elementary, 25 middle and 25 high-school-aged students in each group. Groups were to remain together for a full year and work on theme-based interdisciplinary projects related to Hawai'i that had social significance for Hawaiians. Through the projects students would demonstrate essential competencies and performance standards, including technology and career explorations, and would contribute to sustaining healthy economy in the community. Each group would spend two days each week at a lab site—either the main campus, the forest or the dry-land ocean site. They would spend the other two days documenting their projects. On Fridays, students would participate in Student Development Workshops where they would explore careers, engage in community service, and work with mentors in the community on personal development such as health and fitness. Every Monday through Thursday students would: (1) use the Hawaiian language for opening and closing protocol; (2) have twenty minutes of Total Physical Response exercises that emphasized both the Hawaiian language and physical fitness; (3) do a problem of the week to ensure that students engage in problem solving and record their work in a journal; and (4) engage in sustained uninterrupted reading for pleasure.

However, when the school opened, the teachers found that it was difficult to meet the needs of K–12 students within a single group. They modified the grouping so one group consisted of K–5th grade and two others of 6th–12th grade students. In the morning, eight to ten students grouped by ability work with a teacher or aide to develop basic skills. Each student is pretested in reading, writing, and math and placed in a multiage group according to skill. In the afternoon, students engage in cross-age projects. This is an interesting example of the intrusion of educational reality on even the purest educational philosophy.

The school opening is very similar to that described for MSC. Students form lines (boys on one side and girls on the other) for each grade level, with the faculty facing them at the front. Although the medium of instruction at the KCS is English, the students chant to their *kumu* (instructors) in Hawaiian, reaffirming their commitment to the principles of the school and requesting permission to enter. This protocol is followed by the Hawai'i state anthem, sung in Hawaiian. The older children seem completely socialized to this activity and exhibited neither embarrassment nor inattention, although several of the youngest students had to be admonished to pay attention.

The curriculum is essentially divided into two parts: project-based learning conducted by multiage teams of students (K–5 or 6–12) and skills classes where students are divided into ability groupings. Skills classes (language arts, math, and science) are quite traditional. For example, the mathematics program is a highly structured, "back to the basics" curriculum with emphasis on computation. The reading program is also structured but includes both phonics and comprehension exercises. These are supplemented by more creative activities through their projects.

One formal English class we visited consisted of eight 2nd–6th graders who were all on about the same level studying English sight words, copying them on one page and using them in sentences on another page. Some students have come to KCS from language immersion programs and others from regular DOE schools, so varying skill levels in English and Hawaiian make instruction a challenge for KCS teachers. Children from the two classes in the hut gathered outside on the lawn before lunch to *pule* (pray), an important activity at any gathering of Native Hawaiians.

While the lessons themselves were conducted in English, both teachers and students sprinkled much of their communication with Hawaiian words. These were especially evident as teachers managed the class, frequently employing Hawaiian words such as *ma'ema'e* (cleanliness) or *lokahi* (harmony) or *laulima* (cooperativeness). When asked about this, teachers responded that even children who entered the school with little or no knowledge of Hawaiian readily learn the words from the context.

The learning projects depend heavily on group responsibility (a basic Hawaiian principle) and learning by seeing and doing (a basic Hawaiian epistemology). For instance, at the developing woodland campus, students physically laid out ropes and computed areas and volumes in anticipation of the pouring of cement foundations which would take place the following day. The point to be made is that the school doesn't talk about relevance; it demonstrates it.

Case 3: Hilo Charter School

Seventy students, five core teachers, and many volunteer community members conduct classes on an undeveloped fourteen-acre site and several subordinate sites, all located within about a mile of each other in a community with one of the highest populations of Hawaiians and, not coincidentally, one of the lowest economic levels in the state. Ironically, the location of the sites, some of which front directly on the Pacific Ocean, make the land on which the school sits some of the most valuable in the state. As with KCS, the location of these sites reflects the importance that Hawaiian place on the land (*aina*) and the ocean (*kai*) and their need to be close to both. As the beneficiary of its sponsoring foundation, Hilo Charter School will, in the future, enjoy facilities beyond the reach of many schools. For now, however, the site is largely undeveloped and classes are held in various structures ranging from a large undifferentiated room in a brand new community hall to an open air structure constructed of pipe frames and agricultural tarpaulins. Students play in an open field combining breathtaking beauty with a total lack of recreational facilities. The campus, as is the case at KCS and several other ethnocentric Hawaiian schools, is heavily planted with indigenous plants, most of which have economic, cultural, or spiritual significance to the Hawaiian people. Agriculture (and aquaculture), genealogy, and navigation/astronomy form the core of the educational experience at KCS and in Hawaiian culture, which places emphasis on the relationship of people to each other and to the land and the sea.

The school conducts classes for children from 7th through 12th grade. A preschool operated separately by the foundation occupies a site at the far end of the campus. A separate large room, similar to the office at MCS, with few partitions and no interior walls, serves as school office, staff workroom, lunchroom, meeting room, and so forth. Multiple activities are conducted in the single-room community hall. Four or five classes simultaneously meet in corners of the room. One portion of this large space is given over to fifteen new laptop computers on low, Japanese-style tables in heavy use by students. The contrast between the rustic nature of the site and the enviable array of technology is striking.

The relative quiet and calm demeanor of the students at the school, even during lunch and recess, was noteworthy. With few teachers in evidence and no intrusive adult supervision during recess free play, students seemed happy and self-directed. The end of recess was announced by the blowing of a conch shell (a traditional Hawaiian call) by one of the teachers. It was interesting to observe the relative ease with which the students finished their field games (most involving a dodge ball-type game) and returned without complaint to their lessons. Just as during the start-of-the-day protocols at the other two schools, students at HCS tend to know where to go without prompting and seem to exhibit an unvoiced respect for the fact that they are in a school in the presence of their teachers. Familiar boy-girl posturing often observed on 7th–12th grade campuses was not in evidence. In traditional local fashion, everyone removes their shoes at the door. Lessons are conducted (in English) with the students sitting on the floor. In some cases, the students were arrayed in semicircles around the teacher. In others, the classes were obviously more diffuse, with the students reclining at short-legged tables and the teacher moving from group to group.

Observers used to traditional classrooms might find the room unsettling. There are no chairs and few tables. There was not a blackboard in sight. No walls separated one class from the others. Surprisingly, however, the room was not chaotic. Noise level was at a minimum because there was very little off-task talking between the students in different groups. In fact, it was difficult to find a student whose face was not intently directed toward either the teacher (in those classes where teachers stood at the front) or at his or her work (in those classes where the teacher moved from group to group).

Lessons cover traditional topics. Ultimately state legislation requiring evidence of adherence to Hawai'i's Performance and Content Standards both motivates instruction and limits the extent to which innovation can occur. However, there was obviously a project-based flavor to the classes. One group, for instance, combined art, science, and language as it worked on landscape plans for the campus. Other groups study the Hawaiian approach to astronomy, their relationship to the land and the sea, ecology, and Hawaiian health.

The principal gave us a tour of the campus and then sat down for an extensive interview and discussion. "Hawaiianness" at this school manifests itself primarily in two ways: focus on Hawaiian-related, project-based instruction and respect for the Hawaiian environment and community with which the school closely relates. Subject matter selection is driven largely by the Hawai'i Content and Performance Standards and is, therefore, not that dissimilar from other, nonethnocentric schools.

"Regular" classes for students take place on both the main campus and two nearby sites, one for agricultural projects and the other for ocean-related activities. Teachers teach from Monday through Thursday and meet together on Fridays. On Fridays, the school imports local resource persons to provide an enriched elective environment with heavy emphasis on Hawaiiana (hula, fishing, canoeing).

Perhaps the most significant evidence of the ethnocentricity of the school, as reported by the director, is its situation within the local native Hawaiian community. Relations with parents and community leaders are very close, with parents and, importantly in the Hawaiian community, grandparents being seen as members of the holistic educational team. The importance of *kupuna* (Hawaiian elders) is infused throughout the school.

HCS is eligible for a variety of federal and private supplementary funds without which it would not survive. The school is also fortunate because its sponsor foundation has access to significant land (of the three schools studied, Hilo is the only one with its own campus for which it can make permanent plans) and sources of funding. This means that HCS can focus its energies on educational development, not finding and funding facilities.

Discussion

This chapter seeks to compare Hawaiian ethnocentric charter schools with their traditional counterparts. This is made difficult because of the plethora of features that distinguish any small school from any other. What characteristics truly distinguish Hawaiian ethnocentric charter schools from others?

It is easy to identify each of the schools described herein as charter schools by their clear legal relationship to the state chartering agency, the Hawai'i State Board of Education. Assigning the appellation *ethnocentric*, at least in Hawai'i, requires a closer inspection. Each school clearly declares itself a member of the Hawaiian ethnocentric school subset. In 2000, the leaders of one of the three schools founded Na lei Na'auau, an organization of identifiably Hawaiian ethnocentric charter schools that has grown to include twelve such schools in the state. Lacking objective criteria, the organization's membership is self-selected.

The DIPs of Hawai'i's ethnocentric schools all, in one way or another, decry the failure of the traditional school system to serve ethnic Hawaiian students, but the manner in which they propose to do better varies from school to school. Among several, the key is the preservation and resurgence of the Hawaiian language as a vehicle for the preservation and resurgence of the culture. This emphasis on language has been enriched by interaction with Ka Haku'Ula O Ke'elikolani, the College of Hawai'an Language at the University of Hawa'i at Hilo, which offers the only undergraduate degree in an indigenous language in the country. In addition to its educational programs, it houses an institute which translates primary and secondary texts into Hawaiian and provides a teacher certification program. A growing number of teachers in Hawai'i's ethnocentric charter schools are graduates of the college.

Among other members of Hawai'i's ethnocentric education community, it is through the resurgence of culture and cultural pride, rather than language, that Hawaiian children will rediscover their roots and, thereby, succeed in school and in twenty-first-century life. This group has had to struggle to find a way of preparing students to compete in a world of technology and globalism while devoting time to preserving a history and culture of which most of the world is largely unaware. Members of this group focus their attention on the history of Polynesia and the Hawaiian people. The curriculum includes Hawaiian ethnobotany, ethnogeology, Hawaiian religion, agriculture, and aquaculture. Hawaiian music and art form an important part of the schools' curriculum. Studying these subjects helps students to develop esteem for themselves and their culture.

Overlying this pedagogical spectrum is one of attitude. Each of the Hawaiian ethnocentric charter schools (as, indeed, all of Hawai'i's charter schools) reflects the philosophy of a set of founders. The impediments placed in the way of aspiring Hawaiian charter schools by the state mean that the groups which have succeeded are characterized by strong determination and strongly held views. Each of them is dissatisfied with what the traditional school system has provided for Hawaiian students. They share a determination to shake off the past and to fashion a better future for the children. Within each of these schools there is a mix of striving for a better future and repudiating an unfortunate past. Where each school places itself on this positive/negative spectrum is reflected both objectively and subjectively in the curriculum and the ethos.

Given the diversity of these ethnocentric charter schools, what conclusions can we draw? Just as Lomotey (1992) identified three essential elements of Afrocentric schools, we found that the "Hawaiian" feature common to all three was values. More than other characteristics such as use of the Hawaiian language, ethnic homogeneity of the faculties, and emphasis on ethnically traditional subject matter, we find Hawaiian values throughout the ethnocentric schools at a time when the state Department of Education eschews all mention of values in its quest for universality (and, it might be said, for insulation from litigation from groups objecting to one or another philosophy). For example, state DOE regulations require that before any teacher can introduce a topic that might be considered controversial, the teacher must send a note home to parents soliciting their individual approval. Parents who refuse such approval are entitled to insist that their children not be present when such material is discussed.

Hawaiian values manifested themselves both explicitly in the behavioral expectations which the school placed upon the students and parents and implicitly in the selection of subjects, the meaning attributed to the facts presented, and the emphasis on group responsibility and experiential learning.

Such expressions of belief are unthinkable in the public schools run by the Hawai'i Department of Education. The fear of litigation from individuals or groups objecting to the use of the schools to advocate individual points of view has resulted in a school system where values are the province of the home and school is the place for facts. In an effort to articulate the values of everyone, the public schools in Hawai'i have devolved into an organization that articulates the values of no one. Arguably, within the state, charter schools are the only public institutions allowed to stand for anything at all. Hawaiian ethnocentric charter schools stand for Hawaiian values. Some have argued that this return to educational separatism (championed by rather than forced upon those with minority views) is a case of "separate but better," rather than the discredited "separate but equal."

If values are the thread which distinguishes Hawaiian ethnocentric charter schools from the Department of Education, how, then, do they manifest themselves?

The word *values* appears in the DIPs of all three schools. These values appear in several ways. First, Hawaiians pride themselves on being intensely spiritual. A high percentage of ethnic Hawaiians practice traditional organized religions and many believe literally that the volcano and the sea are live gods deserving respect. Indeed, a significant portion of Hawai'i's population has no trouble in simultaneously adopting both belief systems. This spirituality is found in each of the three Hawaiian ethnocentric charter schools. *Pule* (prayer) begins every significant activity at each of the schools. Children are constantly reminded of their obligation to their elders and to the Hawaiians who have gone before them. They are made aware of the extent to which Hawaiian culture has been submerged beneath Western practices and of their obligation to "right the wrong." And, indeed, all three ethnocentric charter schools place significant obligations on the families which choose to send their children to such schools:

"We look to our *Kupuna* (community elders) to share valuable Hawaiian cultural practices and precious moments, artists and cultural experts to share their skills and knowledge and anyone else willing to pass on their knowledge and expertise to future generations" (Kua O Ka La Public Charter School brochure, 2002). "We envision this 'kauhale' (learning center) to be designed and constructed by the students, parents and community members and to be as self-sustaining as possible . . ." (Kanu O Ka Aina brochure, 2002).

Values also appear in the subject matter of the ethnocentric schools. Fundamental to the Hawaiian world view is a connection with the *aina* (in this context, nature). Indeed, traditionally, Hawaiians viewed nature as a living thing in symbiosis with man. Traditional Hawaiians lived *with* the land; they didn't own it. The Hawaiian concept of *apu'aha* speaks to the land providing whatever is needed for the people who live on it but rejects the concept of private ownership of the *aina*. In such a world, nature is very close to every person and such subjects as agriculture, oceanography, geography, and meteorology take on spiritual as well as factual meaning.

Within the curriculum of all Hawaiian ethnocentric charter schools can be found significant *aina*-related instructional modules. All feature fishing and agriculture as media within which to teach both Hawaiian values and Western facts. Biology becomes a study of indigenous Hawaiian plants, of recycling to protect the land, of fish and birds and farm animals. Physics becomes a study of wind patterns and the eruption of volcanos (within which the goddess Pele is said to live). History becomes a study of the way in which Hawai'i was settled by voyagers from Polynesia, established a tribal culture in the islands, was united into a single nation by Kamehameha I, and was eventually absorbed into the United States of America. Political Science becomes a study of the interaction between the Hawaiian peoples and the Western civilization of whom they (reluctantly, to some) became a part.

Finally, values are found in the pedagogy of Hawaiian ethnocentric charter schools. Current thinking (Meyer, 1998) is that Hawaiian learning is substantially more inductive than deductive. In fact, many argue that that public education's failure to serve Hawaiian children is based on the imposition of Western epistemology on the Hawaiian mind. Hawai'i's ethnocentric charter schools all contain major project-based components. In all the schools, students "get their hands dirty" planting crops, building structures, landscaping campuses, performing traditional Hawaiian music and dance, and decorating classrooms and campuses. Projects are communicated through language arts: reading, writing, listening, and performing. Math and science classes often are directed toward solving practical problems associated with the projects. Not only does such a pedagogy allow students to "touch" what they learn, but it encourages group activities and group responsibility, integral features of the Hawaiian mind-set.

One doesn't have to look far into the way things are done in state Department of Education schools to see how different they are. Indeed, parochial values (either articulated for their own sakes or integrated into the curriculum and pedagogy) are against the rules, lest they offend one or another subset of the educational community. There are a number of reasons for such a situation. One is certainly that years of budget cuts have resulted in a department that seeks to offend no one. Another is the growth of militant parent groups who demand that public schools avoid advocating any values out of fear of having their children exposed to views contrary to their own. The Department has adopted a "controversial issues" policy which requires that parental consent be obtained for a growing list of instructional topics. What has resulted is a generation of Hawai'i's children who have moved through the public school system with a virtual *aversion* to values.

For students from the ethnic mainstream such a situation is unfortunate. For students whose ethnic identity places them *outside* the mainstream, the result is doubly problematic. The lack of congruence between their school and their home when it comes to values tends to remove behavioral norms which they need in their development. And the failure of public schools to teach *any* values means that there is nothing to replace the void. What results puts children from Hawai'i's ethnic minority in a no-win situation: their own ethnic identity is ignored and there is nothing offered as an alternative. It is no surprise that alienated students and parents result, and that the attraction of ethnocentric schools is growing.

Not only is the Hawai'i Department of Education failing to meet the needs of children of color within the traditional public school setting, but it is using its authority to erode the progress made in ethnocentric charter schools. In response to the recent No Child Left Behind federal legislation, the Hawai'i state Department of Education has announced its intent to translate existing objective tests into Hawaiian to make sure that they can measure Hawaiian language schools against Western standards. The announcement included nothing about the cultural content within which the questions are created. One might have thought that they would have learned from the experience of Educational Testing Service.

We conclude with an observation about the statement that the history of charter schools in Hawai'i is too short to permit an objective evaluation of their effectiveness. It might well be that the information we seek is already here. Standardized performance tests can be expected to measure exactly those things from which these schools have fled, while providing no information about the effectiveness with which the schools have instilled the values which lie at their core.

References

Asante, M. K. (2002). Imperatives of an Afrocentric curriculum. From http://twist.lib.uiowa.edu/tenthree/afroc.htm (For additional information see http://www.asante.net/articles/index01.html).

Berv, J. (1998). Charter schools and the compromise of equity: An evaluation of Colorado's charter school legislation. (ERIC Document Reproduction Service No. ED 437 459).

Bolick, C. (1997). School choice, the law and the constitution: A primer for parents and reformers. The Heritage Foundation: Roe Backgrounder #1139. Retrieved from http://www.heritage.org/library/categories/education/bgl139.html.

Buchanan, N. K. (1998). Education. In S. P. Juvik & J. O. Juvik (Eds.), Atlas of Hawai'i (3rd ed., pp. 278-281). Honolulu: University of Hawai'i Press.

Buchanan, N. K., & Fox, R. A. (2002). To learn and to belong: Case studies of emerging ethnocentric charter schools in Hawai'i. Education Policy Analysis Archives, 11(8), n.p. Retrieved from http://epaa.asu.edu/epaa/v11n8.

Capozza, K. L. (1999). Education innovation: Indian alternative schools. American Indian Report, 15(7), 24-25.

Center of Urban and Public Affairs at the University of Texas–Arlington, Texas Center Educational Research and Center for the Study of Educational Reform at the University of North Texas, & Center for Public Policy at the University of Houston. (2000). Texas open-enrollment charter schools: Evaluation 1998-99. Retrieved from http://www.tea.state.tx.us/charter/eval99/index.html.

Cervantes, R. A. (1984). Ethnocentric pedagogy and minority student growth: Implications for the common school. Education and Urban Society, 16(3), 274-93.

Cobb, C. D., & Glass, G. V. (1999). Ethnic segregation in Arizona charter schools. Educational Policy Analysis Archives, 7(1), n.p. Retrieved from http://epaa.asu.edu/epaa/v7n1.

Cobb, C. D., Glass, G. V., & Crockett, C. (2000, April). The U.S. charter school movement and ethnic segregation. 2000 Annual Meeting of the American Educational Research Association. (ERIC Document Reproduction Service No. ED 445 414.)

Coffey, A. J. (2002). Magnets of many colors: Ethnocentric answers to education. Retrieved from http://www.kip.jcomm.ohio-state.edu/ethnocentric_education.htm.

Crockett, C. M. (1999). California charter schools: The issue of racial/ethnic segregation. Unpublished dissertation available at UMI ProQuest Digital Dissertations. Publication Number 9923864 or ISBM 0-599-23428-8.

Dotts, C. K., & Sikkema, M. (1994). Challenging the status quo: Public education in Hawai'i 1840–1980. Honolulu: Hawai'i Education Association.

Education Commission of the States (1999). Charter school equity. Retrieved from http://www.ecs.org/clearinghouse/13/70/1370.htm.

Fusarelli, L. D. (2000, April). Texas: Charter schools and the struggle for equity. 2000 Annual Meeting of the American Educational Research Association. (ERIC Document Reproduction Service No. ED 444 254.)

Gill, B. P., Timpane, T., Ross, K. E., & Brewer, D. J. (2001). Rhetoric versus reality: What we know and what we need to know about vouchers and charter schools. Santa Monica, CA: RAND Corporation.

Hanaoka, Y. (1927). The Japanese Language School: Is it a help or hindrance to the Americanization of Hawai'i's young people? The Friend, 97, 79–80. Reprinted in D. M. Ogawa, (1978) Kodomo no tame ni [For the sake of the children]: The Japanese American experience in Hawai'i (pp. 180–182). Honolulu: University of Hawai'i Press.

Harris, M. D. (1992). Afrocentrism and curriculum: Concepts, issues and prospects. Journal of Negro Education, 61(3), 301–316.

Hawai'i State Department of Education Planning, Budget, and Resource Development Office. (2001). School status and improvement reports. Retrieved from http://doe.k12.hi.us.

Hawai'i State Department of Education. (2002). School Community-Based Management Homepage. From http://www.Hawai'i.gov/scbm/scbm.html.

Hlebowitsh, P., & Tellez, K. (1997). American education: Purposes and promise. Belmont, CA: Wadsworth.

Kanu O Ka 'Aina Charter School. (2002). Informational brochure. Kamuela, HI: Kanu O Ka 'Aina New Century Public Charter School.

Kape'ahiokalani, M., Benham, P. A. N., & Heck, R. H. (1998). Culture and educational policy in Hawai'i: The silencing of native voices. Mahwah, NJ: Erlbaum.

Kapono, E. M. (1998). Hawaiian language renaissance. In S. P. Juvik & J. O. Juvik (Eds.), Atlas of Hawai'i (3rd ed., p. 199). Honolulu: University of Hawai'i Press.

Kelly, M. (1982). Some thoughts on education in traditional Hawaiian society. In College of Education, University of Hawai'i at Manoa, and the Bernice Pauahi Bishop Museum, To teach the children: Historical aspects of education in Hawai'i (pp. 4–13). Honolulu: Author.

Kolbert, E. (2000, October 9). Unchartered territory: Is there money to be made off the failure of public education? The New Yorker, 34–41.

Kua O Ka La. (2002). Informational brochure. Pahoa, HI: Kua O Ka La New Century Public Charter School.

Langlas, C. M. (1998). History. In S. P. Juvik & J. O. Juvik (Eds.), *Atlas of Hawai'i* (3rd ed., pp. 169–182). Honolulu: University of Hawai'i Press.

Lomotey, K. (1992). Independent Black Institutions: African-centered education models. *Journal of Negro Education, 61*(4), 455–462.

Meyer, M. A. (1998). *Native Hawaiian epistemology: Contemporary narratives.* Doctoral Dissertation, Harvard University.

Moersch, C. (1994). *Labs for learning: An experiential-based action model.* Corvallis, OR: National Business Education Alliance.

National Commission on Excellence in Education. (1983). *A nation at risk: The imperative of educational reform.* Washington, DC: U.S. Department of Education.

National Study of School Evaluation. (2002). Retrieved from http://www.nsse.org.

Nelson, B., Berman, P., Ericson, J., Kamprath, N., Perry, R., Silverman, D., & Solomon, D. (2000). *The state of charter schools 2000: Fourth year report.* Washington DC: Office of Educational Research and Improvement, U.S. Department of Education.

Noblit, G. W., & Corbett, D. (2001) *North Carolina charter school evaluation report.* Evaluation Section, Division of Accountability Services, Instructional Accountability Services, North Carolina State Board of Education. Submitted November 2001.

Office of the Superintendent/Planning, Budget, and Resource Development Office. (2001a). Hawaii opinion poll on public education 2001. Honolulu: Department of Education. Retrieved from http://doe.k12.hi.us.

Office of the Superintendent/Planning, Budget, and Resource Development Office. (2001b). *The superintendent's eleventh annual report on school performance and improvement in Hawai'i.* Honolulu: Department of Education. From http://doe.k12.hi.us.

Peterson, P. E. (1998). Top ten questions asked about school choice. In D. Ravitch (Ed.), *BPEP Conference on the State of Urban Education in America* (pp. 57–62). Washington DC: Brookings Institution, Brown Center on Education Policy.

PRB/KIDS COUNT (2002). Children at Risk: State Trends 1990–2000, Special Report. Retrieved from http://www.aecf.org/kidscount/c2ss

Public Sector Consultants, Inc., & MAXIMUS Inc. (2001). Michigan Charter School Report. Retrieved from http://www.voyager.net/psc/charter/index.html.

Ravitch, D. (1990). Multiculturalism: E Pluribus Plures. *The Key Reporter, 56*(1), 1–4.

Rebus Planning Associates, Inc. (1994). *The work sampling system* (3rd ed.). Ann Arbor, MI: Author.

Reyhner, J. (1992). American Indian cultures and school success. *Journal of American Indian Education, 32*(1), 30–39.

Rees, N. S. (2000). *School choice 2000 annual report.* Heritage Foundation: Roe Backgrounder # 1354. Retrieved from http://www.heritage.org/library/categories/education/bg1354.html.

Schellenberg, S. J., Osorio, C., & Porter, C. (2002, April). Changing students, changing purposes: The evolution of a school choice system in an urban school district. 2002 Annual Meeting of the American Educational Research Association. New Orleans. April 2002.

Schmitt, R. C. (1998). Population. In S. P. Juvik & J. O. Juvik (Eds.), *Atlas of Hawai'i* (3rd ed., pp. 183–197). Honolulu: University of Hawai'i Press.

Shokraii, N. (1996, November/December). Free at last: Black Americans sign up for school choice. *The Journal of American Citizenship, 80.* Retrieved from http://www.policyreview.org/nov96/backup/shokraii.html.

Stueber, R. K. (1982). An informal history of schooling in Hawai'i. In College of Education, University of Hawai'i at Manoa, and the Bernice Pauahi Bishop Museum, *To teach the children: Historical aspects of education in Hawai'i* (pp. 16–34). Honolulu: Author.

Tyack, D. B. (1974). *The one best system.* Cambridge: Harvard University Press.

UCLA Charter School Study. (1998). *Beyond the rhetoric of charter school reform: A study of ten California school districts.* Los Angeles: Author.

Wells, A. S. (2000a, November 2). In search of uncommon schools: Charter school reform in historical perspective (Part 1): Revisiting the ideology of the common school. *Teachers College Record.* Retrieved August 11, 2002 from http://www.tcrecord.org.

Wells, A. S. (2000b, November 2). In search of uncommon schools: Charter school reform in historical perspective (Part 2): Revisiting common association. *Teachers College Record.* Retrieved August 11, 2002 from http://www.tcrecord.org.

Wells, A. S. (2000c, November 2). In search of uncommon schools: Charter school reform in historical perspective (Part 3): Charter schools as uncommon schools. *Teachers College Record.* Retrieved August 11, 2002 from http://www.tcrecord.org.

Wells, A. S., Lopez, A., Scott, J, & Holme, J. J. (1999). Charter schools as postmodern paradox: Rethinking social stratification in an age of deregulated school choice. *Harvard Educational Review, 69*(2), np. Retrieved from http://www.edreview.org/harvard99/1999/su99/s99wells.htm.

Whitty, G. (1997). Creating quasi-markets in education: A review of recent research on parental choice and school autonomy in three countries. In M. W. Apple (Ed.), *Review of Research in Education* (pp. 3–47). Washington, DC: American Educational Research Association.

CHAPTER 4

Native American Charter Schools: Culture, Language, and Self-Determination

MARY JIRON BELGARDE

"Only the tribe can really determine the needs of the Pueblo."
—Vincent A. Toya, tribal program administrator
and former tribal governor, Pueblo of Jemez, New Mexico

"What is valuable about this charter school is that we have the opportunity as Native peoples [to] have the ultimate control in how we educate our children, what we educate our children and what standards we set for them to learn by and live by. I see students graduating from high school as an achievement. The real accomplishment comes from students receiving their bachelor's, their master's, and their doctorates."
—Charlotte Romero Garcia, school board member,
San Diego Riverside Charter School,
Pueblo of Jemez, New Mexico

Introduction

Vincent Toya and Charlotte Romero Garcia are involved in local efforts to change the outcome of education for the children who live in the Pueblo of Jemez in New Mexico. Toya's assertion that "only the tribe can determine the needs of the Pueblo" conveys some of the passion that tribal leaders feel about the historic tension that has existed between schools and American Indian[1] communities. Romero Garcia shares her optimism about the role she and other school board members play in establishing their local charter school along with national Native leaders and educators working toward achieving better quality schooling for Native students. In this chapter, I explain the unique power and authority of tribal governments, provide a brief overview of Native charter schools in the United States and a short history of American Indian education, and present a case study of how one tribal community is asserting control over education through charter school laws. Finally, I present a critique of how Native charter schools are affected through institutional and government policies, and then I offer some policy recommendations.

This chapter draws from my own personal background as a San Juan and Isleta Pueblo Indian from New Mexico, a graduate of Stanford University and a Native professor at the University of New Mexico. I teach graduate courses on the history, policy, and issues of American Indian education after working in Native schools for thirty years. The thrust of my work has been to rethink the structure of schooling for Native students and help Native communities deal with education-related issues (in Native communities, this is referred to as "giving back"). Thus, I serve on two boards for Native schools. I have served on the San Diego Native Charter School Board since its inception in 1999 and for the three years prior while the school transitioned from mission school to charter school status.

I do not categorize my position as ideological nor consider myself as a political progressive or Leftist, because I understand the notions of categorizations or classifications, per se, as belonging to a European rather than Native framework. Through the nature of my work, however, I am attempting to create seminal changes in schools, helping to transform an educational system that has historically marginalized Natives' perspectives and helping Natives gain control over the ownership of schools for their children. My efforts might be in alignment with the ideas of many political progressives and social reconstructionists, as I argue for community-based empowerment activities that totally rethink the structure of schools and determine who, how, and what we teach our children through charter school options.

Native Charter Schools

Charter school laws have helped establish creative and innovative schooling options for Native communities in Wisconsin, Minnesota, Michigan, Arizona, New Mexico, Alaska, Oregon, Utah, North Carolina, California, and Hawaii. Tribal officials, parents, and educators are now developing schools that serve the unique circumstances, needs, and aspirations of their children and creating a positive school climate where their culture and lifestyles are respected. Moreover, these schools serve to reverse the historic legacy that downgraded their Native languages and culture. Charter schools, then, represent the potential for Indian communities to restore educational governance and decision making at the local level.

The Ayaprun Elitnaurvik Charter School in Bethel, Alaska, for example, aims to strengthen Yup'ik language and culture with its Yup'ik immersion program. The school works closely with local organizations such as the Association of Village Council Presidents and the Bethel Senior Center. Waadookokaading, or "The Place Where We Help Each Other" in Hayward, Wisconsin, provides students in the early grades with grounding in the local Ojibwe language, culture, and traditions. The Native Arts High School in Minneapolis, Minnesota, provides a curriculum that incorporates drama, painting, music, and creative writing into each academic discipline. The Four Directions Charter High School, also located in Minneapolis, has a culturally based curriculum that includes American Indian history, language, and culture, basic skills, computer skills and experiential learning through media arts. The Nah Tah Wahsh Public School Academy, a K–8 school in Wilson, Michigan, and the Bahweting Anishnabe Public School Academy, a K–12 school in Sault Ste. Marie, Michigan, integrate native culture and language into the curriculum to foster self-esteem. These charter schools were developed after tribal members experienced the devastating effects of decades of school failure through mission, government, and public schools.

Unique Tribal Authority and History of American Indian Education

Through treaty agreements and public laws, the U.S. federal government granted tribes "sovereignty"—the right and power to act and be regarded as sovereign nations. In essence, the U.S. government agreed to grant tribes the right and the authority to make decisions for themselves and to enter into agreements with other government agencies as equal partners (Prucha, 1990; Russell, 1997). The Indian Self-Determination and Education Assistance Act of 1978 (P.L. 93-638), for example, paved the way for tribes to take control over healthcare and housing services on reservations while supporting the right of tribal governments to control the educational activities of its members (Snyder-Joy, 1994). New Mexico State Senator, Leonard Tsosie, stated:

> Self-determination, the way I understand it, is making decisions for yourself and then trying to pursue public policies to that end. Charter schools in a way do that. It allows the schools to determine a curriculum . . . and then

pursue that. In that sense, Indian self-determination and the charter school concept are compatible. (Belgarde, 2002, n.p.)

American Indians have been formally educated through religious missions, the U.S. government, and state public institutions since the mid-seventeenth century. One study conducted by the Brookings Institution in the 1920s revealed that Indian children attending the U.S. federal and mission boarding schools were living under horrid conditions (starving, being used for child labor, dying from diseases, or running away) (Adams, 1995; Connell-Szasz, 1999; Meriam, 1928; Reyner and Eder, 1989). In all of these schools Indian children experienced a deficit approach to assessment, were punished for speaking their Native tongue, and were taught rote memorization and simple cognitive and vocational skills that kept them in low-paying and subservient occupations and ultimately financially dependent on others. Furthermore, until the late-twentieth century, most teachers and administrators knew little about the students' culture and assumed that everyone had to learn English and adapt to Western institutional norms. It became the students' responsibility to learn what was expected of them, and if they wanted to progress to the next level, they had to follow militartaristic and formalistic rules. Native children remained illiterate, learned to feel inferior, denigrated, unchallenged, and became torn between their own culture and that of the dominant society. Therefore, in most recent studies, when Natives were compared to their non-Native counterparts, it was no surprise that Indian children had the lowest achievement scores and secondary school and college completion and retention rates (Adams, 1995; Belgarde, Mitchell, & Moquino-Arquero, 2002; Connell-Szasz, 1999).

These studies indicated that American Indian students, when forced to assimilate into the dominant mainstream culture, experienced cultural discontinuity, suffered from low self-esteem, and performed poorly in academe (Fuchs and Havighurst, 1968; Indian Nations at Risk Task Force, 1992; Kennedy, 1969; Meriam, 1928; White House Conference on Indian Education, 1992). Most teachers knew little about the culture, language, values, ontology, and learning styles of their students. The textbooks and curricular materials were developed for mainstream White students and assumed to apply to all students. Many school buildings were in poor condition or in need of repair. There was a shortage of American Indian teachers, counselors, and administrators to serve as role models. The Kennedy Report (1969) examined the education of Native students in public schools. Many non-Indian educators admitted to disliking the American Indian students. Teachers attributed their poor academic performance to the lack of innate intelligence and parental involvement, cultural deprivation, laziness, and language barriers. Thus, in their view, the Indians kept themselves in low socioeconomic status occupations, poor health, on welfare, or in prison.

All of the major studies on Indian education since the Meriam Report of 1928 have recommended the hiring of Native faculty and staff and incorporating culturally relevant curricula. But most schools have been slow to change (Adams, 1995; Deyhle and Swisher, 1997; Fuchs and Havighurst, 1968; Indian Nations at Risk Task Force, 1992; Kennedy, 1969; Meriam, 1928; Swisher and Hoisch, 1992; White House Conference on Indian Education, 1992).

True Native Education

Cajete (1999) argues that we need to prepare students to live in competing worldviews, philosophies, and expectations. Benally (1994) and Cajete (1999) suggest that we incorporate Native philosophy and ontology into our curricular designs. Most researchers conclude that unless the conditions of schools and teacher education colleges adapt to the individual and community, few positive outcomes will occur. As a result, there has been an outcry for Native educators and community leaders to take control over the education of their students (Belgarde, Mitchell, & Moquino-Arquero, 2002).

Charleston (1994) noted that most schools have implemented a deficit approach to educating Native children by offering remedial, "drill and kill," and unchallenging academic programs. He described three types of education programs provided to them: pseudo Native education, quasi-Native education, and true-Native education. Pseudo Native education, he said, consists of additive programs like tutoring and presenting historical facts during selected times like Thanksgiving. Quasi-Native education consists of adding courses to curricula like Native language and beadwork classes. True Native education means that we should make all the subject matter relevant to Native children all of the time. Native educators and tribal leaders should make decisions on behalf of Native children. Making curricula relevant to children's lives was the major tenet suggested by the philosopher John Dewey in 1916 and fostered by many progressives since his time. There is something wrong with the current educational paradigm. Major culturally relevant changes must be made within the organizational structure of schooling. Cultural relevancy incorporates how one learns and understands the world. Thus, Native learning styles, Native ontologies, and philosophies are key ingredients of this

recipe. It also involves adequately training teachers and providing professional development to teachers and teacher educators of Native children.
Cajete (1994) writes:

> We have to facilitate our children and ourselves in that ancient journey to
> find our face (to understand our true character), to find our heart (to un-
> derstand and appreciate the passions that move and energize our life), to
> find a foundation (work that allows us to fully express our potential and our
> greatest fulfillment), and to become a complete man or woman (to find our
> Life and appreciate the spirit that moves us). We must again create the kind
> of education that creates great human beings. . . . We are the ones who must
> choose the path of our own learning. (p. 68)

Moving Forward to Cultural Relevance: A Pueblo Case Study

As Pueblo Natives, we are working toward transforming the nature of
schools, making them culturally relevant for children. In developing the
charter school, we incorporated the Charleston and Cajete models in the
charter schools developed at the Pueblo of Jemez. The Pueblo is located
fifty-five miles northwest of Albuquerque and is nestled in the Jemez
Mountains. Regarded as a traditional community by other tribes of this re-
gion, the tribe serves approximately 3000 of 3400 members living on the
reservation and continues to practice centuries-old dances, songs, and ceremonies. Tribal officials and elders are determined to have an unwritten
tribal language and to have cultural traditions taught by the families and
through religious ceremonies, rather than through the schools.

Most of the children attended federal government and mission-op-
erated schools located on the reservation. One government school operated by the Bureau of Indian Affairs serves grades K–6, and another K–8
school was once a mission school and is now a state charter school. The
children feed into either a district school located adjacent to the reservation or an Indian boarding school located in Santa Fe, approximately
eighty miles from the community. The Santa Fe boarding school is nationally recognized for offering Native-based curricula, but the children
have to live in Santa Fe for distance reasons. The children who feed into
the adjacent public school experience Eurocentric-based curricula, insen-
sitive and poorly trained teachers, and inadequate and inappropriate instructional materials. The relationship between the tribe and the public
school system has been characteristically difficult and dependent on the

leadership styles modeled by authority figures at the district level. There were sufficient reasons for the Pueblo of Jemez to create their own schools and so, when New Mexico created the mechanism, they established two charter schools.

Pueblo of Jemez Native Charter Schools

The San Diego Riverside Charter School was once a Catholic school, called San Diego Mission, operated by the Franciscan Fathers and the Sisters of St. Francis for about one hundred years, but it closed due to a lack of funds. The school transitioned from being a mission school to a non-profit corporation, called San Diego Riverside School, Inc. The nonprofit corporation raised enough money to sustain the school for two years or until the board explored options for keeping the school going. The parents, community members, and tribal leaders wanted to retain some of the characteristics found in the Catholic school, such as small classes and high teacher expectations. Board member Benny Shendo, Jr., states:

> The Board took a proactive approach, and looked at the senate bill on charter schools, and developed their application based on the language of the bill and so when the bill was finally signed into law, they were ready with their application. They had run a school, had the buildings and children, a vision of what they wanted in the school, and all they needed were the resources. The timing was right. The New Mexico charter school law allowed the Pueblo of Jemez to take ownership over their children's education. (Belgarde, 2002, n.p.)

The children renamed the school San Diego Riverside.

San Diego Riverside currently serves approximately ninety students and uses cultural and linguistic components of the community to develop culturally supportive curricula and is working to exceed state and national standards. It became the first Native American charter school in the state and the first school to be chartered under the 1999 Charter School Law. The majority of the faculty are Native and from the community and serve as role models for students. The school facilities, which were once considered substandard, are now receiving a makeover. The hallways of the school reflect the local traditional Pueblo artistry.

Walatowa (which means "The People" in Towa) High School is also located on the reservation and opened in the fall of 2003. It offers a college preparatory model to promote community integrated learning through language preservation, community wellness, and leadership by academic rigor and experiential learning. What makes this high school different from other college preparatory models is that the school is built around community rather than individual values. Traditional and cultural values, such as taking care of one another and looking out for the well-being of the whole community, serve as the foundation for an integrated curriculum. Community-integrated learning accentuates the interrelatedness of the disciplines and advances a holistic view of knowledge. Students are encouraged to develop intercultural awareness, along with genuine understanding of their own history and traditions. In emphasizing communication, community-integrated learning stresses the fundamental importance of achieving a firm command of one's own language and the acquisition of a foreign language for effective communication. It also aims to develop awareness of the media and competence in information technology. Finally, Walatowa offers a program designed to build strong, well-educated leaders, rooted in traditional and cultural values, from which students will build their personal foundations on pillars of respect, self-discipline, responsibility, community leadership, and high achievement.

Walatowa received some opposition from the school district because the new charter high school was perceived as taking away children (and money) from the public high school. District officials also tried to argue that by using language and culture as its base, the school would secretly teach religion. The tribe appealed to the state and won. The high school opened its doors by offering outdoor experiential education activities.

The San Diego Riverside Curriculum

The curriculum at San Diego Riverside values children's native language and culture and is striving to recognize the giftedness of all students. Over 95% of the children in the community hear the Towa language spoken on a daily basis. The Towa language is encouraged and spoken in the halls and classrooms of the school. Hence, a majority of students are English language learners. The curriculum strives to help students become proficient in both languages, as well as content areas. Board member Benny Shendo, Jr., stated:

> Nowhere else in the world will you find this language. . . . [T]he language gives us the songs and the prayers and our communication with our creator—the way we were intended to pray and once that [language] is gone, then who

do we turn to? When you think about that, [we] don't want to give that up. (Belgarde, 2002, n.p.)

The Towa-speaking educational aides help the non-Native teachers by checking for comprehensive understanding in Towa and English. For example, after the children have read a book in English, the aides ask students, in Towa, to identify the main characters, restate the purpose or moral of the story, or to orally rewrite an ending. The goal of the program is to use the Towa language as a tool to help the children in the learning process—to teach them the concepts in all subject areas using the Towa language. The children could not continue this kind of experience in the Santa Fe school because the teachers do not generally have command of the Towa language or Jemez culture. Therefore, it is critical to ground the students in the Jemez language and culture at an early age.

The Towa culture forms the foundation of the school and is used to determine the curricula with innovative activities coordinated across grade levels. For example, teachers in the school developed an agricultural-based curriculum that spans all grade levels and disciplines. During the planting and harvesting seasons, with the help of elders in the community, the children planted, studied, wrote, harvested, and prepared meals from the main crops grown in the community. The school took full advantage of its physical surroundings as a living laboratory. Scientific experimentation, measurement and data collection and analysis were taught through experiential activities involving growth, nature observation, crops, and weather cycles. The teachers do not attempt to teach the children about culture but use the culture to teach them.

The curriculum honors the local culture while providing an understanding of different cultural perspectives. Students are given opportunities to improve the school and greater community environment. The teachers also work together to create a minimum of four schoolwide thematic units each year that emphasize reasoning and problem-solving skills. The school also provides experiences in leadership, citizenship, life skills, and community service (SDRS Charter School Application, 1999). Students are then able to construct meaning for themselves based on Pueblo values and lifestyles.

Ontological Differences and Performance Measures

The Pueblo communities of New Mexico offer a comparison of ontological differences in living and learning. They have survived thousands of years by living within a belief system that has a distinctly non-Western orientation. Western ontology for example, emanates from an inductive thinking process that helps define, clarify, identify, articulate, separate, and dichotomize thinking habits. Native Pueblo ontology is primarily a deductive thinking process. The mindscape is basically holistic and integrative and the actions that necessarily emanate from this perspective are usually collective rather than singular. When traditional Natives speak about the spiritual ecology of learning, they are speaking in terms of the whole process—plugging into a greater whole. Linear thinkers can only see one thing at a time and not necessarily in relationship to other things (Cajete, 1994; LoRé, 1998; Romero, 1994; Suina, 1992).

The Pueblo people come from an oral tradition, which perpetuates and supports a nonlinear thinking process. The sharing of story, metaphor, and imagination, therefore, is in support of that process. Context is critical to the story and to understanding, but context is not simply stating what is evident; it is creating a visualization of a whole series of events. Nothing is in isolation and therefore nothing can be treated separately from another thing. Suffice it to say that when we think of Native Pueblo ontology we are thinking about a value system that is in conflict with many of the core values of Western thinking. We speak in America about individuality, independence, ego, material gain, aggressiveness, and external reward. And Americans find a way to get monetary compensation for their skills, whether developed or God given. To Pueblo Indians these are necessarily alien values. They speak of community, interdependence, intrinsic reward, humility, and the group. And talent and skills are viewed as gifts from the Creator and should be treated as such; their explication is to be shared for the benefit of all. There are problems, however, in capturing the ontological differences and the mission of this charter school through standard measures (Cajete, 1994; LoRé, 1998; Romero, 1994; Suina, 1992).

Indicators of Student Performance

San Diego Riverside participates in a statewide testing program that assesses individual student progress against common statewide performance standards, including administering New Mexico Content Standards and New Mexico Statewide Student Assessment System requirements. These include the New Mexico Achievement Assessment Program (NMAAP), Comprehensive Test of Basic Skills (CTBS), TerrraNova Survey Plus Exam (CTBS5/TerraNova), New Mexico Writing Assessment (NMWA), and the New Mexico Reading Assessment for its newly funded Kindergarten Literacy Program. The Stanford 9 also provides additional grade-level data.

The school has been struggling to meet state and national expectations on standardized tests. Kaumo (2003), a private consultant, and the Synergy Group, a firm contracted to analyze all charter schools in the State of New Mexico, found that, overall, the students scored below the 50th percentile in all subject areas for three consecutive years. They both agree, however, that the analysis of the data is problematic due to the low number of students enrolled and that the range of scores on standardized tests waxes and wanes due to these low enrollment numbers. Vogel (2003) confirmed their findings and reported that the school's low test scores on the NM CTBS-Terra Nova had resulted in the school being placed on Performance-Warned Status for the year 2001 and Probationary status for the year 2002. Vogel said,

> [T]he school devoted greater attention and resources to standardized testing and testing skills. This year (2002), faculty noted our middle school students had reached "saturation point" on the subject of standardized testing. Teachers concluded that many older students did not perform as well as they could because they lost interest and focus on the day tests were administered.

The school was devastated because its efforts to reinforce language and culture as a means of improving schools could not be captured through standardized measures.

The tribal officials, school board members, and parents want to "follow their heart" or, as suggested by Cajete (1999), develop the kind of education that creates great Jemez beings. They all agree that their vision for the school is appropriate for their community and they must look internally and to other sources of information to assess progress.

School Board and Community Evaluation

The Synergy Group described the curriculum as being unique, meaningful, and enriched, building relationships between students, parents, and the school personnel. They said that the children were demonstrating progress on nonstandardized measures and feel supported on language and culture issues: "The principal reports a 98% attendance rate, which is a positive accomplishment. Students were actively engaged in classrooms observed; they were polite, proud and responsive when asked about their school and teachers" (Synergy Group, 2001, p. 4).

The parents who responded to a Synergy survey indicated great satisfaction with the teachers and the small school and class sizes:

> Parents interviewed indicated they are proud of having a voice in the curriculum of the school and have wanted that for many years. . . . [T]hey have contributed a great deal to the school . . . time, money, and hundreds of hours of labor in preparing the school—with no return except that they proudly say: this is "our school." (Synergy Group, 2001, p. 5)

The parents also noted that not all teachers have the materials they would like and were waiting for additional resources to support their work. They stated that when a school accreditation visit was made, there were some areas identified for improvement, such as a science laboratory for the middle school, and defined health and employment procedures, but the bilingual program and the cultural components of the school received commendation. This was gratifying to everyone involved in establishing the school (Synergy Group, 2001).

Synergy summarized their 2002 report:

> As year three comes to a conclusion, San Diego Riverside is showing progress in developing their curriculum as envisioned in the charter application. The struggle with conversion and change has given way to more cooperative efforts toward meeting all school requirements. . . . Integration of subjects and maintaining a community focus are evidenced in classrooms and school-wide programs. . . . The rich environmental, cultural, and community resources are helping a unique school identity to develop. A parent stated, "We see San Diego Riverside as successful and a good school. The 'smell of memory' is present in San Diego Riverside since many of us went here before. It is going in the right direction to be a collaboration between the school and the parents." (Synergy Group, 2002, p. 5)

The School Improvement Plan also reveals that the faculty members are working toward completing English as Second Language (ESL) and bilingual education requirements. The report states, "The school staff is working hard to refine our curriculum, methods, classroom environments, pedagogical styles, behavioral management strategies, and school climate with a primary focus on reading success for all students" (SDRS Charter School Reauthorization Application, 2003).

I used the San Diego Riverside Charter School to describe a unique educational environment—a place not commonly found in the regular public school systems in New Mexico. Nevertheless, the school bears resemblance to other Native charter schools as they seem to share features that make them characteristically Native. All of these schools have Native language and culture as their base. In the next section, I offer a critique of this particular case study on the San Diego Riverside School and the development of Native charter schools in general.

Summary and Discussion

Numerous scholars and studies acknowledge that we have lived through centuries of colonized oppression and silence. We have been forced, they say, to adhere to European-based institutional frameworks, thereby hindering academic achievement and graduation rates. Charter school laws help establish creative and innovative school options for Native schools in at least eleven states in the United States. We are developing programs to serve the unique circumstances, needs, and aspirations of Native children and creating school climates with teachers and administrators who understand and appreciate their culture and lifestyles. Charter schools represent the potential for Indian communities to restore educational governance and decision making to the local level and to change the course of history in Indian education.

Institutional Framework as a Paradigm

Institutional structures at all organizational levels have impeded the implementation of Native research findings and recommendations. For example, throughout history, someone within the federal or state government has had final authority over the education of Native students. Even when tribes have entered treaty agreements affording them tribal sovereignty, tribal officials have had to seek permission or final authority from the Bureau of Indian Affairs, U.S. Department of Interior, and the U.S. or state Department of Education officials. These governmental officials have had final authority over whether schools have met state and national standards and benchmarks and teachers have met teacher certification requirements. Most often, the agency representatives who developed the guidelines have had the same paternalistic spirit that the federal government displayed toward Indians at their first encounter. These institutional frameworks that were first intended to help strengthen all schools have resulted in inhibiting innovation and change because these agencies have not responded to the research and expertise of Native authorities. They seemed to know what was best for Natives regardless of their own limited knowledge and expertise. The institutional paradigms were not developed for Native communities. Hence, there continued to be a clash of cultures, priorities, and accountability systems replete with shortcomings.

Issues of Cultural Discontinuity and Bilingual Education

The San Diego Riverside School and Walatowa High School are designed to be culturally sound, in concert with the values of the community, and to allow students to speak their own language. Native language and culture are strongly valued in other Native charter schools as well. Researchers suggest that using native languages in schools can reinforce student learning in English and proficiency in both languages (Belgarde, 2002). By complying with the No Child Left Behind Act and making sure all students score above the 50th percentile, penalizing teachers for not meeting testing requirements for second language learners marginalizes the use of Native languages and culture in schools. It rejects ontological differences as I discussed earlier. Cultural discontinuity becomes reinforced when we try to fit a square peg in a round hole. San Diego Riverside is struggling to stay alive. It is on the cusp of losing its charter because its mission cannot be revealed through short-term assessments. It is difficult for the children at Jemez to cognitively think in the Towa language before translating into English—all within a time limit. Even the Chief Administrative Officer overseeing charter schools in New Mexico admitted:

> Having Native American kids participate in standardized testing does not really give an adequate picture of what Native American kids know. Their particular learning style is very different from the teaching style that we have in schools at the current time—even in charter schools. And without appropriate professional development they are never going to make that bridge. (Belgarde, 2002, n.p.)

No Child Left Behind proponents overlook the fact that Native researchers have been able to show that grounding Native students in language and culture will translate into higher academic achievement, retention, and graduation rates, but it takes time. We have to remember that most Eurocentric-based schools for Native children have been a dismal failure since the mid-seventeenth century. The act requires that students become English proficient within a short time and the New Mexico charter school law requires that all schools, including San Diego Riverside and Walatowa, comply with all federal and state legislation. Furthermore, it suggests that schools reward and punish teachers for noncompliance. What incentives, then, are left for Native educators and community leaders to develop their own models of education?

Native experts should help teachers develop authentic assessment techniques that help measure site-based objectives and student mastery of those objectives. We need to train the teachers in portfolio assessments and rubric-based evaluations that are more holistic and analytical compared to other performance-based benchmarks. However, there have been no local Native professors with this kind of expertise available. We currently lack the financial resources to provide professional development training opportunities to teachers as well. This relates to some other accountability issues of No Child Left Behind.

Issues of Accountability

The No Child Left Behind Act of 2001 was intended to "insure that all children have a fair, equal, and significant opportunity to obtain a high-quality education and reach, at a minimum, proficiency on challenging state academic achievement standards and state academic assessments" (United States Government, 2001, n.p.). The act requires that limited English proficient (L.E.P.) students be mainstreamed into all-English content instruction and tested through English after three years in schools. In the end, the teacher is held accountable for enabling L.E.P. students to meet the act's imposed requirements and timelines. This will have a devastating effect on charter school initiatives.

My concern is that the act undermines the goals of American Indian education and the possibility of what Native charter schools have to offer in particular, because Native language and culture is the driving force in Indian-based community education. Prior Indian education history forced many tribes to lose their languages and culture. We will not allow this to happen again. This means not repeating the old education paradigm. This means fighting the rampant use of standardized tests.

This means not having unknowledgeable politicians or bureaucrats dictate what is best for Indian communities. This means that, as Natives, we bear responsibility for revamping the legislation that does not flexibly accommodate community standards on culture and language integration. The community of Jemez will not devalue Towa or suggest that its language comes second to the English language. As Native educators, we need to provide guidance on how children should learn English. No Child Left Behind suggests a "one-goal-fits-all" national education policy in the name of equal access to quality learning. The act provides no vision or room for experimentation to teachers regarding *how* to accomplish its mandated goal of successful performance by English learners on high-stakes standardized tests in English. If we, as Native educators, value language and culture, desire to incorporate Native philosophy and ontology into our curricular designs, hope to prepare students to live in competing worldviews and philosophies, and aim to develop higher expectations through rigorous standards, then we need to provide some guidance and training on this. We need to provide guidance on teacher education training and professional development opportunities to Native and non-Native teachers and administrators in schools.

So, where do we go from here?

The Educated Native and Issues of the Political Left

As I actively reflect on my own personal experience, I can no longer remain complacent, a passive player in the design and outcome of schools. I want to become more actively engaged in the process to create social justice and social change for Native students. Until now, I have not been aggressive in telling it like it is—as many political progressives do. I want to encourage other Natives to complete their formal education, even though the institutions have been slow to change, as we need them to think critically, create a vision, and make decisions for the betterment of others. I want to encourage others to be advocates for developing other Native charter schools, always incorporating the Native perspective into their design. As Native communities, we need our own lawyers, doctors, engineers, business owners, teachers, and administrators. And as Natives, we need to put a name to the problem, identify any institutional shortcomings, and actively work toward changing the course of history.

Note

1. Throughout history and in much of the literature, many different terms have been used to describe this group of people: *American Indian, Native Americans, Natives, First Nations People,* and *indigenous populations,* for example. In this chapter, I use the terms *Native American* and *American Indians* interchangeably to reflect the institutional designations of students and the names of the programs serving them.

References

Adams, D. (1995). *Education for extinction: American Indians and the boarding school experience, 1875–1928.* Lawrence: University Press of Kansas.

Belgarde, M. (2002). *From mission school to State charter school: Indian education in the 21st Century* [CD-ROM]. Washington, DC: U.S. Department of Education.

Belgarde, M. J., Mitchell, R., & Moquino-Arquero, A. (Summer 2002). What do we have to do to create culturally-responsive programs? A story about American Indian teacher education. Special Issue: Indigenous Perspectives of Teacher Education: Beyond Perceived Borders, *Action in Teacher Education.*

Benally, H. (1994). Navajo philosophy of learning and pedagogy. *Journal of American Indian Education, 12*(1), 23–31.

Cajete, G. (1994). *Look to the mountain: An ecology of Indigenous education.* Durango, CO: Kvakiʻ Press.

Cajete, G. (1999). *Igniting the sparkle.* Skyand, NC: Kivaki Press.

Charleston, G. Mike (1994). Toward true Native education: A treaty of 1992 final report of the Indian Nations at Risk Task Force, (draft 3). *Journal of American Indian Education, 33*(2), 1–56.

Connell-Szasz, M. (1999). *Education and the American Indian: The road to self-determination since 1928.* Albuquerque: University of New Mexico Press.

Dewey, J. (1916). *Democracy and education.* New York: Macmillan.

Deyhle, D., & Swisher, K. (1997). Research in American Indian and Alaska Native education: From assimilation to self-determination. In M. Apple (Ed.), *Review of Research in Education* (pp. 113–194). Washington, DC: American Education Research Association.

Fuchs E., & Havighurst, R. (1972). *To live on this earth: American Indian education.* Albuquerque: University of New Mexico Press.

Indian Nations at Risk Task Force. (1992). *Indian nations at risk: An educational strategy for action.* Washington, DC: U.S. Department of Education.

Kaumo, B. (2003). San Diego Riverside charter school state mandated testing results 2003. Pueblo of Jemez, NM: San Diego Riverside School.

Kennedy, R. (1969). *Indian education: A national tragedy, a national challenge.* Washington, DC: United States Government Printing Office.

LoRé, R. K. (1998). *Art as development theory: The spiritual ecology of learning and the influence of traditional Native American education.* Ph.D. dissertation, University of New Mexico.

Meriam, L. B., Brown, R. A., Roe Cloud, H., Dale, E. E., Duke, E., Edwards, H. R., et al. (1928). *The problem of Indian administration.* Baltimore: John Hopkins Press.

Prucha, F. P. (Ed.). (1990) *Documents of United States Indian policy* (2nd ed.). Lincoln: University of Nebraska Press.

Reyhner, J., & Eder, J. (1989). *A history of Indian education.* Billings: Native American Studies, Montana State University-Billings, and Council for Indian Education.

Romero, M. E. (1994). Identifying giftedness among Keeresan Pueblo Indians: The Keres study. *Journal of American Indian Education, 34,* 35-58.

Russell (1997). *American Indian Facts of Life: A profile of today's tribes and reservations.* Phoenix: Author.

San Diego Riverside School. (1999). Charter school application. Pueblo of Jemez, NM: San Diego Riverside School.

San Diego Riverside School. (2002). School improvement plan: Improving the future of our children. Pueblo of Jemez, NM: San Diego Riverside School.

San Diego Riverside School. (2003). Charter school reauthorization application. Pueblo of Jemez, NM: San Diego Riverside School.

Snyder-Joy, Z. K. (1994, Fall). Self-determination in American Indian education: Educators' perspectives on grant, contract, and BIA-administered schools. *Journal of American Indian Education.*

Suina, J. (1992, January). Pueblo secrecy result of intrusions, *New Mexico Magazine,* 60-63.

Swisher, K., & Hoisch, M. (1992). Dropping out among American Indians and Alaska Natives: A review of the studies. *Journal of American Indian Education, 31*(1), 3-23.

Synergy Group. (2001). Evaluation of New Mexico Charter Schools, 2000-2001. Santa Fe: New Mexico Department of Education.

Synergy Group. (2002). Evaluation of New Mexico Charter Schools, 2001-2002. Santa Fe: New Mexico Department of Education.

United States Government. (2001). PL 107-110, No Child Left Behind Act of 2001. Title 1: Improving the Academic Achievement of the Disadvantaged. Section 001: Statement of Purpose. Washington, DC: U.S. Government Press.

Vogel, I. (2003). Personal Conversation. Pueblo of Jemez, NM: San Diego Riverside School.

White House Conference on Indian Education. (1992, January 22-24). *One heart, many nations: The White House conference on Indian education.* Atlanta: John Dennis Productions.

CHAPTER 5

Independent Black Schools and the Charter Movement

PATTY YANCEY

Introduction

Over a decade after the first charter schools opened in Minnesota, charters across the country enroll only 1% of the total national public school population. Nevertheless, the charter movement is a major player in the school reform field, and still triggers spirited debate on the national, state, and local levels. Parents appear generally in favor of the idea; unions and school boards remain wary; and the teacher/principal camp straddles both sides of the fence with some educators eagerly seizing the opportunity to abandon the traditional system and start their own schools.

The appeal of the charter concept is broad. Schools are being founded in low-income urban communities of color, in suburban White neighborhoods, and among rural home schoolers and American Indian populations. And according to recent national surveys, the most common reason across charter populations for wanting to found a school is the desire to realize an alternative vision of schooling. Almost 60% of charter schools cited vision as the most important reason for founding. For one-quarter of charter start-ups, this vision includes serving a special target population, such as at-risk African American students, fine art students, dropout youth, and Limited English Proficient students (RPP International, 2000).

It was predicted that charter schools would be elitist schools, creaming White students and high-achieving students of color from public schools. National and state studies indicate statistically that this prediction has not materialized. Presently nationwide, charter schools serve a population that is demographically similar to that of all public schools. Approximately seven in ten charter schools have a student body that is racially and ethnically similar to their surrounding district and 18% of charter schools enroll a larger percentage of students of color than their surrounding district. Connecticut, Illinois, Louisiana, Massachusetts, Michigan, Minnesota, New Jersey, North Carolina, and Texas enroll a much higher percentage of students of color than all public schools in those states. As far as the representation of students eligible for free or reduced-price lunch, charter schools served a slightly higher percentage of low-income students in 1998–99 than all public schools in twenty-seven charter states—39 versus 37% (RPP International, 2000).

Looking more closely at the make-up of individual charter schools state by state, however, the picture blurs. In Arizona, charter school enrollment patterns reveal a much higher percentage of White students than the nearby public schools.[1] In the diverse state of California, minorities are underrepresented in its charter schools. In the states where charters serve a larger number of students of color than the rest of the public schools, a number of charter schools have enrollments of all or predominantly one race or all low-income, mixed race—for example, all African American; all Latino; all low-income Latino and African American; all low-income American Indian and White. Some states have enacted caps or formulas that disallow the practice of charter schools serving one race, but charter advocates have cried foul. They argue that because of magnet configurations, tracking, and White flight, the public system is already racially and socioeconomically segregated (Mayes, 1998). Advocates also cite the well-documented track record of the public education system in its failure to meet the needs of low-income children and youth of color.

Of the students of color served in charter schools, African Americans have the highest numbers, with charter schools in fifteen states enrolling a greater percentage of African American students than all the public schools in those states (RPP International, 2000, p. 32). In some of these states, there are a number of charter schools that have enrollments that are 85–100% Black or have an Afrocentric philosophy and curriculum. Most of the predominantly Black charter schools are located in large cities and have been organized in response to the underachievement, overcrowding, and lack of accountability experienced in traditional public schools. In North Carolina in 1998, 12 out of 33 charter schools served predominantly African American students (Schnaiberg, 1998, p. 22). In Michigan, 69 percent of charter school students are African American compared to the general Michigan K–12 population of 14 percent (Bulkley and Fisler, 2002, p. 16).

In addressing the predominance of African American charter schools in Michigan, Jim Goenner, former director of the charter school office at Central Michigan University, argued that these charter schools are not promoting segregation and don't attract families simply because of their African American focus. Goenner believes that the motivation for parents is the opportunity to participate "in a smaller, more intimate, more responsive system. [Parents are] showing us that [professional educators] need to put back the family atmosphere in schools and that schools have to be more responsive in meeting the needs of African Americans" (Mayes, 1998, p. 7A).

Carl Candoli, a former superintendent of schools who was hired to implement desegregation in the Lansing public system, opposed charters but conceded, "African Americans were forced into the charter school movement by years of rejection from the system. I see the reason for it. They can say, 'We're doing our own thing' and more power to them, I guess" (Mayes, 1998, p. 1A).

In an attempt to further understanding of the proliferation of U.S. charter schools organized and operated by ethnic minority populations to serve their own communities, this chapter explores the African American charter school experience as one example of the phenomenon. Using qualitative methods, field research was conducted in 1997 and 1998 at three charter schools—Umoja Charter School, a private conversion in Michigan, Clarkville Elementary, a start-up charter in Florida, and Denton College Preparatory, another private school conversion in Arizona.[2] All three schools were in their third year of charter operations when site visits were made to the schools. Documents analyzed included local news articles, official charter documents, school-to-home communication, and annual reports. Research studies from the Policy Analysis for California Education (PACE), the U.S. Department of Education's National Study of Charter Schools, and the national news media provide state and national data and political context.

Preceding the case studies, an overview of the African American independent school movement follows in the next section. This historical information broadens the context by situating the charter schools in the educational experience of marginalized groups in the United States.

History of Independent Black Schools

Parents choosing to enroll their children in Afrocentric or predominantly Black schools is not a new phenomenon. Even though the 1954 Supreme Court decision was heralded as the messiah of educational opportunity for African Americans, its implementation was contested, circumvented, and undermined for decades by state and local authorities, as well as many White parents, across the U.S. In Lansing, Michigan, for example, White citizen groups successfully blocked implementation until 1976 through a myriad of court battles and recalls of board of education members who backed desegregation plans. In other public school districts, African American parents and teachers became discouraged by the desegregation strategies employed, such as busing and tracking of Black students. Black teachers lost their livelihoods as Black schools were closed and the hiring practices of the new, desegregated public system revealed a preference for White teachers over African Americans. In a nationwide study conducted by Joan Davis Ratteray and Mwalimu J. Shujaa in the 1980s, African American parents interviewed strongly stated that integrated public schools were "out of sync" with Black family and cultural values, and that White teachers often had low expectations for Black students (Ratteray, 1992).

In the 1960s and 1970s, groups of African American parents sought alternatives to the public school and turned to leaders in their own community for educational alternatives specifically designed for their children. As far back as 1798, independent Black schools had been in existence in the northern United States because Whites harassed and threatened African American students who tried to attend village schools. After Reconstruction, the founding of independent Black schools spread across the South and continued throughout the United States until the *Brown* decision appeared to wipe out the need for continuing the practice. The responsibility of educating African American children appeared to be out of the hands of parents and Black teachers and nestled in the capable arms of the federal government. Anything that promoted "separate" or "segregated" facilities or programs was regarded with suspicion and those African American educators who continued to support independent schools fell out of favor with the Black mainstream population (Ratteray, 1992).

As mentioned, the reality of the African American experience in the integrated public education system (that is, busing, low expectations by White teachers, lack of reinforcement of cultural and family values in school policies, overcrowding, tracking) triggered a renewed interest in the Black independent school. In 1972, the Council of Independent Black

Institutions (CIBI) in Buffalo, New York, established a formal network of African American alternative schools known as "independent Black institutions," or IBIs (Shujaa, 1992). Some of the IBIs employed a more traditional Eurocentric approach in their curriculum, organization, and pedagogy. Others, inspired by the Black Power movement, infused their curricula and pedagogy with African-centered philosophy and content and created the Afrocentric model. Researcher opinions vary on the curricular and pedagogical boundaries of the moniker IBI, but the common element of all member institutions is the organizing philosophy of the "independent neighborhood school"—a neighborhood-based, self-help response to the educational needs of its families (Shujaa, 1992). The developmental style of politics, which emphasizes the cultivation of efficacy in those most affected by a problem, is central to the IBI philosophy and vision. Strong parent involvement and "creating a family-like atmosphere" within the schools, the incorporation of an explicit value system into all aspects of the organization, and the reliance on the African American community for leadership and financial support are the key components of the philosophy (Lomotey, 1992).

This developmental style of politics is reminiscent of the educational philosophy of the Highlander Folk School in the Tennessee Mountains, where many civil rights activists gathered, trained, and prepared for the voter registration drives across the South. The Highlander School, cofounded during the Depression by Myles Horton, was initially conceived as a school for the Appalachian poor. The Highlander mission was based on the belief that if the poor and oppressed knew how to analyze what their experiences were and generalize what they know, they would be able to draw on their own resources and collectively affect change (Payne, 1995). In the 1930s, Highlander taught and organized coal miners and small farmers; in the 1950s it was a meeting place and training ground for civil rights leaders. Among its most famous students and teachers was Septima Clark, who was instrumental in establishing the Citizenship Schools. The mission of the Citizenship Schools was not only to promote Black voter registration, but to create involved citizens and to develop local leadership. In *I've Got the Light of Freedom: The Mississippi Freedom Struggle* (1995), Charles Payne argues how critical this philosophy was to the Civil Rights Movement:

> Over the long term, whether a community achieved this or that tactical objective was likely to matter less than whether the people in it came to see themselves as having the right and the capacity to have some say-so in their

own lives. Getting people to feel that way requires participatory political and educational activities, in which the people themselves have a part in defining the problems—"Start where the people are"—and solving them. (p. 68)

It is important to point out that IBIs founded in the late 1960s and 1970s were not that popular because they relied primarily upon tuition and financial support from middle-class Black families, churches, fraternal organizations, and sororities for sustainability. The schools were not a choice for most low-income, poor, and/or marginally educated African American families. But it now appears that with some state charter laws making it possible for charter school founders to serve targeted populations and for established private schools to convert to charter status, independent Black schools may gain a stronger toehold in the mainstream educational system.[3]

An example of an established private Afrocentric school that converted to charter status is Umoja Charter School in Michigan. Umoja was initially founded as a Saturday K–2 private school by African American parents, teachers, and community activists in 1974. The founding of the private school was sparked by a busing plan being implemented by the district at that time, which some African American teachers strongly opposed. There was also a high level of dissatisfaction in the African American community about perceived academic, cultural, and political gaps in the educational programming of the public schools serving their children. In the following section, school life at Umoja is described. After Umoja, the stories of Clarkville Charter and Denton College Preparatory follow. In all of the case studies, the leading questions that guided the investigation were:

- Why was the school organized? Who were the founders?

- What is the organizational structure and governance of the school?

- What is the educational philosophy and program?

- What outside support bases—financial and informational—does the school have? What is the role of the local community in the charter school?

- What is the role of parents at the school?

- How is what is happening in the charter school related to how teaching and learning is approached or viewed in other institutions outside the charter school (for example, school district, teachers' union, federal and state government)?

Umoja

In 1982, with the help of an Episcopal ministry, Umoja's educational program expanded from its initial K–2 Saturday configuration to a regular five-day week, serving preschoolers through 8th graders. Umoja added a secondary school component to its program in 1992; and just two years after that, the private school was invited by its surrounding district to convert to charter status under district sponsorship. The district invitation to convert was met with substantial hesitance on the part of the Umoja community because of the fear of losing autonomy. However, on the plus side, converting to charter status afforded Umoja a stable public funding base which allowed the school to broaden the population it served to lower-income and poor families. Public funding also provided students with better instructional materials and resources, and increased teacher salaries, benefits, and professional development services. As a charter school they could not restrict access to anyone that wished to enroll, but they were not required to alter their African-centered educational philosophy or curriculum as long as state standards were met. The fact that all Umoja teachers had to be credentialed or working toward a credential was viewed as a plus by the director, who remarked, "Continuing education for staff is always a positive thing."

The faculty and board welcomed the opportunity to serve a larger and more economically diverse population, but they were apprehensive about the increase in numbers and about opening their doors to families with conflicting philosophies of learning and rearing children. And it turned out that these were the main reasons that the first years of operation under the charter were so difficult. So many children who entered were operating at a far lower level of academic achievement than the continuing Umoja students. According to the director and teachers, they were initially unprepared for these new students who lacked respect for adults and were used to relationships based on conflict. The staff had to do "a lot of talking" that first year to solve conflicts and acclimate students and parents to the value system. The director and the assistant director laughed when they recalled their first year: "All we did was talk, talk, talk, and then we'd talk some more."

As a charter school, Umoja graduated its first class of seniors in 1996. The preschool retained its private status but was still housed in the same main school building at the time of my site visit in 1998. A mental health center at one time, the red-brick building was a one-story, rather drab looking structure with safety bars on the windows. My first impression was drastically altered upon stepping in the front door. A massive spray of fresh tropical flowers on a small table in the entryway, the smell of incense burning, and the sound of African drumming instantly replaced that first snapshot of the cheerless, institutional exterior.

The Educational Program

In the Afrocentric educational program, the Western experience and system are not ignored, but utilized as a framework or impetus for exploring a phenomenon or particular subject in the context of Africa or as it relates to African people worldwide. Umoja's mission outlined in its annual report lists seven tenets:

- Creating and developing a K–12 African-centered learning model that encourages academic excellence, self-determination, entrepreneurship, and social responsibility;

- Producing a new activist leadership for the redevelopment of the African American community;

- Reinforcing group identity, pride, and self-esteem through the daily use of exemplary deeds and virtuous thought from African people throughout history;

- Instilling a sense of belonging in parents, students, and teachers by emphasizing the concept of extended family;

- Developing strategic thinking based on past and present successes and creative possibilities for the future;

- Preparing students for higher learning; and

- Examining the effects and benefits of extended exposure of learners to Afrocentric education. (Umoja 1997 Annual Report)

The Umoja philosophy was rooted in the development of the whole child. Early attention to the physical, social, cultural, cognitive, and emotional needs of children was emphasized in the school's educational program and the role of parents in the child's education was considered paramount. Umoja's educational program differed from the traditional model of public education in the following ways:

- Afrocentrism guided the curriculum, instruction, discipline policies, parent involvement, governance, culture, and climate of the school.

- Schoolwide monthly themes integrated the curriculum across grades and subjects.

- Students were organized in multiage, cross-grade groupings that were based on ability, interests, and social maturity.

- There was a strong sense of family and community.

- There was a parent involvement requirement and contract.

There were 192 students, 12 full-time teachers (7 certified), 8 assistant teachers, 3 adjunct teachers, one director, and one assistant director. Students wore uniforms: brown shirts and pants or skirts with African Kente cloth trim for lower grades and black pants or skirts and white shirts with vests of African cloth for upper grades. The majority of faculty and staff wore African-style clothing—colorful print dresses, loosely fitted patterned shirts, and head wraps. Adults were addressed as "Mama" or "Baba," followed by their first name. There was a large communal kitchen located in the center of the building, separating the preschool from the upper grades.

The school was organized in three divisions: preschool through grade 3, grades 4 through 7, and grades 8 through 12. Each division was staffed by a team of teachers, assistant teachers, and adjunct faculty under the direction of a head teacher. The teacher teams worked collectively planning and evaluating curriculum, setting goals, and assessing student progress. Within each division, students were assigned to cross-age, cross-grade groupings (Work/Study Circles) which were based on individual ability, interests, and social maturity, rather than traditional grades. At the beginning of each semester, placement tests were administered in all academic subjects and plans of study were designed for students. The organization of classroom time was a mixture of traditional and block scheduling. Class sizes ranged from six (upper grades) to ten (younger) students. At times, the combination of aides and volunteers in the classroom brought the student teacher ratio down to 1:1.

In the middle grades (4–7), students were separated by gender for the majority of class time. This policy resulted from the Umoja teachers' own observations of their students. They found that girls and boys "learn and concentrate better" in separate groups during the upper elementary and middle school years. So students were organized coeducationally for their enrichment classes and extracurricular activities, and separated according to gender for their academic courses for those grades.

On a typical day at Umoja, high school students would begin earlier than the rest of the students with a Tai Chi session before the morning assembly. A drum call alerted the school community to assemble for the opening ritual at 8:00 AM. The whole school—all adults, students, parents, visitors, faculty, staff—participates; however, due to the limited space, students and adults were clustered in the open spaces in classrooms, hallways, and offices throughout the length of the main building. Roll was taken; pledges and oaths were voiced in unison (facing East); the African American anthem was sung; inspirational messages were delivered, and a short silent meditation period ended the ceremony. Because the building was small, the groups could hear each other clearly from room to room. The assembly ceremony was repeated after lunch to refocus for the afternoon and at the close of the school day at 4:00 PM.

In a focus group with the upper grades, a number of the students recalled their initial resistance to enrolling in the academy and the difficulty of their first years as students. The new Umoja recruits believed that the academy was too far "away from everything" and their friends from other schools teased them about going to an African-centered school. As far as what changed the opinions and attitudes about the school, some of their responses included:

- I like the African culture.
- I like the standards.
- They push you to be yourself.
- The school is okay even if there are no sports because academics are important.
- It's like a family type of environment.
- I can get individual attention.
- There is a sense of familyhood, brotherhood.
- I stay for the people as much as the academics.

Curriculum, Instruction, and Assessment

The charter school curriculum addressed the core requirements of the state of Michigan, organizing courses into five major components: math, science, culture (social studies, art, music, and dance), communication skills (English, foreign languages, creative writing, journalism), and physical development. There was also a computer literacy program. The curriculum strands were integrated through schoolwide themes such as

Ancestors and Family Month (October), Life in America (November), and We Are All Scientists Month (coincides with district preparation for the science fair).

Although the curriculum was guided by state requirements, the content centered around Africa and African people worldwide. For example, in government class, Umoja students studied the structure of the U.S. government, while comparing it to systems of government in past and present African nations. When the subject was the Declaration of Independence, the students also researched why and how the peoples of African nations have sought independence from colonial rule. Students had to research the declarations, learn about reparations, and write their own declaration. In the arts, offerings ranged from African drumming and dance, classical music, blues and jazz, to theatre. For the annual science fair, students designed and produced a science project—collectively or individually—that explained and displayed a problem that impacted the growth and development of African people anywhere in the Pan-African world (famine, drought, dams, industry, and so forth).

Teachers employed different instructional approaches, including small groups, whole classes, and individualized instruction. They taught across grades, as well as team taught. Students were encouraged to research, express original ideas, and create new ways to express their ideas through projects, debates, and presentations. Tutorials were provided after school in math, reading, and test-taking skills, and science and field trips that reflected the schoolwide themes were arranged monthly.

Student progress was measured by observation of student interest, originality and quality of work, oral and written examinations, portfolios, and standardized tests (MEAP and MAT). Book tests, essay exams, interviews, research papers, and exhibitions at the end of thematic units provided the data. Four years of science, math, social studies, and language arts and two foreign languages were required for graduation. Every student performed in two annual public performances, as well as poetry and dance recitals, debates, and public speaking programs throughout the school year. There was also a Rites of Passage program for students from grades 4 through 12 that met after school and on Saturdays during the spring semester. The program offered age-appropriate classes in such subjects as health and nutrition, assertiveness vs. aggression, career development, financial management, sexism and racism, and home and family management. The yearly culminating event, the "Passage" ceremony, marked the progress of individual students on their path to graduation and adulthood.

Parents

Umoja's schoolwide commitment to parent involvement was rooted in the Afrocentric mission and was in place prior to charter conversion. Parent contracts were a school policy and parent orientation sessions were mandatory for parents of entering students. There were four formal parent-teacher conferences held throughout the school year and in addition to volunteering in the classroom and for school functions, parents raised funds for the charter school and chaperoned for in-school activities and field trips.

Each semester, Umoja distributed course of study outlines to parents of the students in the upper grades for every subject that their children were taking. For the youngsters in the primary grades, course outlines were distributed monthly to parents. Umoja also provided an array of services to parents and the larger community such as evening and weekend classes for adults (for example, Black studies, health and nutrition, fitness and martial arts, Kiswahili, genealogy, and home study.)

The Umoja faculty talked earnestly about their attempts to reach out to all of their students' parents. They'd found it to be more difficult, since becoming a charter, to reach out and effectively connect with parents who were more marginalized and at risk. These parents avoided meetings and encounters with the teacher and did not answer school-to-home communication. The teachers remarked, however, that the parents "eventually came around." Parent participation at the charter school was high. Ways that parents were involved included making and selling lunches to raise money for the prom, classroom volunteering, clean-up and hospitality for events, and committee work. Parents who served as committee heads formed a council that meets periodically with the director and advises on policy and programs. Parents, faculty and staff, and students were members of what was known as the Family Network, which met monthly for a potluck dinner and discussions or guest speakers. The average attendance was ninety-six.

Teachers

Teachers were employed "at will" at Umoja; at the end of each school year they were offered a contract to return the following school year. There was no collective bargaining agreement. Teacher turnover was minimal when Umoja was a private school, and since it has converted to charter status this has not changed. Starting salaries were only about two-thirds of the starting salary for teachers in the district, but benefits were comparable. The teachers found out about Umoja through word-of-mouth or Ms. Makeda Carter, the director, recruited them for their positions. Seven of the twelve full-time teachers are certified, and the rest are working on their certification. All are African American.

Many of the teachers had or have had children or grandchildren who were enrolled in the school. One of the teachers was the daughter of the founding director and attended the private school as a student. She was one of the first graduates of Umoja.

Teacher collaboration was the norm at the school and their approach to the organization of their work was not traditional. For instance, grades 4 through 7 were taught by two full-time teachers and one assistant teacher, with adjunct faculty teaching physical education, French, and Kiswahili. In another example, the three science teachers developed the science curriculum together and often team taught across grade levels. All teachers acted as student advisors, worked with parents on committees, shared in the daily decision-making with the director, and were involved in leading or participating in after school groups or activities.

As mentioned, professional development was a top priority at the school. Teachers engaged in approximately twelve to twenty workshops, inservice training, and conferences throughout the year. Topics for the professional development sessions included block scheduling, portfolios, affirmative learning, individualizing instruction, attention deficit disorder, assessment, how to make use of test scores, charter school development, and multiple intelligences. Because the school is a member of the Council of Independent Black Institutions (CIBI), it was required to host a summer teacher training institute on theory and practice every other year. The teachers and Carter described the CIBI network as "invaluable" for professional development and collegial support.

Leadership

The original founding director of the private school was still in place as the director of the charter school. A former public school teacher and college professor, Ms. Carter visited and researched Black independent schools in the East and Midwest and networked with other alternative schools before opening the private school. In the first five years of operation, she did not receive a salary. In describing Carter, one of the Umoja teachers said, "She is a master of compromise and consensus, . . . also a master at culture-centered decision making." Parents and students agreed, citing Carter as an "inspirational" and "spiritual" leader.

Although Carter definitely wielded much power in the school community (for example, teachers were hired and retained at her discretion; she was the founder of the original school), the Umoja faculty, parents, and board did not impart the feeling that they were disempowered. Carter also did not appear to separate herself or operate above the everyday life at the school. As I roamed through the school, I encountered her presence everywhere—participating in the kitchen preparing meals for the students, comforting a crying preschooler, leading reading groups, and assisting teachers in the classroom.

The charter school's board of directors was composed of five community and local business people, two parents, and two teachers. There was also an active advisory board of sixteen community members. All members of the governing board were involved prior to charter conversion and as one board member remarked, "We're all intimately connected to the school." The chairperson had been serving on the Umoja board for more than ten years and was instrumental in assisting the conversion. The board met once every other month and its duties included policymaking, monitoring finances, troubleshooting, and community networking. Decision making was through consensus. The day-to-day decision making and educational program were in the hands of the director and faculty.

The Umoja Community

The years of operating prior to charter status and its membership in CIBI appear to have provided Umoja with a solid foundation and close-knit environment that facilitated the integration of large numbers of students and families who were not knowledgeable about Afrocentrism or did not buy into the philosophy. CIBI provided the staff with professional development in discipline and behavior problems, and in working with families who were not likeminded in their views on raising and educating children. Other factors that contributed to Umoja's stability and success by the third year of charter operations appear to be: strong leadership, buying into the vision and philosophy by the majority of the school community, and a high degree of internal accountability.

There was also a pattern of openness and frankness among the school community in discussing their difficulties and struggles. All of the adults cited student discipline as the most serious issue that they "have ever had to deal with." Finding new facilities was the second. As a private school, Umoja always struggled financially, but because of their conversion to charter they were finally achieving financial stability. The one thing that was negatively impacting the school budget, however, was vandalism. As a result, the parents organized and began patrolling the premises to send a message to the surrounding community that the Umoja families were concerned and proactive about their school.

Except for the inordinate amount of paperwork, Carter reported that the district did not monitor the activities of Umoja very closely. Internal accountability was strong, however. There was a personal interest—exhibited across the membership of the community—in the success of the school and its constituency.

Clarkville Charter School

In contrast to Umoja, Clarkville was a start-up charter school conceived collaboratively by a prominent African American community leader and civil rights activist and a White conservative Republican politician with an eye on the governorship of Florida. Both wanted to increase the capacity to succeed for the low-income children at risk in a high impact urban area and welcomed the charter law as a means to operationalize their vision. In July of 1996, the district approved their charter—the first charter granted in the state of Florida. A month later, the two founders hired Ms. Faith Jefferson, an African American sixteen-year Dade County veteran teacher, for the position of principal. Ms. Jefferson had been "very content" in her teaching position and was reluctant to take on "a situation that didn't have a blueprint," but she explained:

> My high school students were so turned off to school. I often dreamed [of how] I would change this if I had my own school. . . . [T]he focus needs to be on making productive citizens—you don't have to go to college to be a productive citizen. The charter school was an opportunity to see if I could really make a change . . . see if my ideas about how to educate children really work.

The two founders "really pushed for Jefferson," because they believed her educational vision matched their own; and because "she was creative and flexible and could handle the challenge." The first challenge that Jefferson faced was opening the school in a month's time. The founders located and rented a former school site that had been closed for many years (and according to Jefferson "was a horrible mess"). With their families and friends assisting, the three washed and painted walls, laid carpet, and cleaned restrooms to prepare the facility for students. In twenty days, the school was open for business. Sixty children, representing forty-seven family units, were enrolled in grades K–2 one week before school began. In the first year 99% of the children were African American, and 80% were eligible for free or reduced lunch. English was the first language for the majority, and four children were identified with special needs.

The Educational Program and the Students

Clarkville's original plan was to add one grade level per year, stopping after the middle school grades were reached. The principal felt strongly that if the students could remain at Clarkville through middle school, they would be able to handle anything.

By 1998–1999 the school had expanded according to plan, from K–2 with 60 students to K–4 with 189 students, 18–20 per classroom. The school operated on a typical 180–day year for students, and the teachers worked year-round. Classrooms were single grade and instructional time was organized in two-hour blocks for language arts, math, and science. The arts, critical thinking, and problem solving were important components of the curriculum, but "core knowledge" formed the backbone of the Clarkville curriculum. According to Jefferson, "Most of our children have missed the basics so we can't ignore—Can you read? Can you write? If you can't then it's hard to get to the next level, whatever that is." Measured by portfolios and standardized testing, the schoolwide goal was to improve at least five percentage points above the previous year or from where the child was upon enrollment in the charter school.

While the curriculum content observed was traditional and fact driven—workbooks, worksheets, pretests—the pedagogy was caring and energetic, and embodied the "bob-and-weave" metaphor of teaching. During a visit to the 3rd grade class, the teacher, a young Latino man, was coaching students while they answered questions and solved problems in their language arts workbooks. He walked around the room while giving instructions: "You have five minutes to complete questions two and three." He continued walking around the room during the writing, stopping often and bending down beside desks to consult with students. . . . He checked his watch. "Time's up. [rustling of papers, students chatter, exchange papers with partners] Jeremy, number two please." After the student answered correctly, the teacher asked the class if any one had another answer. Hands went up quickly. The teacher encouraged students to think of comical, yet appropriate adjectives to substitute in the sentence. They giggled and squirmed as they gave their answers. Questionable answers were discussed and analyzed. The teacher coached the students with comments such as "Learn from your mistakes" and "There's nothing wrong with making a mistake if you learn from it." The process—writing answers individually, exchanging papers with a partner, whole group discussion—was repeated for twenty minutes until the class broke for recess.

The school adhered to district guidelines for standardized tests—the SAT-9, Epcott, and the Florida Writing Test—and voluntarily opted to administer the Metropolitan (K–2) and Brigance Tests (K). Improving performance on standardized tests was a schoolwide mission, as the head teacher explained:

> We do a LOT of preparation for standardized tests. For instance we hold Saturday workshops for the students and their parents or grandparents. It's not required but most parents send their kids. . . . We coach kids and teach the parents how to coach their children at home. . . . Teachers work overtime to do this . . . and yeah, we complain a lot beforehand sometimes, but it really pays off and parents appreciate it so much. Last year parents volunteered eight Saturdays to prepare for the SAT-9.

In the first year of operations, the students scored at the bottom of the list of county schools on the SAT-9. But by 1998, Clarkville ranked at or above the countywide average, scoring higher in reading, writing, and math than eleven other elementary schools with matching demographics. A large display in the school office highlighted the local major news headline: "Fledgling Charter School Excels."

The majority of students observed appeared happy and engaged in the classroom, at recess, and at lunch. When I encountered them outside of class, going to the office or running an errand, they were purposeful in their actions, but helpful and eager to shake hands and introduce themselves. Approximately 10% of the students hailed from residential areas, but most were from the inner city. Due to the principal's insistence, bus transportation was provided. About 60% of the students take the bus and the rest are brought to school by parents. School uniforms were required: red shirts and black pants or skirts. Boys wear ties on Mondays and Fridays.

The first time I visited the school, I stumbled upon an impromptu assembly, convened due to inappropriate behavior by students on the buses. I had arrived early for my appointment and found everyone in the cafeteria. As I entered the room, only the teachers turned to look at me. The students were seated and silent, looking straight ahead at Ms. Jefferson. Teachers were scattered around the room, standing near their group of students. Jefferson was speaking at a medium-low voice level, but it was easy to hear her because the room was so quiet. Jefferson was very solemn and looked from face to face as she spoke:

> I couldn't believe what Mrs. Dukes was telling me. [pause] The only thing I could think of was that she was not talking about MY kids. I know my kids know how to act in school, out of school, on the buses, at home, at the mall, on the playground. [pause] Or do we?

The "talking-to" continued for only a few minutes more. Jefferson ended with the statement, "I think you owe your bus drivers an apology and a thank you for picking you up and driving you to school and back home safely every day." The students were then dismissed to go to their classrooms. As they left the cafeteria, they had to walk one-by-one past Jefferson. She touched the children on their shoulders, and addressed them by their names, individualizing her comments as they filed by. She stopped one boy, who had his arms folded across his chest and his brow furrowed, and said to him, "I don't think we should go to class with a face like that. You're going to stay with me until I find out about that face." He stood by her side until all the children were gone and then the two went into Jefferson's office.

Relationships

The relationships among the school community—board, administrator, staff, faculty, students, and parents—were described as "cohesive," "like-family," "comfortable," and "open." There were nine credentialed teachers at Clarkville in the 1998–99 school year, four full-time aides, and two office staff. All teachers had an aide for a half day. The majority of the staff were women. Two of the teachers were African American, one, Anglo, and the rest Hispanic. The office assistants were Hispanic and African American, and the aides were all African American. Staff and faculty turnover was low—only one teacher had left by the third year and that was because of the twelve-month work schedule.

Summers were used for professional development, reviewing and planning, working on their rooms, and talking to parents. In addition to school holidays, teachers received two weeks of vacation in the summer. Professional development was available throughout the school year: An educational consultant was on site for individual teachers Monday through Thursday and mini-workshops were scheduled after school when needed. Teachers had one hour during the school day specifically for planning with their grade-level partner. No teachers served on the governing board.

When the charter school opened, teacher salaries were below the district salaries. By the third year, Clarkville teacher salaries were higher than the district's, but benefits were still less. Most teachers found out about Clarkville via newspaper ads or word-of-mouth. Some were personally recruited by the principal. The two men on the faculty—one Hispanic and one African American—explained, "Ms. Jefferson came looking for us." While acknowledging that their jobs are time consuming and demanding, all the teachers seemed to genuinely love their job and their school community. Even with the financial drawbacks, teachers said they would not go back to work for the district. Note some of their comments:

"We love what we're doing."

"When you walk on campus you feel the love we have for each other and for our children."

"We're competitive as far as our individual classroom performance, but there's a lot of team spirit that goes into that."

"We complain a lot about all the hours we put in, but we wouldn't have it any other way."

"Ms. Jefferson is invaluable, awesome. . . . We're very fortunate that this all is really happening."

"Ms. Jefferson is a miracle worker. When I worry about how much something is going to cost, she always says, 'Don't worry about the money.'"

As far as parent involvement, Clarkville requires that parents sign contracts at the time of student enrollment that detail the parent involvement expectation of thirty hours per year. The principal reported that the school was "quite successful" in getting parents to participate because

we allow parents to meet the requirement in so many different ways—one father cuts the yard and one helps in the kitchen, two parents sit on the board, some volunteer for the Girl Scouts or the Boy Scouts, some give money, one father came and cooked ribs for the Christmas party. Talk about being in the zone—he was in the zone. . . . Last year we figured involvement to be at 80% . . . and that's without consequences for those that do not meet the requirement. Peer pressure and the kid pressure on parents keep the involvement up.

The parents interviewed credited Ms. Jefferson for the high level of involvement: "She's right here with whatever is happening. She's really involved . . . it makes you feel good seeing her so involved and she makes you want to be involved. She'd spend the night here if she could."

Leadership and Accountability

As with Umoja, the head of the school factored strongly in the positive climate and performance of the organization at this early developmental stage of charter operations. Students, teachers, parents, staff, and board claimed Jefferson to be the key to their success. Her vision aligned with the vision of the founders, she was a seasoned veteran of the home district, she had allies in the community, "she was a thinker, as well as a doer," and she was a risk taker. She was also willing to learn on the job and be flexible:

I didn't realize that my role would be so broad—not just being an administrator but also cleaning up the yard, mopping the floors. It's really a mom and pop organization—nothing's traditional about the roles. I also had to learn to contract out for services, be entrepreneurial . . . manage a business.

According to Jefferson, the reason for the school's success was that "everyone holds everyone accountable." Because her job entailed so many unknowns, she emphasized how important it was for the board of directors to hold her accountable. In addition to the two founders, the governing board was comprised of two parents, a community college president, a private college president, a member of the local business community, and a former principal. Jefferson and the head teacher attended the monthly meetings, but were not members of the board. Although faculty and staff interaction with the board was minimal, the two founders were very visible during the school day and at functions. They would often drop by and bring visitors, and act as community liaisons—securing donations and volunteer labor from local businesses.

As far as sponsor oversight, the district scheduled two official site visits and approximately four informal visits per year to the school. Jefferson was candid that she didn't always comply with the district officials' informal visits and requests for "unnecessary" paperwork. She curtly stated, "I don't have enough staff to be doing a bunch of busy work" and explained that in order to make her work life somewhat manageable, she studied the ins and outs of the district reports and regulations so that she would not get "jacked around." She knew the system well after being a district employee for sixteen years and was considered an "efficient and savvy charter school director" by her district colleagues.

Denton College Preparatory

Denton was also in its third year of charter operations during my site visit in the spring of 1999. The Arizona school was first founded as a small private school serving seventy African American children, and in 1995, the school converted from private to charter status. In the first year of charter operations Denton served 248 K-8 students. By the third year, it was serving 280 students. Denton was the brainchild of the founding director, Dr. Lawrence Marshall, a former journeyman printer and elementary school principal. Marshall, an African American man, was well known in the Black community as an educator and advocate for underserved children and youth. He worked with students in church summer camp and tutored in after school programs and in juvenile detention facilities. He explained that he had improved the scores, attendance, and behavior at one dysfunctional district school in a predominantly Black neighborhood, but the district did not seem to care about this and gave him no support. Marshall's tenure with the district was very rocky, and he was exasperated with the public school system's failure with "problem kids." He decided to leave the district and start a small private school to serve African American families.

In the first and second years as a charter school, Denton operations encompassed one campus, which was formerly the headquarters for the state teachers' union. In year three, the charter school opened a sister school and hired a dean for each site who was in charge of day-to-day operations. Marshall's official title was president of the corporation and CEO.

The students on the main campus were 90% African American; on the second campus there was more diversity—65% African American, 30% Anglo, and 5% Hispanic and other races. Marshall's target populations for the charter school were children who were not performing well academically or were not challenged in traditional school settings. According to Marshall, he'd never had to advertise for enrollment for the charter school. His status in the Black church and his reputation as an educator, coupled with word-of-mouth communication, were all the advertising needed for the Black parents in the community to respond and enroll their children.

Educational Program

While a district principal, Marshall formulated and began marketing his own teaching and learning approach and study kit, "Learning How To Learn." He formed a for-profit company to manufacture the study kits and began to use the strategy in all of his tutorial work. The "How to Learn" study kit was a plastic box that held learning tools: a dictionary, a thesaurus, a specially designed notebook, a learner's manual and study skills guide; a pencil and pencil holder, "How to Learn" videotape and audiotape, and word cards.

The study kit was featured prominently in brochures publicizing the school and listed as a key element of the charter school's educational program. The Denton College Preparatory's vision and philosophy read:

> We believe that all children can learn when provided with the tools and the opportunity to utilize them. The underlying principle of Denton College Preparatory's educational program is the concept of Confluent Education, which is a merger of the cognitive and affective domains of learning. We also believe that a child's education involves a collective effort by parents, the Academy, the student, and the community. Denton College Preparatory's program of study seeks to maximize the contribution and effort of each of the above parties. Our vision is to be an innovative model of superior education that produces academically prepared and socially responsible citizens. (Denton College Preparatory Information Brochure, n.p.)

A two-week intensive training program was held every summer for the Denton teachers on the How to Learn approach and two workshops per semester were offered for parents. The study kits were mandatory for the 5th through 8th grade students and Marshall's for-profit company donated the kits.

The Academy was organized into single-grade, traditional multiple-subject classrooms at the elementary level, and in subject matter classrooms for the middle school grades. A traditional nine-month schedule was followed by students and teachers and the average class size was twenty-two. Students were enrolled on a first come, first served basis and were required to wear uniforms. Every student had an Individual Learning Plan and was tracked into either college preparatory, learning enrichment, or special needs. Students in the learning enrichment classes were those who were working below grade level or were categorized as disruptive students.

Each school day began with a ceremonial gathering with the whole school participating, featuring inspirational songs and recitations. After this, students returned to their homeroom and the upper grades attended their mandatory How to Learn class. Reading was scheduled for seventy minutes a day (same time for all grades) with students organized in mixed-grade ability groupings. Homework was assigned four nights a week and Friday mornings were earmarked for tests. Music and art were not part of the core curriculum.

Teachers

The Denton teaching staff was not covered by a collective bargaining agreement and many were not certified. Their contracts were year-to-year. In the 1996–97 school year, eleven out of fourteen classroom teachers were not certified. Turnover—both student and teacher—was an issue. Marshall explained that in the first year of the charter he had had an "extremely difficult time" with his teaching staff:

> There were a bunch of young teachers that tried to take over. They didn't share the vision and complained about the lack of materials and resources all the time. I had to fight to get rid of them. I learned from it, though. . . . I don't leave hiring up to anyone but me now. You have to surround yourself with people that think like you and share your vision.

At the end of the second year, in a phone survey, staff conflict, burnout, and turnover were indicated as three of the four barriers the school was experiencing. In the third year, four of the teachers said that the charter school was still struggling with high turnover. The school had gone through five 5th grade teachers in one month that year. Three 8th graders complained that they "haven't had a math teacher for most the year." A 2nd grade teacher remarked that the teacher turnover in the upper grades "has affected us a bit" but that morale was "pretty good." However, she also reported that only 40% of her class were returning students.

Professional development opportunities in the third year were described by teachers as "slim." The offerings were primarily created in house and the teachers found the overall quality of these "so-so." There were Marshall's two-week summer workshops on Learning How to Learn and Wednesday after school staff meetings were earmarked for professional development, but teachers "wished there were more" professional development offerings generated from "outside of the school." Marshall had sent four teachers to a standards workshop that year, but that was all as of April of that school year.

In interviews, teachers mentioned the lack of resources at the school. They named this issue as the "biggest drawback of the job." During observations, the lack of books and instructional materials was noted in some of the Denton classrooms. For example, in the science lab, the shelves and worktables around the room were bare. No books, equipment, or tools were visible. The English and social studies teacher remarked that there were "few good literature books" so he "xeroxes material from newspapers, teacher manuals, and magazines." But he explained that he found this to be a "mixed blessing" because it forced him to be more creative.

During my site visit, the Learning How to Learn philosophy and study kit were enthusiastically endorsed and championed by the founding director, but there appeared to be minimal buy-in on the part of teachers, students, and parents. Although Dr. Marshall conducted a two-week summer workshop for teachers, four orientations throughout the school year for parents, and daily classes for students, Denton's educational program seemed fragmented and serendipitous, dependent on faculty strengths and what supplies and resources were available. The teachers interviewed did not speak of a common pedagogical or curricular vision.

Students and Parents

As in the case of Umoja, the conversion to charter status meant that the number of low-income families enrolled in Denton increased. In the second year as a charter serving 288 K–9th graders, the ratio of low- to middle-income families was 50:50. In the third year, only 30% of the students were from middle-income families. Behavior problems increased at the school with the rise in numbers and the change in the socioeconomic demographic.

According to Marshall, some of the parents were "surprised and upset" to find that their child, upon enrollment at the charter school, was not automatically on a college preparatory track. The parents believed that because the name of the charter school was Denton College Preparatory, all enrollees would be taking college prep classes. Marshall explained that "a lot of parents (were) looking for a quick fix" when they enrolled their children. Some of the new charter school students had "real behavior problems" and were achieving far below grade level so they were tracked into the Learning Enrichment Center (LEC). There were conflicting perceptions among the school community about the nature of the Learning Enrichment track. Marshall emphasized that this track was for students operating below grade level, but the Denton dean said that the track was for disruptive students. Denton students said that the Learning Enrichment Center was "supposed to be" a temporary in-school suspension track that students rotated out of after eight weeks. However, it was their perception that if students were tracked into the LEC, they stayed there for most of the year. In the Denton Disciplinary Due Process Procedures, the LEC was described as a temporary in-school suspension track:

> Should the student be suspended to the [Learning Enrichment Center], and should the student's behavior not improve significantly enough to return him/her to class, the student becomes subject to an extended stay in LEC until the behavior improves. Prior to release from LEC, the student will meet with the Dean of Students to discuss his/her period of LEC and to review and discuss the student's plan for Self Correction. (Denton College Preparatory Disciplinary Due Process Procedures, p. 2)

As mentioned, many of the parents enrolled their children because of their personal connection to Marshall or knowledge of his reputation. While teachers in the lower grades reported that their students "love being here" at Denton, four 8th graders who participated in a focus group spoke disparagingly about the school and Dr. Marshall. The girls had been enrolled at Denton for two years and were identified by one of the deans as high achievers as far as their grade point averages, standardized test scores, and extracurricular activities. The students did not mince words about their frustration with the school. Their major criticism was that they were "not learning anything" and that the substitute teachers (who were numerous) didn't teach, but "just sat there." The teacher turnover issue was affecting them greatly and all four were looking forward to graduating that year and going off to 9th grade elsewhere. They felt strongly that the teachers at the school could not "control" the problem students' behavior and as a result, the school was "noisy and dirty." The girls were particularly harsh about Dr Marshall's "How to Learn" approach and found the daily sessions on using the kit a waste of time. They were adamant in their criticism: "We hate the study kit" and "We've been hearing the same things over and over (in the daily sessions)." The girls claimed that a lot of students' study kits were empty and they carried the boxes around because it pleased Marshall. Upon exiting the focus group, the girl who had the least to say during the session turned to me and said, "Most of the kids don't want to be here. After I graduate, no one else in my family will ever come to this school."

However, some of the parents of younger students praised the Denton teachers and the school. One of the mothers lived in the neighborhood of the main campus and was a former student of the dean. She was particularly pleased with the smaller class sizes and the one-on-one support that her stepson was receiving. He had had "a lot of academic problems" before coming to Denton, but he had improved and was presently achieving at his grade level. Her son's teacher contacted her every week about his progress. Another parent remarked that Denton even had a dedicated office for parents at the school.

Individual teachers reported that communication was good between them and the parents of their students, but also remarked that schoolwide parent communication was inconsistent. The school did not have a policy of mailing out information to parents, but distributed it to students to take home, which was inefficient. Nevertheless, one of the new teachers remarked that he found Denton's parent involvement attitude and philosophy far more collaborative than what he had experienced at the Catholic school he had just left. He described the Denton parents as "very cooperative," but agreed that "a good minority" were "totally uninvolved." Marshall blamed this high level of uninvolvement on the fact that his original plan for parent contracts and requirements for enrollment had been rejected by the sponsor when he was petitioning for the charter. He also mentioned that many of the parents "want a quick fix" and don't view involvement as necessary and that "teachers don't understand the importance of communicating with parents."

Leadership and School Climate

While comments describing school life as "like a family" punctuated almost every focus group and interview at Umoja and Clarkville, this was not the case at Denton. The overall climate at the school was a marked contrast to that of the other two schools. There was high teacher turnover and high student turnover, overall morale was mediocre, and the physical environment exhibited a lack of care (for example, soiled and ripped carpets, holes in bathroom walls, and classrooms without resources). Although Marshall was a charismatic personality in the community, his leadership style was hierarchical and distant from his school population. While some of the classrooms, connecting hallways, and student restrooms were unkempt and rather sad looking, Marshall's office was large and immaculate, resembling that of a successful, high-powered CEO.

Upon being confronted with some of the issues raised by teachers and students, Marshall answered that the problems the charter school were experiencing stemmed from the following:

- Some parents want a quick fix.
- Teachers don't understand the importance of communicating with parents.
- Some of the kids are discipline problems.
- Teachers come to the job for just a paycheck.
- Staff members have not bought into the vision.
- People can't deal with start-up dissonance.

Approximately a dozen parents assisted Marshall in founding the school, but the visionary and driver of the charter was Marshall. He used his own money for start-up funds and was in charge of all major decisions, from founding through operations. After problems in the first year with disgruntled teachers, Marshall abandoned a "team hiring approach" and assumed sole responsibility for recruitment and hiring. He explained that in that first year, some of the young teachers who were hired tried "to take over the school." Marshall felt that the teachers did not share his vision and were upset by the lack of textbooks and teaching resources.

As with the teaching staff, Marshall had experienced problems with his board of directors in the first year of charter operations. The unrest resulted from a parent complaining to the board about her son being physically restrained by a classroom teacher. According to Marshall, some of the board members challenged him about his handling of the incident, with one member warning Marshall that the board had the authority to fire him. This did not go over well with Dr. Marshall. He explained that "this is my charter" and "the board is not my boss." In the third year of the charter school, all members of the board of directors were appointed by Marshall. The board acted in an advisory capacity rather than as a governing board, and as Marshall explained, "They don't interfere." There were seven members: six were parents and the seventh member was Dr. Marshall's wife. Their power was limited to approving the charter school budget and overseeing expenditures.

The issue of accountability surfaced repeatedly as an issue at Denton. Unlike Umoja and Clarkville, the responsibility for holding members of the charter school community accountable was not shared among the Denton College Preparatory membership. There was no one at the school overseeing Marshall's performance. By the third year of Denton's charter operations, Marshall had risen to prominence in school choice circles as an African American charter founder and choice advocate who had improved the academic performance of low-performing Black students at his charter school. He was often off campus, speaking at national and state charter conferences and education-related seminars and events.

In 1998, the Arizona State Department of Education put Denton College Preparatory on notice for ninety days because of its "lack of responsive to state paperwork requirements and fiscal auditing." The Center for Education Reform reported:

> [Denton College Preparatory] has improved student performance, fosters an atmosphere of order, and engenders a sense of community. Its sister school . . . has replicated the success, scoring higher composite scores than the district averages on the 1997–98 Stanford Achievement test in grades 3, 5, and 7. However, its expansion (to two campuses) and a lack of responsiveness to state paperwork requirements and fiscal auditing requirements has [sic] landed it in the hot seat. (Center for Education Reform, 2002, n.p.)

As a result, Marshall explained that he "now take(s) responsibility for making all major decisions," often staying up "past 2:00 in the morning, going over the books."

"So what?"

Although all three of the charter schools in this study served an all or predominantly African American population, they are quite different in their founding stories, educational programs, organizational climates, and behaviors. What they all shared, however, was that their founding visions were responses to the performance of the traditional public education system in serving African American students. The specific context—the state public education system and charter law, district regulations, and the local community and its resources—and the individual founders shaped how each of the visions were operationalized (Yancey, 2000). Parents and families were made aware of the charter schools primarily through word-of-mouth communication and newspaper ads. Relatives, neighbors, churches, and beauty parlors were the key conduits of the word-of-mouth information and the reputations and personal knowledge of the charter school principals were the beacons.

As noted previously, African American parents turned to the educational leaders in their own community back in the 1960s and 1970s for solutions to the poor achievement and perceived ill treatment of their children in the public schools. But there's an interesting twist at the turn of the twenty-first century. Black parents are not confining their options to educational solutions formulated by members of the African American community. Nor are they restricting their choices to schools created or operated by liberals or the political Left. Take Clarkville, for example: cofounded by a conservative White politician, there is a long list of Black families waiting to enroll their children in the charter school as soon as space allows. This White politician is not a popular figure among African American Floridians, but his belief that low-income Black students could succeed if provided with the right school environment was shared by Black leaders and parents in the community. His joining forces with a well-known Black community leader was a strategic move to broaden his political base, but his founding partner viewed the venture as ultimately beneficial to everyone involved: "People say he's using me. Well, he may be, but what a great cause. . . . The more we talked, really there were no philosophical differences, just a difference of ethnic perspectives. . . . We had the same message, but people reacted differently" (Staletovich, 1997, p. 1A).

Their reasons and perspectives for pursuing the partnership were different, but both men shared the goal of improving the education of low-income Black children. Neither cared whether it was done in an all-Black setting or an integrated one. The politician even argued to reporters that "there are more important things than integration."

> If we're successful teaching children to read and write and calculate math and they learn character, their character is formed in a way that makes them productive citizens when they're older, does it really matter? . . . Social policy shouldn't be imposed on children. (Staletovich, 1997, p. 1A)

Statements like these shock and disturb progressive educators and charter opponents. They continue to sound warning bells about the charter movement fostering a return to a segregated public education system, but Black charter parents appear not to buy into one-race charter schools as a negative thing. This was the recurring theme during my interviews with African American charter school parents, along with the fact that Black parents had lost faith in the traditional system of public education and no longer believed that the sanctioned educational leaders in our country—teacher unions, district superintendents, school boards—whether conservative or liberal in their political persuasion, cared about Black children succeeding in life. The cry of "Resegregation!" by charter opponents was answered by parents with, "So what?" Poor and low-income Black children are already being educated in public schools that serve a predominantly low-income Black population. As one Michigan mother explained, "No one seemed to care about that until the charter school came along. So what does that tell me?"

This theme surfaces across the nation from Los Angeles to Dayton, Ohio, to Washington, D.C. When the NAACP and the U.S. Justice Department were challenging the legality of Louisiana charters in 1999 because of the racial make-up of some of the schools, the Baton Rouge *Advocate* reported:

> [A]n African American father said the Justice Department and the NAACP "stand in the way of education and equality for our children by opposing charter schools. They do so in the name of desegregation. We feel that desegregation has not been a savior for our children that it was meant to be." Children have been bused to schools that are now "raggedy, run-down," and "due to demographics and parental movement from the inner city to the suburbs, the type of desegregation we first hoped for seems unlikely. . . . We want the (desegregation) lawsuit to stop destroying our children's education. We want charter schools." (McKinney, 1999, p. 1-A)

Charter organizers argue that they are not purposefully seeking segregated schools. As public schools, charters cannot restrict access or deny enrollment to any family seeking to enroll their child. Operators of predominantly African American charter schools report that it is the location of the schools in Black neighborhoods and/or the nature of the educational program that lead to the racial composition of the student body. When the Healthy Start Academy was organized in North Carolina, there were forty White students who were initially enrolled. When an affordable facility was located for the charter school in a mostly Black neighborhood in Durham, all of the White families withdrew their children. The charter opened with a majority of African American students who came from the immediate neighborhood. Schnaiberg of *Education Week* reported that the founding director (a White former New York state school administrator) maintained that his chief priority, and the priority of the parents he served, was to offer a quality education to his students:

> True integration, he argued, comes from the upward economic mobility gained through education. "I hear parents say: 'My kid is reading a year above grade level. And I don't care whether he's sitting next to a white student or not.'" (1998, p. 22)

Conclusion

The three charter case studies offer examples of the varied success of individual charter schools that serve African American students. Umoja, with its long history and strong network of support in the Black community, is a stark contrast to Clarkville and Denton. Umoja's history and connection to a wider network definitely offered the charter school a better foundation for academic success and district support. Clarkville students were also making improvements as far as achieving academically, but even with their close ties to the Florida governor, they received a D rating from the state the same year they made significant gains in their standardized test scores. Nevertheless, both schools are still in operation in 2002 and remain popular with their constituencies.

Denton College Preparatory is no longer in business in Arizona. Although charter proponents lauded the charter school in its early years as a shining example of the movement's ability to meet the educational needs of an underserved population, it appears that the publicity may have contributed to its downfall. Dr. Marshall became a "celebrity" in charter school and voucher circles as an African American choice advocate, traveling across the country for speaking engagements. He was cheered and embraced by the movement, which desperately needed to disprove the prediction that charter schools were going to be "White flight" schools. With Marshall's attention directed away from his school, and without the buy-in from his faculty, staff, and parents for his educational vision, the charter school floundered.

It is important to emphasize the critical role that the lack of buy-in plays in a charter school's struggles. In each of the charter school case studies, "struggles" and "rough times" were a part of their stories. But it was only at Denton that the solutions to problems appeared to rest solely with the founding director. As Marshall stated, "this is MY charter." Internal accountability—formal and informal—was minimal. Although the charter sponsor eventually red-flagged the school's lack of responsiveness to state paperwork and fiscal auditing requirements, the Denton community's lack of buy-in and internal accountability appeared to underlie its downfall.

As the charter school movement develops, we find that within the stories of its achievements, failures, supporters, participants, and opponents, a highly nuanced, conundrum-filled world of educational policy and decision making comes into focus. School choice, as in all school reform, has deep historical roots that are often trivialized, hidden, or ignored because of the significant political stakes for Democrats and Republicans, conservatives and liberals, the Right and the Left. Traditionally, educational policymakers are distanced and removed from the local impact of their decisions. By the time their bitter fights yield a school program that is experienced in the daily lives of the marginalized and low- to middle-income families, students, and teachers, it often bears no resemblance to the vision that launched the idea.

Through different states' interpretations of charter law, and local districts and sponsors implementation of "what is possible" locally, we witness in the charter movement a participatory political and educational activity in which the people are "credentialized" to play a role in defining and attempting solutions to society's problems and institutional inadequacies (Payne, 1995, p. 333). And yes, there are major duds among the "thousand flowers blooming." However, as CORE's James Farmer argued in the 1960s, there is a desperate need to involve the people themselves—individually, personally, actively—in the struggle, if we are ever going to achieve change (1966, p. 17). Without active participation by the people, the public education debates and solutions will continue to be shaped by educational researchers and policymakers whose decisions are colored by their own everyday realities, their positions as observers, and their self-identification as saviors of the marginalized and underserved.

Notes

1. The May 27, 1998, evening edition of the *Arizona Republic* reported the results of an Arizona State University study that compared the percentages of White students attending 62 Valley charter schools to the enrollments of Whites

in neighboring public schools. In central Phoenix, Khalsa Montessori charter school enrolled 82% White students, compared to three district schools which enrolled an average of 10% White students. In east Phoenix, Villa Montessori Main, Meadowbrook, and Campbell charters enrolled an average of 87% White students, while their three district neighbors enrolled an average of 36%. The pattern of larger numbers of White students enrolled in charters than in their neighboring district schools was echoed in the following cities:

- Mesa: Sequoia Charter 90% White, 2 neighboring district schools average 58%; Benjamin Franklin charter 96% White, 2 district schools average 55%.
- Tempe: Tempe Prep charter and Montessori Day charter average 85% White, 3 district neighbors 68%.
- South Phoenix: Tertulia charter school is 1% White, which mirrors both districts. Copper Canyon Academy, by comparison, is 60% White. Two of its neighboring district schools average 64.5% and the other two 45.5%.

2. Pseudonyms have been used for all charter schools and their faculties, parents, and students who are primary sources in this paper.

3. In 2000, twelve states allowed the conversion of existing private schools to charter status. Approximately 10% of all charter schools in the U.S. were preexisting private schools, 18% were preexisting public schools, and 75% were newly created (RPP International, 2000).

References

Center for Education Reform. (2002, February 4). Arizona puts school on notice to fish or cut bait: Phoenix case demonstrates power of charter school accountability. Retrieved from http://www.edreform.com/press/981215az.htm.

(Denton College Preparatory) Disciplinary Due Process Procedures.

(Denton College Preparatory) Information Brochure.

Farmer, J. (1966). *Freedom when?* New York: Random House.

Mayes, M. (1998, April 5, 6). Resegregation in Lansing schools. *Lansing State Journal*, 1A, 4A.

McKinney, J. (1999, October 15). Charter school interference hit: Opposition to program denied. *The Advocate* (Metro Edition, Baton Rouge), 1-A.

Payne, C. M. (1995). *I've got the light of freedom: The organizing tradition and the Mississippi freedom struggle.* Berkeley: University of California Press.

Ratteray, J. D. (1992). Independent neighborhood schools: A framework for the education of African Americans. *Journal of Negro Education*, 61(2), 139–147.

RPP International, (2000). *A study of charter schools: Fourth-year report.* Washington, DC: U.S. Department of Education, Office of Educational Research and Improvement.

Schnaiberg, L. (1998, August 5). Predominantly Black charters focus of debate in N.C. *Education Week*, 22.

Schnaiberg, L. (1998, September 24). Michigan tests show charter schools lagging. *Education Week*. Retrieved February 4, 2000 from http://www.edweek.org

Shujaa, M. J. (1992). Afrocentric transformation and parental choice in African American independent schools. *Journal of Negro Education, 61*(2), 148–159.

Staletovich, J. (1997, June 16). Area's first charter school ends "rough" year. *Palm Beach Post*, 1A.

(Umoja) Annual Report. (1997).

Yancey, P. (2000). *Parents founding charter schools: Dilemmas of empowerment and decentralization*. New York: Peter Lang.

CHAPTER 6

Voices of Progressive Charter School Educators

MELISSA STEEL KING

S ince the early days of the charter school movement, public debate over the reform has been complicated by the diversity of perspectives among charter school advocates. Motivations for supporting charter schools range from moving toward a privatized, market-driven system of education to strengthening public education by encouraging innovation (Wells, Grutzik, Carnochan, Slayton, & Vasudeva, 1999).

On the national stage, the charter school debate usually centers around one end of this spectrum. The loudest voices in support of charter schools are often those of political conservatives who promote charter schools, like vouchers, as a free-market reform based on choice and com- petition. These voices draw opposition from those on the Left who firmly support public education and view charter schools as inimical to reform within the current system.

The other end of the spectrum is less often heard: liberals and pro- gressives who support the charter school movement as an innovative means of improving public education. This chapter broadens the public debate by highlighting the experiences of several charter school educators who identify as politically progressive. Six educators from charter schools around the country were invited to respond in writing to questions prob- ing their motivations for working in charter schools and their experiences as progressive charter school proponents. Their responses, compiled below, represent the critical reflection of educators who are committed to charter school work but not necessarily to the agendas of the more visible, conservative charter advocates.

The educators included in this discussion were selected to represent different types of charter schools—expeditionary learning, for-profit, and culturally grounded—and a range of roles within the school—teachers, founders, and directors. The participants operate schools in California, Arizona, Pennsylvania, and Massachusetts; their experiences are thus shaped by the different historical and political contexts of charter legislation in their state. All six practitioners identify as politically progressive. These diverse participants were brought together in an informal roundtable conversation with the goal of letting progressive charter school practitioners speak for themselves about a variety of issues that inspire and challenge them.

Although the participants in the discussion are similar in their hopes and in their willingness to discuss the limitations of the charter school movement, they are not of a single voice. Most describe being drawn to charter schools by the desire to provide a quality education for students who are traditionally underserved, and by the promise of rethinking educational purpose within community-based institutions. They speak candidly about such challenges as finding and maintaining facilities, securing adequate funding, providing appropriate special education services, and sustaining vital autonomy against encroaching accountability reforms. However, they differ in their views of issues such as standardized testing and the necessity of participation in the broader charter school movement. Their disagreement over for-profit schools, in particular, is one example of how policy context can shape the experiences of charter school practitioners. The educators in Arizona, a state with a disproportionate number of charter schools run by education management organizations (EMOs) (according to CorpWatch [2003], EMOs manage or operate about 19% of charter schools in Arizona, compared to 12% of all charter schools nationwide), have much stronger opinions about for-profit schools than the other participants. Taken together, the voices of these progressives reflect the possibilities, limitations, and contradictions faced by those who support charter schools as a means of promoting social justice through publicly funded education.

Discussion Participants

Two of the discussion participants, Alison Reeves and Donna Braun, were founding members of the Ha:sañ Preparatory and Leadership School in Tucson, Arizona. The two women are currently Co-Directors of Ha:sañ, which opened in 1998 in a renovated church near the University of Arizona. Ha:sañ's mission is to serve as an academically rigorous, bicultural, and community-based high school for Native youth. Nearly 100% of students are Native American—primarily from the Tohono O'odham Nation, with a growing percentage from the Pasua Yaqui Nation and other Southwest Tribes—and all aspects of the school's curriculum are infused with elements of O'odham language, traditions, and Native history. Their four-day week with block scheduling (three long periods and an academic support period each day) allows for professional development and teacher preparation on Fridays, and helps relieve the stress of traveling for many of the students who commute long distances from nearby reservations. Before helping to found Ha:sañ, Braun worked as a high school science teacher and as an instructor and teacher trainer in environmental education. Reeves, who is currently working on a doctorate in teaching, teacher education, and educational leadership, previously coordinated a district gifted education program and taught for nine years—every grade from preschool to college.

Marjorie Wilkes joins the conversation from the West Oakland Community School (WOCS) in West Oakland, California. At the time she was interviewed, Wilkes was the part-time Development Director at WOCS while completing a master's degree in theology. During the first three years of the school, she served as the codirector for operations and external relations. In 1996, Wilkes initiated the founding of WOCS by convening a group of concerned educators, community members, and education advocates to research and write the school's charter. This WOCS Working Group designed a college preparatory middle school program that serves one cohort of 50 students at time, following them from 6th grade through 8th grade. Located in the historic Bethlehem Lutheran Church, the school features a 1:5 adult-student staffing ratio (with class sizes of 25 students at the most), a biweekly reading and writing enrichment course, and an extended day that includes study hall and extracurricular enrichment classes. All of the students are African-American (96%) or biracial (4%), and 75% of students are residents of West Oakland or nearby communities. Before helping to found WOCS, Wilkes's career included positions as budget lobbyist and program developer for the New York City teachers' union, director of two nonprofit organizations, grantmaker for Pfizer, Inc., and education consultant for foundations and nonprofits in New York and Oakland.

From the East Coast, Meg Campbell and Thabiti Akil Brown of the Codman Academy Charter School (CACS) in Boston both contributed to the conversation. Campbell, one of the founding members of CACS, is currently the head of school. She is also a lecturer at the Harvard University Graduate School of Education, and was previously executive director of Expeditionary Learning Outward Bound, as well as a teacher and active parent in Boston and Chelsea Public Schools. Brown is the founding humanities teacher at CACS. Having earned a master's degree in the teaching of social studies from Columbia University Teachers College, he student taught at the Beacon School in New York and then spent two years teaching at the International School of Panama. Their charter school, opened in 2001, is an expeditionary learning community that aims to prepare students for full participation in the intellectual, economic, and civic life of our society. The CACS "campus" is located in several buildings in the Dorchester neighborhood of Boston. Besides walking between classrooms, meeting spaces, and the fitness center in Codman Square, CACS students spend at least one full day a week in an off-campus course—for example, at the Huntington Theatre Company or the Museum of Fine Arts. The school includes an extended day and mandatory Saturday morning classes.

The sixth participant is Andrew Danilchick, from the Mariana Bracetti Academy Charter School (MBA) in Philadelphia. Danilchick is the expressive arts teacher, 6th grade Village Lead, and technology integration coordinator. The school, whose management partner is Edison Schools, Inc., was founded in 2000 by LULAC, a Latino community development nonprofit in North Philadelphia. Currently serving grades 6-9, the school plans to grow each year to eventually include both middle and high school (6-12). Located in a renovated, warehouselike former railroad station, MBA's mission is to prepare students for academic success and leadership in today's knowledge economy. The school curriculum follows the Edison design, and the schedule includes ninety-minute classes for students and ninety minutes daily of professional development time for teachers. The student body is 65% Latino, 30% African American, and less than 5% White. Prior to coming to MBA, Danilchick taught at a private Quaker school and a suburban public school.

Responses: Experiences of Progressive Charter School Educators

Personal Politics

In discussing their personal politics, the participants voice a concern for social justice and civil rights, as well as a desire to work outside of and transform the existing educational system. They cite this desire as a key difference between the liberal and progressive agendas. The two African American participants also talk about moving from a Democratic Party allegiance—traditional in the African American community—to affiliation instead with the Independent Party, reflecting their dissatisfaction with the move of the Democratic Party toward the center.

Q: How do you identify politically and why? What are the movements or issues that concern you or that you have worked on? Ultimately, what makes you a progressive?

ALISON REEVES: *I am probably "progressive" due to my concern with social justice issues. For the most part, I became an educator as an activist endeavor. I have spent the bulk of my career working on issues associated with equity for Native American students and communities.*

MEG CAMPBELL: *I identify with a long tradition of social justice, which for me has its roots in the Catholic Left. I was shaped and inspired by the civil rights, antiwar, and feminist movements and my maternal lineage were FDR Democrats of a devout nature, with strong admiration for the labor movement. I identify myself as a deeply political person, who sees much through a political lens, but realizes it is still just that—a lens. There are others. [What makes me a progressive?] My heart and mind being connected through my deeds [and] my choices in how I use my time and skills—whose interests I am trying to serve.*

MARJORIE WILKES: *I am a registered Democrat, as is everyone else in my family and as are most African American people. As the line between Democrats and Republicans has blurred to the point of indistinguishability, I will probably become an Independent before year's end. Regardless of party affiliation, I am what most people would regard as progressive, which means that I do not believe that we can create real and meaningful change within the parameters of our current political and economic systems, but neither do I have the revolutionary courage to work toward completely dismantling those systems. Much of my work (including my work at the West Oakland Community School) is about staging mini-revolutions at the edges of existing systems. It's not quite as useless as rearranging deck chairs on the Titanic, but it's probably no more useful than inflating a life boat and rowing like crazy, praying that we won't be pulled under by the force of the sinking ship.*

*Please forgive the hyperbole and melodramatic metaphors. . . . We're
in the midst of the biggest budget crisis California has ever faced, and my
disgust with politics and politicians has reached a level that even I find
alarming. Oakland is the largest city in Alameda County, which spends
$134 per youth per day to lock up juvenile offenders. The West Oakland
Community School receives $22 per child per day to educate middle school
youth. Call me an alarmist, but there's something deeply, deeply wrong and
corrupt about a country that uses its resources in this fashion. There is
something deeply wrong with a country where people consume and consume and consume, without regard for how their consumption destroys the
environment and helps to create poverty in so many other parts of the
globe. . . . [As] you can probably deduce, my interests outside of education
include economic development, environmental justice, prison reform, and
restorative justice.*

DONNA BRAUN: *I honestly don't have a description for my political identity.
The main movements or issues that I have worked on have been mostly
centered on ecological issues, environmental education, and Native American education. I feel strongly that the earth and human societies need ecological and human diversity to survive and thrive. This is what has
directed my actions in both my environmental activism and in my work to
help create our charter school. I believe that in working in multiple ways
(i.e., education, political activism, science, law) toward encouraging this
diversity to remain and grow, remains the hope for positive change.*

THABITI AKIL BROWN: *I am a recent convert from the Democratic party to an
Independent. Following the path that many African Americans before me
followed, I registered as a Democrat when I turned eighteen. [However,] as
a person who believes in working for social justice, who sees the current incarnation of the capitalist economic system in the U.S. as fatally flawed,
and who has until recently always voted against another party/person instead of for a candidate, I can no longer claim to be a Democrat. There
just isn't much space for a leftist in a two-party system where both parties
have moved center and right. As a Left-leaning person, with increasingly
less liberal and more radical notions, I have been trying to rethink my
political stance.*

    *In the realm of education I am a progressive because I am inter-
ested in building nontraditional schools that seek to educate students to
critically analyze the world towards effecting social change. I envision this
type of school as a center of community and learning where students are*

constantly engaged in a variety of "real-world" experiences as a counter-point to their classroom time. While teaching towards both—classroom time and real-world time—is a necessity, my focus is less on "learning how to play the school game" and more in line with looking at concepts, people, historical events and discussing/brainstorming ways to improve the world that we live in.

Q: What do you see as the difference between liberals and pro-gressives in education policy?

BROWN: I believe that liberals are interested in working within the status quo to effect change, whereas progressives are more content to work outside of the system, more interested in trying to remake the "this is school" model. The liberal camp in education policy in public schools works to maintain the present structure of schooling, while tweaking the content to meet Left-leaning aspirations. The progressive camp recognizes the benefits of the lib-eral stance, but is interested in making more fundamental changes to the structure of schooling. Instead of implementing a unit on the civil rights movement and the struggle for fairness and equality, a progressive may be more interested in building a school around these ideas.

WILKES: Liberal education reformers believe that we can create change within existing schools and school systems. They believe in the value of such ex-periments as school-based management and other efforts that are truly top-down in nature but often masquerade as bottom-up reform. Progressive education reformers are more skeptical about the possibility of creating change within existing schools and systems. Most of us are trying to create new types of schools with as much autonomy and distance from the exist-ing school system as we can muster. I believe that most, but not all, charter schools are examples of progressive reform.

REEVES: I think that the biggest distinction here really is one of purpose. Liberal policy seems more concerned with making sure that everyone has equal ac-cess (although we know even this isn't the case) to an already agreed upon definition of student achievement, that the purpose of schooling is to facil-itate equal access and participation in our global corporate economy. Pro-gressive policy can seek to upset the current balance of power, and to promote different views of a just society. Progressive policy can seek to ex-tend our idea of the purpose of education.

Entry into Charter Schooling

The participants had varying initial impressions of the charter school move-ment. Some thought of it as a new option for addressing the educational needs of traditionally underserved populations—an option with the poten-tial to have a broader transformative effect on public schools in general. Others viewed charter schools simply as a mechanism to achieve their im-mediate goal of creating an academically rigorous, community-based local school. Regardless of their different impressions at the outset, all of the par-ticipants were spurred to become involved in charter schooling because of their frustration, even "outrage," with what they viewed as the substandard education being provided to public school students in their communities.

Q: What were your initial impressions of the charter school reform movement and of charter schools?

BRAUN: *My initial impressions of the charter school movement was that it was an option capable of creating opportunities to improve education for un-derserved populations that was actually within reach for seldom empow-ered stakeholders, like parents and teachers, to effect and implement their own ideas for change. I also had the impression that it would provide an opportunity for diversity to flourish in incubators of creative problem solv-ing and that this could ripple out to affect the rest of the education system.*

DANILCHICK: *I first thought that primarily parent groups in a community who wanted a different experience for their children formed charter schools. I guessed that in any given charter school, you would see many parents in-volved in the daily life of the school. When I learned a bit more, I thought that charter schools were like lab schools where innovative practices could be tried out and public schools could learn from them. I originally thought mostly conservatives, some of them religiously motivated, backed charter schools.*

REEVES: *I did not have an initial impression before I got involved. We were look-ing for some way to improve the absolutely dismal prospects our students faced in terms of school choice. My initial efforts to help students to try and push for reforms at the district I was working for were going nowhere. When efforts to reform within the district system failed, we started explor-ing the idea of a charter school as an avenue for doing something better and different for the students. At that time, the literature about charter schools was scant. I was aware of the NEA [National Education Association] stance at that time, and the negative responses from colleagues. Several professors in my program told me that they couldn't support my work on the charter because they supported "public schools."*

WILKES: *I have never been impressed with charter schools as a reform "movement," and I have never viewed them as a panacea for the failures of public education. We chose to become a charter school because there appeared to be no other mechanism for creating a small autonomous school that would hold itself accountable to the identified needs of its children and families.*

Q: What factors (community, political, cultural, professional, personal, etc.) led you to become involved in charter schools?

REEVES: *Pure and unadulterated outrage led me to become involved. I realized I couldn't in good conscience participate in a system where failure was considered normal. Yes, there were a lot of concerned educators in the schools I worked in, but it was rare for anyone to really question what was going on. The community from which our students come has been disrupted for five hundred years and there are many challenges due to this disruption. The schools on the reservation tend to blame the students and parents for their own failure. I was told when I started my job there (by several other educators) that the students and parents didn't care about education because their culture didn't value it. This was not my lived experience. I saw a lot of students who did care very much and wanted to do well. They wanted to finish school, go to college, and work in the community. Parents were very supportive of efforts made on their children's behalf. This idea that no one cared was more like a convenient excuse for not making efforts to change things.*

I had the unique perspective of previously working on a different reservation for several years where the schools were more geared to student success. This helped me to realize what could be possible. Additionally, when we wrote our charter, we used data that had been collected in the community. Community members were very clear about what they wanted: college preparation and inclusion of language, history and culture. It seemed so simple to me to just do what was needed and wanted by the parents and students.

Unfortunately, it was clear that this wasn't going to occur in the local school district. We were led to charter reform simply because it was an available option. We took advantage of the option to create an alternate reality, one stripped of many bureaucratic constraints.

WILKES: In 1996, when we first began planning WOCS, charter schools were the only mechanism for creating a small autonomous school in Oakland. Having worked in New York City, with its delightfully robust alternative school movement, I was shocked to find so few alternatives to traditional public schools in Oakland. The school district now sponsors a Small Autonomous Schools Initiative, which Superintendent Dennis Chaconas describes as "internal charter schools."

CAMPBELL: I'm a single mom and I've lived in Dorchester for twenty years. I've long been outraged that we don't have a college prep public high school and when my own daughters seemed safely launched (they are now twenty-two and twenty-four), I decided I'd give it my best shot. I considered a Boston Public Schools pilot school, but wanted more freedom, frankly.

DANILCHICK: I don't think that public education as it exists today is serving the needs of our nation's young people. There are too many interest groups (school boards, unions, community groups, parents, etc.) who are forgetting a very important question that all schools should focus on: How do we serve our students and give them everything that they need so that they can develop the tools they need for life? Essentially, many of the problems in our schools reflect this lack of value for education and children. I believe that the charter school and homeschooling movements have potential to shift the focus back to the child and lead to transformation of the American educational system, but the movements are struggling against strong forces that resist any change.

I also had personal and professional reasons for choosing to work at my charter school. As a biracial Latino I feel a need to work in a school with a significant Latino population. Students of color need teachers of color as role models. My experiences as a biracial man from an urban working class family and my education at some of the nation's most elite colleges give me the tools to support my students in developing the skills needed to have success in dominant culture, while at the same time staying connected to their own cultural identities. I also crave a dynamic, progressive working environment where I can collaborate and build with other adults. At a charter school, my merit, skills, energy, and willingness provide me with leadership opportunities that would be unavailable in a traditional school. At charter schools, leadership is much more about *creativity and innovation since culture is being built out of a void (or what the teachers and students bring to it from their prior experiences).*

Experiences as Progressive Educators in Charter Schools

Upon becoming involved in charter schools, participants found that the movement is diverse, encompassing conservative, corporate, and progressive agendas. They describe a variety of reactions from their colleagues. Some have received support from activist peers who recognize their charter school work as an effort to create systemic change. However, more than one respondent notes that whereas moderately Left or liberal colleagues tend to be supportive of their reasons for involvement in charter schools, their progressive peers tend to be more distrustful of the charter school movement. Their political mismatch with many other charter school advocates is a tension for some of these educators—often coupled with a concern that the potential for innovation in charter schools to affect the broader public school system is not being realized. However, despite skepticism about the politics and potential of charter schools as a broad reform movement, each of the participants reports consistent satisfaction with their involvement in their particular school because of the positive impact they are able to have on their students and communities.

Q: How have your initial impressions changed now that you have been a charter school practitioner?

Danilchick: *I have learned that family involvement at charter schools in Philly, although much better than public schools, is not as great as I hoped. . . . At the beginning of lots of charter schools, tons of parents attend opening events and there is much promise of a "school with transparent walls" where parents are deeply connected to the daily life of the school. In practice, it's hard to integrate parents. With limited resources, time restrictions, and the overwhelming task of building a school, it's easy not to work to cultivate a different model of parental involvement. . . . I've also learned that there is a tremendous amount of diversity and specialization among charter schools.*

Braun: *When I first became involved with the movement, I didn't realize the opportunities that I saw opening up for parents and students were also openings for corporations to focus on innovations in turning profits. To me,* these corporate schools are the strings attached to the opportunities being given to progressive charter schools. It is strange that two polar opposite concepts exist under the same legislation and interesting how flexible that legislation is to allow for both.

REEVES: It is a disparate movement. There are those trying to stifle democratic aims and turn the entire system of public education into a market place. There are also those who are utilizing charter reform because they are outraged at what is being offered in the public schools and this provides their best option for meaningful reform. There are lots of stances in between these two extremes. Being a progressive charter practitioner is a pretty tough spot to be in politically. The charter movement is dominated by extremely conservative market zealots who see charter schools as the gateway to their ultimate agenda of privatizing public education and installing a voucher system. Progressive educators tend to not support charters for these reasons. As a progressive educator who is a charter practitioner, you don't fit in with either group.

DANILCHICK: My expectations of charter schools acting as lab schools to spur all sorts of reform across all of education were also very much let down. Charter schools, for the most part, are autonomous from the public school system and each other. Knowledge, ideas, and resources are not shared at all. I believe that my school could help other schools improve and vice versa. By not connecting charters to the public system or each other, a tremendous opportunity to uplift all education is lost.

BRAUN: My impression is that the change that the charter school movement can effect, while still having strong possibilities for many communities, is being hampered by bureaucracy and by the fear of change felt by traditional public schools as a result of charters. These roadblocks and obstacles need to be eliminated to allow the movement a real chance to thrive.

I feel confident that our school is innovating and having a positive effect on our students and their community; however, the challenges to survival have been immense. The city, state, and federal hurdles to simply exist and secure money for innovative programs have taken Olympic efforts to maneuver around. At times, these hurdles have left us too exhausted to continue improving our efforts to innovate and our services to students. These struggles to strive, coupled with the backlashes we have faced from the public school system that many of our students have left to attend our *school, have made me feel that the strong innovative incubator impact our school should have is still in the distant future.*

Q: How have other colleagues on the Left responded to your charter work?

CAMPBELL: *I live in a community with many activists—environment, peace, housing, etc.—and they've been quite supportive overall. People see the connection.*

BROWN: *I've found that the responses I get from colleagues on the Left regarding my work in a charter school are mostly favorable. Many of the folks who I gravitated towards as an undergraduate and graduate student shared my sentiments in terms of creating new schools that asked students to be students in a different way. Some have gone on to make change within more traditional public schools while others are working in a variety of more progressive schools (charter schools, pilot schools, alternative schools, etc.). The folks who work in schools similar to CACS are often excited to participate in an exchange of ideas. This larger community of innovative educators helps to nourish and sustain our smaller school community.*

REEVES: *When we started our charter, we were working in a traditional school district. Mostly my more progressive colleagues (who weren't already working with me on the charter) responded that the school would never open or it wouldn't work. [In the district,] people questioned my ethics for wanting to work outside the system, and associated our project with some of the more questionable aspects of charters such as for-profit schools. We were working in a failing system, and [the charter founders'] decision that it couldn't be changed and that it wasn't tolerable or reasonable to continue trying really made even our most progressive colleagues uncomfortable. The idea that our charter proposed a major shift in the way things would happen was threatening.*

Usually in my university classes, there is an initial "leper" period also. Just like most prejudices that people have, however, when they find out more about our project, the reasons for it, and the successes, they are pretty open minded and supportive. I have had a few professors tell me that although they support my work, that they don't support charters in general. The most oft mentioned reason is the problematic nature of legislation that allows for increasing privatization of something we believe should remain public. In

general I agree that privatization has very dire potential consequences for
education. However, in my opinion it is important to realize that business
has historically had undue influence on public education, both in terms of
content and in terms of guiding its goals, structure, etc. In this way, it does
not seem such a huge leap. Again, familiarity with our project usually allows
people to see that in at least this case, it makes sense.

BROWN: After relaying his experiences in a large, underfunded, overcrowded,
poorly managed middle school in Harlem one of my good friends asked,
"When are you going to work in a real public school?" This led to a discussion about what the term "real public school" meant. I explained that
charter schools are real public schools—state funded instead of city
funded—and that we deal with the same population of students as traditional public schools. We are not enemies in this war to educate our children; we have to have movement on multiple fronts. My friend's efforts to
improve the quality of education in his school and my efforts to do the
same in my school both work towards the common goal of improving
education in traditionally underserved communities of color.

BRAUN: [In my experience,] colleagues who might be considered to be moderately on the Left have understood the rationale for our charter school and
have been supportive. Colleagues who would be considered to be on the
far, or really even beyond, Left have respected the work we have accomplished at our school, yet could imagine even more radical efforts to help
the students we work with.

WILKES: Most of my liberal colleagues are also very excited about what we are
doing at WOCS. Most of my progressive colleagues are supportive but be-
nignly skeptical about our chances of success. With the passing of the
years, I find that I pay closer and closer attention to the wisdom of my elders, especially my grandmothers and my older African American neighbors in the "Lower Bottoms," which is the community's nickname for my
West Oakland neighborhood. Not long after my family moved to the Lower
Bottoms, one of our across-the-street neighbors came over to introduce himself. His name is Ron, and he is a longtime community activist, an artist
and poet, and a former member of the Black Panther Party, which got its
start in West Oakland. He asked what I do for a living, and I told him
about WOCS.
        "Wait right here," he told me. "I have a gift for you." He crossed
the street to his house and returned a few moments later carrying a book

that had belonged to his grandmother. The book, titled School History of the Negro Race in America, is probably the oldest Black history textbook published in America. The copyright date is 1891, and the author, Edward A. Johnson, was principal of the Washington School in Raleigh, North Carolina. In spite of my protests, Ron insisted that I accept the book as a gift.

"But this is like a family heirloom or something!" I told him.

"That's right," he agreed. "It's an heirloom and you're the heir. You're a teacher," he said, pronouncing that word with so much reverence that it gave me chills.

And then he patted me on the head as if I were a kindergartner and said to me, very gently, "Now you know they ain't gonna let you get away with what you're trying to do, right? You remember COINTELPRO? That's what happens when Black people try to do something for their own. . . . Of course, that don't mean we shouldn't at least try. You just keep on keepin' on till they stop you."

As I write these words, our school is preparing for charter renewal, and the political climate is uglier than it's ever been. The Oakland Education Association [the Oakland teachers' union] has recommended a moratorium on all new charter schools, and the president of the state school board has recommended that districts reject charter renewals for any school with an API [Accountability Performance Index] score of less than 4 (ours is a 3). I spend a lot of time these days meditating on Ron's advice: "You just keep on keepin' on till they stop you."

Q: Have your experiences with charter schooling affirmed your reasons for becoming involved?

WILKES: *For the most part, they have. We have considerable autonomy and control over our school's curriculum, budget, and personnel. The charter school regulatory environment is changing, however, and we are now subject to new legislation regarding teacher credentialing, participation in the Accountability Performance Index, etc.*

DANILCHICK: *For the most part I agree, although I think charter schools can do better across the board. The challenges that charter schools face of dealing with practical concerns such as resources, behavior management, creating a culture, and supporting new teachers are immense, but well worthwhile to undertake. I'm definitely invested in my charter school and the movement and*

*I am glad that I've chosen this route. It's a hard road, but the satisfaction of
being a part of transforming students, teachers, and communities is great.*

BRAUN: *I see improvement needed in our charter school and many other schools;
however, huge strides have been made with our students academically and
socially. The numerous students I have watched take advantage of their
second chance at our school and flourish, who otherwise would have faded
into a dropout statistic at another school, have affirmed all my reasons for
becoming involved in charter schooling.*

REEVES: *Yes. I am glad that we started our school. It might not be the right answer in every situation, but in this case it has been. We were able to respond to an educational emergency. When less than half of a population
is graduating from high school, and less than 5% of all adults finish college, you are in the middle of an emergency. The public school situation
was also bankrupt from a cultural perspective. We have worked so hard to
create a community of Native scholarship at our charter school. This has
required learning and unlearning so much that we all know about schooling. We are breaking ground every day. At the basis of every decision is
love and respect for the students. As I have already stated, my previous efforts at working with these students in their previous public school were
very unfulfilling. The system was so entrenched in ineffective practices,
negative perceptions, and layers of bureaucracy that no change was possible. To the public school system on the reservation, change was an accusation that someone was doing something wrong. At our charter, we try to see
change as positive.*

The Potential of Charter Schools as a Progressive Education Reform

While not all participants view the charter school movement as a
progressive initiative, they generally locate charter schools' progressive potential in the autonomy from the constraints of the traditional public
school system. Progressive educators in charter schools can use this autonomy to transform entrenched and ineffective approaches to education.
In general, the participants do not view this use of charter schools as conflicting with the cause of public school reform. They are universally
disenchanted with mainstream public school reform—if they believe any
reform is occurring at all—and seem to hope that charter schools can either
become a new movement for change or complement and give life to the

current public school reform movement. They each also report having chosen to work in a charter school that fits with their politics, even if they do not agree with the tenor of the movement as a whole.

Q: What is the progressive potential of charters? How do charter schools, as a progressive education initiative, differ from a liberal approach to education?

BRAUN: *Charters schools that are started and operate with the purpose of work-ing toward some type of justice for their students' situations can be pro-gressive initiatives due to their goal to create positive change. Within the confines their state, federal, and/or private funding allow, charter schools that focus on such change have the potential of creating real improvement in their students' educational experiences. And, hopefully, these improve-ments will have the potential of inducing a positive ripple effect in the way their students experience life in their society, the way they treat others in their society, and, most importantly, the earth in general. This approach to induce real change in the way and reasons students are educated differs from a "liberal" approach in that it strives for the specific purpose of that change. A liberal approach seems more interested in maintaining the cur-rent social structure and therefore focuses on creating the appearance that positive change may someday in the future manifest, while insuring that the present situation remains unaffected.*

BROWN: *Charter schools have the ability to be leaders in education reform in ways that are quite difficult for traditional public schools. Encumbered by layers of bureaucracy, traditional public school have so many existing regulations that educators often lack the flexibility to radically remake their schedules, fine-tune their staff, or adjust the allocation of financial resources. This is where charter schools are at a considerable advantage. The autonomy of charter schools allows educators to have a heightened ability to mold our individual schools for our particular student popula-tions. From this vantage point there is a huge upside to the charter school movement.*

REEVES: *I would have to say that I do not think that charter schools are a pro-gressive initiative. It's a pretty big stretch to view them that way when their underlying premise is a free market approach. That said, I would concede that some educators and parents are utilizing the charter structure to do some pretty progressive things. The progressive potential is there, but with constraints. The most progressive charter school is still faced with reconciling the issues inherent in the accountability movement at large.*

Q: How do you respond to those who charge that charter schools hurt the cause of public school reform?

REEVES: *What public school reform? There is no public school reform occurring, outside of the accountability movement that is extremely problematic. My biggest concern in this area is for-profit schools which try to promote the illusion that charter schools (for-profits) can do things cheaper and better than regular public schools. I think that this hurts the cause of increasing funding for all schools. The idea that the accountability movement can fix the problems faced by public education is very misleading. It also ignores the underlying social problems that need to be addressed.*

BRAUN: *I believe traditional public schools need to change from large institutions that view students as products to places of student-centered opportunities. This can't be done in their current context. There would be no incentive for improvement in traditional public schools if charters weren't pulling students, teachers, and money from them. Charters based on innovative techniques can only help traditional public school to reform and serve students better.*

CAMPBELL: *I invite [opponents of charter schools] to visit my school and meet the teachers and students—or to visit our website and read for themselves what students have to say about the school. We serve a higher percentage of students (82%) eligible for free and reduced lunch than the BPS [Boston Public Schools] district average. I know our students are going to go to college. Also, I ask [opponents] where they enrolled their own child or the child they most love. My dream for Codman Academy Charter School is to be good enough that I'd enroll my own daughters there—or other children I love. As for "public school reform"—that's a grand idea and I have spent the better part of my professional life working on it. Now I'm trying to make a contribution in what I see as an area of need: figuring out small urban college prep high schools. I don't think we've got them figured out. People need compelling examples of what works; what are we reforming public education to look like? We're practical dreamers hard at work.*

WILKES: *In general, I don't even dignify this accusation with a response. Far too many of our public schools, especially those that serve large numbers of low-income children of color, are broken beyond repair. They do a huge disservice to children whose families are already caught in a heartbreaking cycle of poverty and despair. I began my career in public education believing that we could actually reform public school systems. I no longer believe this. I no longer believe that top-down policy imperatives generate meaningful, ground-level change. I do believe, however, that we can create, one by one, schools with talented leadership, dedicated teachers, solid educational programs, and a strong commitment to educating each and every child. Perhaps, in time, we can create a critical mass of these schools, which can drive bottom-up changes in educational policy.*

DANILCHICK: *The variety of answers to this question is very much influenced by one's ideology, experiences, and values. I know that charter schools serve many students who have been expelled from public school or who have had very strong failure experiences in public school. For those students, charters perform an important function. Charter schools may also act to motivate schools to work harder to service the students that they still have and to adopt some of the innovations happening in charter schools. Charter schools can work with public school reform movements.*

I believe that there are other reform movements that hold real promise for transforming public education. My wife and I have begun homeschooling our four-year-old; the resources and networks available for homeschoolers indicate to me that political and educational advancement of the movement may lead to changes in state law and even in how people conceptualize the educational process. I also think the standards movement is offering many positive concepts and practices to modern education. The standards movement stresses that the dependent variable is high student achievement and the independent variable is time and support. If that idea is fully supported then schools would do anything and everything needed to help students grow and achieve. I feel strongly that a new reform movement needs to be created that merges some elements from different reform movements along with some new ones. Take the underlying beliefs of the standards movement, add to that an unrelenting commitment to develop the emotional and social skills of children, and shift society to more fully value children and the resources needed to build a better world, and perhaps a new movement may develop. Any new movement will be greatly limited unless it can find a way into a national dialogue that transforms the level at which children and education are valued.

Q: Do you feel that charter schools are aligned with your poli-
      tics, in general, or your views on public schooling? If not, how
      do you reconcile your work with your politics?

CAMPBELL: *Yes, they are. I hope someday we have a system of education funded
like we fund our highway system—evenly across the nation. I think Aus-
tralia's way of organizing school systems is worth study: five states and
each state in effect gives a charter to every school. Same funding across
each state. No local districts.*

DANILCHICK: *Since I do not really believe that public education is currently serving
the needs of young people, charter schools appeal to me as a possible alternative or a means of spurring reform in public education. One of the unique
features of charter schools is that any organization or group of parents or educators can submit a charter application. As a result, charters schools are extremely diverse. Some have an experiential or adventure-based learning
theme, others are core knowledge schools. There are many charter schools
that, for a variety of reasons, are struggling to provide a good education. The
charter school I currently work in fits me, but the majority of them probably
wouldn't. Our school is privately managed and I am definitely not against
that approach as long as students benefit and are the primary focus.*

REEVES: *To some extent I feel that they are [aligned with my politics]. I do feel
that they allow for more socially just schooling options, and that this is important. Charter schools can bring power and voice to those who previously
didn't have any, or had very little. We have had to reiterate over and over
to parents and students that we need to hear complaints and suggestions,
that we are listening. They are used to being powerless in the school system.*
      *One of the unstated, but generally understood, purposes of public
schools in America has been to define what it means to be an American,
and to promote acculturation into our economic and political systems as
they are. With Native Americans specifically, it has been a primary form
of genocide, erasing their culture and language and forcing them to develop "American" values. Obviously, I think this is very wrong. Charter
schools allow an avenue for redefining what schooling is about for groups
such as these.*
      *I am really torn on the issue of segregation. I am concerned about
the negative aspects of this, but in a situation such as ours, our students
were already segregated (reservation schools) and parents want a school
that can focus on their student's unique needs. A large urban public school*

simply cannot provide a culturally appropriate education to all of the groups attending. It isn't logistically possible. There are other groups who are choosing to segregate through charter schools. I think the interesting question for those concerned with this is, "Why?"

In a larger sense, charter schools are an arm of the accountability movement in general. As such they legitimize the focus on standardized test scores. I don't support this type of school improvement, and feel that it is damaging to marginalized groups. I think that the accountability craze, as it is being implemented through No Child Left Behind, has a lot of power to homogenize schooling, to force charters into the same paradigm that traditional public schools are operating within.

BRAUN: *Public schooling should represent and incorporate what the public/ community wants for students. This democratic ideal does not occur now in large, traditional public schools and has a better possibility for occurring in small, progressive charter schools. I do not support corporate charters; their investment in capitalism and perpetuating a consumer society represent conflicts of interest in empowering youth to critically think about the world around them, which I believe is essential for a real democratic society. At the same time, the students I work with have very little to no hope of receiving even decent treatment as humans, let alone exposure to an innovative curriculum that focuses on them as learners, in the traditional public schools they have attended. They deserve and need a school experience that values them as people and focuses on them as talented learners, and the charter school movement has provided a means for them: our school. Although I don't support corporate, for-profit charters, I can reconcile being part of the same movement because our students so desperately need a school like ours. Other means of procuring funds (e.g. private) would be less stable and still require us to bend to the interests of funders.*

REEVES: *I, too, remain clear on the fact that it is allowing us to do something better for our students, that students and parents want this school. When we started our school, we had opposition from many different factions, including tribal leadership. We strove to define our community as the parents and students. Basically, we took out the middleman, meaning all of the bureaucratic constraints that had limited previous reform efforts. This made things really simple for us.*

WILKES: *Almost any option that promises a better education for low-income children of color aligns with my politics.*

Hopes for the Future

In general, the participants express a hope that the influence of progressive charter schools will grow and create more widespread change in public education. They cite the need for more financial and professional support for charters, more collaboration with public schools, and more investment in charter schools from higher education. Most participants envision themselves continuing to advance progressive politics by working, in some capacity, with their own charter school or with charter schools more broadly.

Q: Ideally, what do you hope will be the future of the charter school movement in this country?

BRAUN: *I hope that progressive charter schools continue to grow in numbers, so that underserved populations have a chance at a better educational experience and so that traditional public schools may learn and change from their innovations.*

CAMPBELL: *I hope [the movement] will mature and become more reflective and self-critical. We have a long way to go before we realize the ambitions of serving all students well.*

DANILCHICK: *I hope that the movement gets stronger with better quality schools. There is such a resistance to change in public education, it would take thousands more charter schools and hundreds of thousands of parents choosing charter schools to really shift our nation's approach to schooling. I hope that charter school legislation is rewritten to provide better resources for schools, especially with special education. I also think that the standards for charter schools should be much higher with lots more support and training provided from the states and federal government. Charter schools need to be invested in to the degree that student needs are being met, not merely as a result of property tax mileage rates. I also hope that charter schools are evaluated on many more measures than only test scores.*

REEVES: *I think that it will eventually have the effect of breaking up the larger school systems into more responsive, less bureaucratic units. We already know that smaller schools are generally better. Charter schools allow an opportunity to demonstrate this. I don't generally support applying a busi-*

ness metaphor to schooling, but I do think that the market-based approach upsets the status quo in potentially positive ways. We know that
there is an effect on districts, that they become more responsive to students and parents when there are local charters. This is a very good
thing. I would like this to be taken a step further and see formal mechanisms put in place for collaboration. We would love to tell other schools
how to help our students—more students win in this way. Charter
schools such as ours can redefine education for Native American students. Nothing would please me more than to see the acculturation
model of schooling for Native Americans disappear completely.

Higher education has chosen to mostly ignore the charter school
movement as if it is going to disappear if they don't acknowledge it. Charter schools are basically laboratory schools and as such could benefit
greatly from collaboration with institutions of higher education. Teachers
and administrators need opportunities to receive training to work at charter schools. There are a few pilot programs around the country, but I
would like to see much more work in this area.

I also hope that we can take the lead in providing more equitable
ways to define student success for all students. Many charters are using
multiple indicators of student success even though they are legislated to
participate in standardized testing. The groundwork is there to move
beyond such narrow indicators; we just have to steer the conversation.

WILKES: To be perfectly honest, I don't devote much time to thinking about the
future of the charter school movement in this country. I devote every wak-
ing and sleeping moment to thinking about the future of WOCS and how
in heaven's name we are going to sustain this one remarkable little school.
Please forgive my tunnel vision.

Q: How do you envision the future of your own involvement
     with charter schools?

CAMPBELL: Critical friend and advocate.

BRAUN: I hope to continue to work with progressive charter schools, as a teacher
or administrator.

DANILCHICK: I hope to work in charter schools for a long time. I feel a deep obligation to serve urban youth so I think I'll remain in the city. I really like

where I work right now and for the first time can imagine myself at a school for more than five years. I see myself involved at different levels of leadership, but I am currently resisting the temptation to be a principal of a charter school or perhaps to even start my own charter school. The personal costs would be too high at this point considering that I want to continue to be a highly engaged and nurturing father for my son. The energy and time needed to start a school is incredible, but the idea very much appeals to me.

WILKES: I have found that launching a charter school has consumed every bit of physical, mental, emotional, and spiritual stamina that I possess. I am taking a sabbatical after this year and looking forward to a well-earned period of rest and reflection!

REEVES: In my particular situation, I am supposed to be working myself out of a job; it is part of our school's charter and mission that the leadership be Native American. I am not sure how I will continue to be involved after this. There has been a great deal of interest in our school from other Native American communities. I am doing some research to help facilitate sharing of information between Native American charter schools. It is clear to me how this can be a great option in this particular situation. I think as a reform option, it has great potential but that it needs to be steered in a progressive direction. The conversation is very lopsided in the literature. We have started to move beyond the "should they exist" debate into more intensive questions. I feel annoyed at the constant focus on whether or not charters are raising test scores. I realize this is the national focus, but like many, I think it is an assumption about schooling that needs to be questioned. How can charter schools promote equitable schooling experiences for marginalized groups? What would that look like and how could it be measured? How can charter schools promote democratic ideals? When students and parents choose to segregate, what are they resisting and why? These are the types of questions I am interested in, and see myself trying to answer in the future.

Conclusion

The above discussion reveals some areas of fundamental agreement among the progressive charter school practitioners who were interviewed. The participants share the belief that charter schools can allow progressive educators to work outside a dysfunctional system, transform stagnated educational practices, and provide a high-quality education to students who are traditionally underserved. In discussing their personal politics, all of the participants frame their educational work within a larger concern for social justice.

Though these educators concur on the ultimate aims of their charter school work, their discussion brings to light a certain lack of consensus around the means by which charter school practitioners should carry out a progressive politics. As evidenced here, the charter school movement supports a wide variety of educational philosophies, so that even those with similar politics may find themselves disagreeing about the types of schools and educational strategies that best serve children. The responses above highlight certain resulting tensions around the market-based nature of the charter school movement, the use of charters as a tool for broader education reform, and the question of whether, ultimately, charter schools should be considered a progressive reform initiative.

The participants differ in their levels of comfort with charter schools as a market-driven reform. Some argue, like Wilkes, that any type of school that provides a quality education to underserved children fits with their politics; for Danilchick, this specifically includes for-profit schools like the one in which he works. Other participants—the Arizona-based Braun and Reeves in particular—emphatically distance themselves from what they see as a corporate, market-based agenda in the mainstream charter school movement, believing that the principles of capitalism fundamentally conflict with the principles of social justice work. Nonetheless, even those who express the latter opinion acknowledge the fundamental premise of the charter school movement that by competing with traditional public schools for students and resources, charters can provide incentive for innovation and improvement in public education. The different stances of the progressives in this discussion provoke the question, Can reforms with an underlying market logic ever effectively serve as a vehicle to promote social justice?

A second tension centers around participants' level of dedication to using charter schools as a lever for broader public education reform. While some of the educators speak hopefully about their schools serving as an impetus, model, or laboratory for educational change, several also express an all-consuming focus on just building and sustaining success within their individual schools. Whether the participants simply wish to create an effective community school or maintain the ultimate goal of creating broader public school change, it is clear that the daily challenges of running a charter school—including securing facilities, strengthening student achievement, and answering to district, state, and federal mandates—largely drain any time and energy that could be used to begin collaborating with other schools. How can charter schools effectively spur innovation and improvement in the public school system if charter school practitioners are either not inclined or too swamped to reach out and share best practices? And how long can progressive educators hold out hope that charter schools will spur broad change in the face of their own observations that in reality, this sort of interchange is not taking place?

Finally, the question remains whether charter schools should, indeed, be considered a progressive reform initiative. While all of the participants agree that charter schools can serve as vehicles for progressive work, the complexity of their views on the nature of the charter school movement raises questions about what in fact constitutes progressive education reform. If an initiative advances the goal of equalizing educational opportunity for historically underserved students, is it inherently progressive—even if it simultaneously aids a conservative agenda of privatizing education? Can charter schooling be considered educational reform, even if change happens only within isolated, community-based autonomous schools rather than throughout the entire public school system? And as these progressives seek to create charter schools that avoid and counteract the perceived failings of traditional public schools, how should the success of their reform efforts be defined and measured, and by whom? Politically progressive educators must increasingly engage with each other, grappling with such questions and forging a deeper understanding of what it means to harness the full progressive potential of charter schools. Through continued discussion, progressive charter school educators like those represented here can learn from and support each other, as well as build visibility so that their voices and views will be heard more often in the national charter school debate.

References

CorpWatch. (2003). Corporations capitalize on for-profit education. Retrieved July 17, 2003 from http://www.corpwatch.org/bulletins/PBD.jsp?article id=5489

Wells, A. S., Brutzik, C., Carnochan, S., Slayton, J., & Vasudeva, A. (1999). Underlying policy assumptions of charter school reform: The multiple meanings of a movement. *Teachers College Record, 100*(3), 513–535.

Part II

FRAMEWORKS FOR
PROGRESSIVE SCHOOL CHOICE
ANALYSIS

CHAPTER 7

The Charter School Movement: Complementing or Competing with Public Education?

ALEX MEDLER

Charter schools have become a significant innovation in American education. Since 1991, legislation authorizing charter schools has passed in forty states and the District of Columbia, and approximately 2,695 charter schools are open, serving more than 684,000 students (Center for Education Reform, 2003). The size and scope of this phenomenon is clear. What these schools are intended to accomplish, how they contribute to change in our broader school systems, and how we can understand them as a collective unit are less clear. This chapter will use Social Movement Theory (SMT) to show that people disagree about the purpose of charter schools. Specifically, they disagree about the relationship between charter schools and the rest of our public schools.

In one sense, charter schools are public schools whose presence expands the range of teaching available within the public education system. They complement public schools. In another sense, charters are intended to prod unresponsive and failing bureaucracies. By competing with the public schools, charters are meant to indirectly fix the public school systems through the application of market pressures. This difference stems, in part, from the unit of analysis. Each individual school adds its own way of teaching to the public system, while collectively the charter movement creates markets of choice. SMT helps us understand whether this movement is more accurately described as the aggregation of individual schools that collectively complement our larger system, or as a burgeoning market

189

sector, with competitive dynamics designed to stimulate widespread change in failing systems. Both interpretations are based on experience. Influential people inside and outside the movement are contesting which approach should dominate.

If one definition increasingly dominates the public perception of charter schools, then the other approach could become more difficult to operationalize. For example, if charter schools are only understood as positive additions to large school systems, and schools that would compete with district schools are not allowed to open, those systems need not make any changes in response to the charters that remain. This would make competition impossible or irrelevant. Alternatively, charter schools could be understood strictly in terms of the competitive pressures they place on districts. Pressure arises when charter schools attract students and public funding that would otherwise go to traditional[1] public schools. In this case, whole communities that would otherwise welcome new public schools designed to better serve particular students may fight charters instead. They would do so to protect the resources of existing public schools that are also trying to serve students they care about. Thus, whether charter schools come to be seen as primarily complementary or competitive (or both) could change the way the public treats them. It could also change the political dynamics of other education reforms, like school vouchers, that use similar frames.

This chapter examines how and why the charter school movement can thrive despite an ongoing fight over its purpose. Do participants' attributes—including their sense of identity, the forums in which they operate, and movement membership—shape the frames they use to characterize the charter school movement? Does SMT and its conceptual tools help us understand these dynamics? These questions raise issues important to people on the Left and Right. If people on opposite ends of a political spectrum use different frames to describe a single movement, how will these frames affect both the movement and its place in society?

Before empirically documenting the dynamics of framing in charter schools, this chapter will define and outline the genesis of these frames. Section 2 justifies the application of SMT to charter schools. Section 3 places the dynamics of the charter school movement into theoretical tools in SMT and describes the major subframes. Section 4 outlines the historical development of the charter school movement and illustrates how the complementary and competitive subframes emerged through this history. Section 5 articulates a puzzle that arises when conflicting subframes operate under a comprehensive master frame and describes the data used in this analysis. Section 6 presents findings and discusses their implications.

Charter Schools as a Social Movement

To the uninitiated, the charter school movement may not even appear to be a social movement. This is a mistake. According to McAdam, Tarrow and Tilly (1996), a social movement is "a sustained interaction between mighty people and others lacking might: a continuing challenge to existing power holders in the name of a population whose interlocutors declare it to be unjustly suffering harm or threatened with such harm" (p. 21).

The charter school movement challenges a public school system of immense scale and might. Approximately 85,000 public schools are operated by 15,000 school districts, serving approximately fifty million students and employing more than two million teachers. The districts administering these schools take their legitimacy from state constitutions and generations of precedence. While state and federal governments support charter schools, the primary power holders responsible for administering public schools are local school districts. The school districts are the power holders that the charter school movement challenges.

Charter school founders are arguably social movement actors who benefit from facilitation by state leaders who codify political opportunities under state charter school laws. Nevertheless, charter school founders themselves are not power holders in the traditional school systems. Parents, teachers, and community groups seek to exercise direct control over a public school. And because of the duration of charters—three to fifteen years—and the creation of new public institutions, the effort put forward by these challengers is necessarily sustained. The families that choose to send their children to charter schools also sustain the movement.

Whether the students attending charter schools have been or will be harmed by the power holders is something that fuels a lengthy debate in the education field (Berliner and Biddle, 1995; Kozol, 1991, 1995). Under some circumstances described below, charter schools are perceived as a solution to harm inflicted on students by a large and unresponsive education system that is failing children generally. Many argue the harm comes to children from a variety of sources outside the schools, and the district's role in furthering that harm is a sin of omission more than commission. In either analysis, the charter schools are seeking to protect and better serve children harmed by the status quo.

In sum, the charter school movement is a social movement. It represents a sustained effort on the part of a traditionally weak population against a mighty group. Other powerful actors, notably state and federal policy makers, have played a role in shaping the political opportunities to forge charter schools. However, individuals and groups from outside the policy-making structure are driving the movement by exercising unique forms of social action. One potential criticism of this attempt to portray charter schools as a single social movement is its diverse nature. But this diversity does not suggest two different movements. Instead, it represents a struggle by those inside and outside the movement to define it.

Theoretical Tools

This analysis uses the tools of Social Movement Theory to define and articulate the competing concepts within the charter school movement. The concepts of framing, identity, movement membership, and arena all help illuminate the charter school movement's dynamics.

Multiple Frames

The charter school movement operates within multiple frames and various participants in the charter movement have disagreed about the construction of its meaning. Snow and Benford's (1992) collective action frame is a concept that captures this process. A "master" frame of *choice* is shared among most participants. The widespread support for choice masks divisions over how full or controlled these choices should be. Beneath the agreement, and reflecting the division, are several competing frames (or subframes) that are determined, in part, by the participants' sense of identity. These subframes include charters as both market actors *competing* with the established system and as sources of educational diversity that *complement* the larger system.

Competitive Charters

As competitors, charter schools are important for their impact on the larger, nonchartered school system. Charter schools create pressure on the broader education system, hopefully stirring a response from traditional bureaucracies that otherwise fail to meet consumer needs. Choice is an instrument to change the larger system (Chubb and Moe, 1990; Kolderie, 1990; Moe, 2001; Rofes, 1998), and charter schools provide an expansion of choice (Peterson and Hassel, 1998).[2]

The competitive frame is based on contention and is often part of a larger policy debate over school vouchers and other market-based education reforms. It is attractive to people on the Right who prefer market mechanisms to public solutions generally and who are skeptical that large public institutions will succeed in solving social problems.

Complementary Charters

Under a complementary frame, the charter schools themselves are the movement's purpose. Charter school founders create alternatives within the larger framework of public education. The public benefits from a large collection of individual schools that collectively provide more options (Nathan, 1996; Dale and Deschryver, 1997; Finn, Manno, & Vanourek, 2000). Schools leaders also benefit from expanded professional opportunities, including those in which educators can work in "learning communities" that may increase student performance (Wohlstetter and Griffin, 1997a; 1997b).

Using the complementary subframe, the traditional public school system's failures are less important. Instead, charter schools provide solutions to unique problems that individual students face. The educational opportunities that charter schools provide to students and teachers create the compelling rationale for complementary charter schools. This frame is attractive to many people on the Left who believe our public institutions should do what it takes to solve the problems children face, regardless of their background. It fits with attitudes that differences among children should be celebrated, and perhaps even reflected in, the public schools teaching them. This subframe also responds to a belief that schools need the flexibility to tailor their approaches to children's differing needs. Rather than making all children fit within a single form of instruction, a variety of schools can address the needs of different children and different communities.

While many progressives believe in the need for deep structural changes in public institutions like our school systems, portions of the Left fear that the market-oriented, competitive aspects of the movement will threaten the larger public school systems they have fought to maintain. These charter opponents often include people and groups with a historical interest in the public school systems like state teachers unions, school boards associations, parent groups, and community-based organizations. Progressive leaders willing to support charters can try to emphasize complementary frames for the charter movement. But they must confront historical allies who are anchored in previous political fights and who now

oppose charter schools. These former allies can manipulate the competitive frame to fight the movement. This fear of the competitive aspects of
charters is exacerbated by charter advocates on the Right who emphasize
the competitive side of the movement as part of political struggles to promote vouchers and other forms of choice that are less complementary to
public education.

The subframes are not mutually exclusive and many charter school
supporters and operators believe both subframes capture important attributes of the concept. For many charter supporters, including progressives, it
is not necessary to pick a single frame. But they must balance or emphasize
different subframes in different circumstances. It is easy to imagine a charter school founder who is motivated to create a charter school by a sense
that the larger public system has failed. This founder may be frustrated by
the larger system's unresponsiveness to children's needs. Once up and running, their charter will compete for children with the district-run schools.
The potential loss of students and revenue could stimulate the district to respond to families' concerns to win back their students. Even if that response is satisfying to the charter founder, he or she must still maintain the
charter school's enrollment. Ironically, a responsive school district improving its own schools to win back students from the charter is harmful
to the charter founder's goals of retaining students. The school leaders' efforts to recruit and retain students will likely involve work to improve the
charter school and communicate its unique attributes to prospective students and their families. This one person can move back and forth between
the subframes and easily reconcile them with their work. Nevertheless, at a
broader level, there is a struggle over which characterization will dominate
the movement and serve as its public persona.

Both frames can appeal to a single person because they share several
ideas. Both frames emphasize the importance of diversity and choice in approach to education. They both hold that children learn in different ways;
each school can succeed best by implementing one form of schooling well,
rather than trying to be all things to all people; families should be able to
match their chosen school to the way their child learns; and small independent charter schools, freed from unnecessary rules and regulations, can
implement their chosen model and meet the needs of individual students
better than larger bureaucratic systems.

The competitive and complementary frames part ways in how they
diagnose the existing system. The competitive frame argues that larger
systems are truly broken and in need of pressure to improve; while the
complementary frame argues that, regardless of the current system's

performance, additional models of schooling will make it better because families will have more choices.

On the ground, much of the distinction between the proponents of the two frames relies on their relative weighting of two broadly held goals for the charter movement. Supporters of the complementary frame acknowledge the positive contribution of market pressures on larger systems, but prefer to emphasize that new schools provide forms of instruction needed locally. Supporters of the competitive camp also believe in the advantages of adding new public schools, but they prefer to emphasize the effects of competition on the larger system.

These subframes are not recent developments superimposed on the movement after a decade of operation. Rather, they reflect the history and development of the charter idea as it diffused among states and educators. As this chapter will argue, more than ten years into the charter school movement there are systematic variations in which frames are applied by whom, and in which contexts.

Identity

The identities that participants embrace shape the frames they apply. Competition among identities is a frequent aspect of social movements (Stryker, 2000). In many cases, individuals can support multiple frames, and differences in approach among participants can be characterized by variations in identity salience (Stryker, 2000). Whether someone in the charter school movement ranks the competitive approach over the complementary frame may be tied to that person's sense of individual identity. And the concept of identity is not shaped by membership in a Social Movement or Social Movement Organization (SMO) alone. According to Styker, identities that are "rooted in outside relationships can subvert collective identities tied to movements" (p. 25). Stryker's point could be used to argue that these identities could also affect which frames participants choose to use within the movement.

Incompatibility between group identity and individual identity may lead people to decline participation (Friedman and McAdam, 1992). This incompatibility will impact the selection of frames, which may be just as important to the long-term viability of the movement. For example, many school founders come from a background in education, and many of those are from public schools. The teachers, principals, and leaders of these schools are likely to identify themselves as *public school educators* or *public school leaders.* Many policy entrepreneurs in the charter school movement do not come from school environments, nor do they consider themselves educators. These leaders may identify themselves as *education reformers.* Still other charter school organizers and policy entrepreneurs may be affiliated with a particular student population or community. For such leaders, their identity may also entail a sense of self as a *community advocate.* Such advocates may primarily be interested in creating safe places for the children they consider underserved in traditional settings (Wells, Lopez, Scott, & Holme, 1999).

These three identities, or combinations of them, may affect how attractive various frames are for understanding and describing the charter school movement. Public educators may be primarily interested in complementary charter schools providing educational diversity; education reformers may be more sympathetic to charter schools as competitive market actors; and community advocates may be able to draw on both frames depending on the circumstance.

Movement Membership—or the Role of Opposition in Definition

These identities are not exclusive to the charter school movement. Whether people support or oppose a movement, they can still play a role in defining it. According to Friedman and McAdam, many groups are defining a collective identity, including "movement opponents, rival SMOs, law enforcement officials, and the media. . . . (T)he survival chances of an SMO often rest on the outcome of just such contests for control of the group's image (Friedman and McAdam, 1992, p. 166).

This act of identification might be worth considering as an act of movement repression or facilitation (see Tilly, 1978). People working in nonchartered schools and conducting advocacy and policy work in the traditional public school arena may also embrace these identities. Their positions vis-à-vis charter schools may indicate which frame they use to characterize the movement. The frames people outside the movement choose may differ from those selected by people with similar identities within the movement. For example, a public educator who works in the charter school movement may attempt to characterize the movement under a complementary frame of educational diversity. A public educator working outside charter schools who believes charters threaten the existing public school system may choose to characterize the movement by what they consider the more hostile frame—the competitive, market-actor frame.

Consequently, the role of identity in shaping the frames people use to characterize the charter school movement may interact with membership in the movement.

Multiple Forums

Another factor interacting with the roles of identity and frames in the charter school movement could be the forum. Advocates may select the forum in an effort to gain support for an idea that is less acceptable in another arena (Schattschneider, 1960). Alternatively, their arena may dictate different tactics, including different frames. The terms of the debate at the school, state, and national level are likely to affect these interactions. It is my hypothesis that proximity to children and teaching increases the saliency of educational diversity as a frame and decreases the attraction of using a competitive frame.

History of the Charter Movement

The complementary and competitive subframes emerged as the idea was created by policy entrepreneurs, through the creation of the initial state laws, and in the political dynamics that took place within states as charter schools opened. This section builds the case for the significance of the two frames by outlining their use through each of these processes.

History: From Intellectual Concept to Concrete Programs

As this section will explain, the charter school movement started with a limited scope and a complementary frame, but over time it evolved to represent conflicting frames and a much larger scale. It began as a limited and complementary notion put forward by an intellectual in the education establishment. A prominent labor leader borrowed the idea and expanded its scope while maintaining its complementary nature. A small group in Minnesota incorporated competitive aspects into the charter concept as they drafted the nation's first charter law, but state politics forced these policy entrepreneurs to limit the scale and potential competition for the initial charter program.[3] As the idea diffused through the states, legislatures put different ideas into law, incorporating both complementary and

competitive aspects in state law. Finally, on the ground the charter programs manifested these different frames through their relationships with
existing public school systems.

Policy Entrepreneurs Introduce the Idea: Budde and Shanker

The idea is credited to Ray Budde who circulated a version in the 1970s.
Budde was writing for the Regional Laboratory for Educational Improvement of the Northeast and Islands. This laboratory is part of a system of fed-
erally supported centers that work to improve and serve the public school
systems. It is not surprising, then, that his proposal was not threatening to
the educational establishment. His first offering was a limited concept emphasizing expanded services under traditional public education operating
under the complementary frame (Budde, 1988, 1989, 1996). According to
Budde, the idea was for a local district to give groups of teachers within an
existing public school three to five years to run their program as they saw fit,
with little interference from the school or district administration. This first
notion did not compete with local schools, but complemented the larger
system by simply augmenting a program within a single institution.

Budde's idea received little attention until Albert Shanker, the late
president of the American Federation of Teachers (AFT), resuscitated it in
1988. While the unions would later balk at the privatizing aspects of the
charter movement, Shanker believed that using a charter to delegate
authority to a group of teachers was a prolabor action. Interestingly,
Shanker proposed the idea of charter schools as a reaction to the growing
standards movement (Shanker, 1988a, 1988b). Shanker feared that the
state's looming standards and assessments would infringe on the profes-
sionalization of teaching and he believed charters presented an opportunity for teachers to protect their autonomy over instruction. Shanker
expanded the notion from departments within schools to chartering entire schools. According to Shanker, charters would be granted, "to teams
of teachers and others to set up their own autonomous public schools"
(Shanker, 1988, p. E7). As the charter concept grew it still vested authority in traditional powers (that is, local school boards) and, by strengthening teachers' rights, it served progressive goals and complemented the
existing system by providing a new opportunity for teachers.

Shanker's advocacy clearly demonstrates the Left's participation in
the genesis of the charter movement. It also expanded the scale of the idea
to include whole schools and continued the complementary role of charter

schools. But Shanker's version also included a diagnosis of problems in the larger system as a reason to allow new schools to go their own way, suggesting a systemic rationale for the movement. Despite this evolution, after Shanker the charter concept still fell short of using competition from charter schools to pressure the larger system to address the problems that created the need for these new options in the first place.

Policymakers Codify Conflicting Frames in Minnesota

In 1991, Ted Kolderie, a nonpartisan policy analyst, brought the concept to Minnesota. He worked with Joe Nathan from the Center for School Change and State Senator Ember Reichgott-Junge to write the nation's first charter school law (Nathan, 1996).

Nathan's background includes a long history of work on progressive causes. He came to the charter movement after working with the bipartisan National Governor's Association on education reform. When asked to define his background, Nathan emphasizes his role as an inner-city educator and founder of an innovative public school. In his extensive public speaking on behalf of charter schools, Nathan frequently recounts his participation in the civil rights movement's Freedom Summer. He was also active in efforts to protest the Vietnam War.

Reichgott-Junge, who eventually became the legislative leader for a multiyear effort to establish charter schools, describes herself as a "mainstream Democrat" (Reichgott-Junge, 2002). The Minnesota teachers union regularly endorsed her prior to her work on charter schools. Based on the speaking and writing of Al Shanker, she expected the local teacher's unions to thank her for sponsoring charter school legislation. She assumed they would agree that charters created opportunities for expanded professional involvement.

Kolderie works as a nonpartisan analyst, specializing in asking "big questions" about the structure of public systems. When asked to describe his background, Kolderie explains that he is "[m]ostly defined by what I'm not; not governmental, not academic, not political, not commercial." Kolderie has worked on issues of public governance and finance of governmental institutions since the 1960s, and began work on state-level education in the 1980s (Kolderie, 2002).

Based on the roles played by Budde, Shanker, and the team in Minnesota, it is worth noting that charter schools were not initiated as a conservative scheme threatening to erode public education. Instead, the charter school movement emerged from organized labor, nonpartisan writers in the education establishment, progressive education reformers, and leaders in the Democratic Party.

The Minnesota team began its work on the first charter law after a speech by Shanker to a Minnesota audience. Kolderie introduced a degree of competition to the complementary version that had been used thus far. For him, charter schools in the aggregate were more important than individual schools. Their significance came not just from adding to the services or increasing teacher autonomy, but in the pressure to improve that charters place on larger school systems. According to Kolderie the charter movement "breaks the exclusive franchise" of the local school district in the ownership and operation of public schools (Kolderie, 1990, p. 1). Thus, even before the first law was passed, policy entrepreneurs introduced two different rationales for charter schools—one complementary, the other competitive.

Despite Shanker's original work and Reichgott-Junge's sponsorship, the Minnesota affiliate of the AFT saw the proposed legislation as a threat to teacher security and benefits and actively opposed the bill. Shanker himself wrote to Kolderie opposing Minnesota's legislation because of its treatment of teachers' pension rights under the new law. To win passage, the proposed Minnesota legislation was altered to deemphasize the competitive aspects of the program and to strengthen the control over the charters by school districts. For example, the law that eventually passed limited the number of schools that could be granted and gave local districts sole discretion over granting charters. While Minnesota later amended its law to allow increasing numbers of charters and to allow applicants to seek charters from entities other than local districts, the dynamics that lead to compromises in Minnesota were present in many of the state debates of charter schools and reflect the varying subframes used for the movement.

It is important to note that there are differences between the explicit policies that states write into law and the implicit politics of charter schools. Many state charter school laws begin with legislative findings that describe the purposes of the law. Legislative findings traditionally serve as a preamble to legislation. They are intended to inform later interpretation of the law if questions arise regarding legislative intent. The legislative findings in most charter laws echo one another as legislation passed in one state was often used to inform bill drafting in another. Organizations like the Education Commission of the States, and this author, played a role in diffusing such language among states. These legislative findings emphasize the complementary nature of charter programs by articulating expectations that charter schools will expand opportunities for parents and teachers and provide forms of schooling that better serve students, including "at-risk" students. Direct mention of competition, or intended effects of charter schools on the larger school system, are generally not included. This failure to include explicit reference to the competitive nature of charter schools in legislative findings does not mean competition was not in the minds of some legislators, or implicit and institutionalized in aspects of state laws. To understand the contention among the frames in the legislative process requires both an examination of components of laws and an interpretation of the implicit meanings of these policy details.

Charter Schools (and the Frames) Diffuse to other States

New charter laws followed Minnesota's in California, Colorado, and Arizona. Voters in both California and Colorado rejected ballot initiatives for school vouchers in the months before charter legislation was introduced. In both states, leaders in the Democratic Party worked in cross-partisan coalitions to pass charter legislation. In Colorado, Governor Roy Romer and Representative Peggy Kerns (both Democrats) worked with Republican Senator, and future Republican Governor, Bill Owens to pass Colorado's law. In California, Democratic Senate leader Gary Hart successfully passed the charter law in an end-of-session maneuver.

In both states there were compromises between leaders (Hassel, 1999). There were those who hoped to head off future voucher legislation or ballot initiatives by providing some choice within the public system, via a complementary version of charter schools, as well as voucher proponents who hoped charter legislation would build momentum for later voucher legislation, through a competitive version. The compromises between these views were reflected in both laws. While districts remained ultimately responsible for granting charters, appeals processes were put in place that allowed charter applicants to receive charters over the objections of local districts. The competitive framing is reflected in these appeals processes, which allow charter schools to compete with hostile districts for students and funding. They also maintained a complementary framing in the legislation's statutory findings by codifying the importance of providing options for parents and teachers within public school choice and by emphasizing charter schools' potential to serve at-risk student populations.

Arizona then passed legislation in 1994 that emphasized the competitive frame. In this case the state legislature, dominated by Republicans, narrowly failed to pass voucher legislation just before the charter bill was debated. The Senate Education Committee chair, Lisa Graham Keegan, introduced a charter bill that allowed private schools to convert to charter status and created three different venues that charter applicants could apply to while seeking approval. For these and other reasons, this legislation has been described as one of the "strongest" charter school laws. The strength of a law is determined by charter-advocacy groups according to the ease of receiving charters and the degree of autonomy the schools receive under state law (Bierlein, 1995, 1996; Dale and Deschryver, 1997). The lack of accountability in the initial Arizona law, and the similarities between voucher programs and charter programs that grant charters to private schools, provided an example of a state with a competitive framing of the movement.

Keegan, who sponsored the original legislation in the Arizona legislature and later administered the state department of education as the elected chief state school officer, initially advocated an approach to charter schools in which school accountability was primarily addressed through the market actions of parents choosing schools rather than external oversight by charter authorizers carefully reviewing charter applications or student achievement. This conservative approach emphasized limited government, which was reflected by an extremely limited staff assigned to charter school oversight by the state department of education.

The initial failures of several Arizona charter schools helped leaders in other states emphasize the benefits of public governance and oversight of charter schools. While potentially limiting charter autonomy, public governance of charters contributes to the complementary frame by grounding the new schools more firmly in the public system, rather than placing them outside the responsibility of public leaders.

In summary, the tensions between the Left and Right were reflected in compromises over the extent to which charter schools were separated from, and thus better able to compete with, the traditional school system. This tension was apparent in the legislative intent and related policies that encouraged schools to serve underserved populations and promote teacher empowerment. While the passage of charter school laws is an example of policy diffusion, rather than a social movement, the thousands of people who responded to this opportunity and created schools is clearly such a movement. The efforts to create and run new schools also illustrate the contending frames used to promote the laws.

Implementation: Local Struggles of Definition

In states that limit chartering activity by retaining district control over the charter review and approval process, the complementary role is practically inescapable. Under laws like those originally passed in New Mexico, Minnesota and Wisconsin, the districts were the only entities that could approve charter applications. Not surprisingly, the districts were most interested in proposals that served at-risk students and others who were difficult to teach within the traditional public schools. The charters that emerged from these programs disproportionately served special education and minority populations or emphasized services for students who had dropped out of traditional public schools.

In Colorado, where rapid growth of Denver suburbs put tremendous pressure on districts to create new facilities, districts were willing to approve charter schools that relieved this pressure by serving students in nontraditional facilities. Meanwhile, the inner-city Denver district and its teachers' union remained resistant to all but the most politically connected charter proposals. Thus, in states with less statutory power for charter applicants, the school districts and teachers' unions remained willing to support charters (or at least oppose them less vigorously), as complementary aspects of their programs. This completion took the form of schools serving difficult-to-teach students or providing low-cost alternatives to building new and expensive school buildings. However, applicants that would compete with the traditional system, by offering to serve "mainstream" student populations or creating schools within shrinking districts, faced strong opposition from districts and teachers' unions, and had little chance of approval without statutory language allowing applicants to seek charters from nondistrict authorizers.

In states like Arizona, where the district is not the only charter authorizer, the dynamics of competition play a larger role. Here districts that are opposed to charter schools serving traditional populations cannot stop these charter proposals from going forward. It is important to note that charter schools incorporate elements of both frames in every state. The tensions stem from the balance between complementing and competing with public education and the emphasis different parties place on each element.

Interest Group Politics

Interest group politics also provide a range of opinions and beliefs about the charter school movement. District leaders and school board members often support complementary functions of charters but remain hostile to competitive approaches. Teachers' unions tend to support complementary approaches to the issue at the national level, reflecting the initial thoughts of Shanker and later politics between the Clinton administration and the national unions. Initially, the National Education Association (NEA) went as far as to promote an initiative that provided technical assistance to local affiliates interested in forming charter schools. At the state and local level, however, the unions maintain strong positions opposed to charters in almost all circumstances.[4]

Meanwhile, despite this organized opposition, approximately 19% of charter schools are converted public schools (RPP, 1998, p. 35), generally led by traditional public school teachers and leaders who consider their charter schools to be part of the public system. Another 10% of the charters are converted private schools (RPP, 1998), operating primarily in states like Arizona that allow this practice. These schools are often run by individuals who consider "their schools" to be hybrid public/private schools, if not entirely private schools operating with state support.

The Research Puzzle, Data, and Measurement

One would expect a master frame to forge a sense of agreement over the general purpose of a movement. Subsumed beneath consensus over the purpose would be disagreement about the details of implementation, tactics, and strategies. A counterintuitive dynamic is taking place in the charter school movement. The location and degree of agreement are reversed between the master frame and its subframes. The master frame of choice is broad enough to allow for the appearance of consensus on policy details. But beneath apparent consensus, at the level of subframes, we discover an important split over the purpose of the movement rather than disagreement about details of implementation.[5] This reversal leads to a fractious movement.

Based on this context, I will examine media coverage about the charter school movement. I will document the use of competing frames, noting the varying approaches used by participants with different backgrounds operating in different forums. I hope to clarify and validate the appropriateness of the frames and identities proposed above. My hypothesis is that the frames used by people inside and outside the charter school movement are affected by their position in the education system and their support or opposition to charter schools. I believe that the closer a person or issue is to a charter school, the more likely they will use a complementary frame for the charter movement. People who are opposed to charter schools, as well as those who promote the idea but who do so from a greater distance from individual charter schools, will frame the issue in terms of competition. Stories that are designed to fuel debate, for example, opinion pieces and editorials, will emphasize competition. Discussions of policy will also emphasize competition more than stories of schools.

The Washington, D.C. Area: A Mix of Schools and Jurisdictions

This analysis includes all articles about charter schools identified by NEXIS in the Washington, D.C., area over a four-month period. This metropolitan area includes the District of Columbia, Virginia, and Maryland. The charter school movement in this area provides a reasonable cross-section of the types of newsworthy events taking place in the charter school movement around the country. Coverage of Washington, D.C., can include national policy, city politics, problems of public education in a large urban setting, as well as a vibrant charter school movement. The district has about 15% of its public school students attending charter schools. The range of issues addressed in the Washington area media makes this analysis more informative because it can cover both policy and practice.

The inclusion of state-based stories in Maryland and Virginia allows for analysis of local and state arenas as well. Maryland just passed a charter school law in 2003. Maryland coverage examined here includes local debates among community members hoping to form charter schools without state law as well as coverage of efforts to establish a charter school law. Virginia has a law that limits competition. Subsequently, coverage includes efforts to promote complementary schools as well as policy struggles aiming to change the state's charter law.

The Media: Reflecting Conflict and Shaping Public and Policymaker Attitudes

Media coverage is important for several reasons. It serves as a mirror, reflecting the dynamics within the movement. It also plays an active role by informing, and thus helping to shape, attitudes and perceptions of the charter school movement among the public and policymakers. It is not that language and discourse around charter schools are, in themselves, determining the nature of the charter movement. The work of school founders, teachers, and children in schools is affected by many aspects of our society that apply greater influence than coverage of these schools in the printed media.

By describing the events taking place, quoting the participants' words, and articulating the arguments taking place in different forums, the media is presenting the ideas floating around the charter school movement. By telling a story, each article is choosing a narrative to capture the complexity. The stories that are told are also important because they provide people who have less concrete experience in charter schools with ways of understanding what is taking place in the movement. Because most people, including policy makers, do not have firsthand experience with the charter movement, the media's interpretation is more likely to shape how they understand it.

Examples of Media Coverage

A cursory review of the articles reveals that individual stories generally reflect one frame or the other—but not both. At the school level, stories tend to emphasize the school's accomplishments, or at least its efforts to help students overcome challenges. At the district and state level, the stories shift to interinstitutional conflict. These stories discuss charter authorizers considering closing schools or struggling to find resources to meet demands placed on the larger system. At the national level, stories are not surprisingly focused on policy rather than school issues. National stories and observers often portray charters as a step in the direction of, or at least linked to, vouchers. A few examples illustrate these topics.

Supreme Court Justice Sandra Day O'Connor connected charters to vouchers in her questions during arguments in the case involving the Cleveland school voucher program. During the arguments voucher opponents argued for separating charters from vouchers for the purposes of the case. O'Connor responded, "Wait just a minute. How is it we can't look at all these schools?" (Murray, 2002, p. A3), implying that charters were part of a larger array of choice education options that needed to be considered together.

Clint Bolick, of the conservative Institute for Justice, favored O'Connor's line of reasoning and illustrated the contentious nature of the competitive frame for the charter movement by explaining that "the groups assembled here (voucher opponents) are out to protect their *stranglehold monopoly* on inner-city public schools" (Murray, 2002, p. A3, emphasis added).

Other supporters of charter schools also emphasize the conflict between the charters and the rest of the system when working at the national level. When describing a growing effort to improve accountability among charter schools, Jeanne Allen, a prominent conservative supporter of charter schools from the Center for Education Reform, reflected the conflict between charter schools and the larger school systems by explaining, "We are at a critical state. . . . Right now, there's a real war going on for the future of charters" (Egan, 2002, p. A15).

State-based, procharter advocates, meanwhile, recognized the benefits of a more conciliatory tone. Speaking for the California Network of Educational Charters, Gary Larsen responded to the same proposals by explaining, "Many of these proposed reforms make a lot of sense. . . . But our fear is that the big baby of charter schools with be thrown out with the bath water" (Egan, 2002, p. A15).

Coding the Data

Each article was coded for a variety of factors. The dependent variable measured whether the article or individuals quoted in the article framed the charter school movement as complementing public education or competing with the system. Independent variables tracked aspects of the participants and the story being addressed. These variables included whether the story was about a school, a school district, a state, or the nation; whether the story was about school activities or policy; whether the story was positive, neutral, or opposed to charter schools; whether the framing contained in the article was attributed to a school-level actor, a policymaker or entrepreneur, or a reporter; and what type of article it was, including announcements, news and feature stories, or opinion pieces.

Each of the independent variables was either dichotomous or trichotomous and was coded with dummy variables.[6] To the extent that stories or participants could be recognized as in favor of or opposed to charter schools, the articles were coded as procharter, neutral, or anticharter. Coding the dependent variable was more complex. The rubric allowed for reliable coding decisions. Articles were coded as complementary when they described:

- the accomplishments of schools, school leaders, or students;
- schools addressing obstacles that illustrate the ability of the charter schools to meet students' needs; or
- the unique needs of students who are served in charter schools.

Articles were coded as competitive when they were based on a critique of the larger school system's failures and emphasized conflict between charters and those systems. Stories were coded as competitive if the articles framed charter schools as:

- part of a larger struggle for vouchers or other forms of school choice;
- a threat or stimulus to the local district or the state system of education;
- engaged in a struggle with their district or authorizing entity over power and resources; or
- required because of failure in the existing public school system.

Findings

The data demonstrate several of the hypothesized results. Multiple subframes are being used in the charter school movement and there are systemic differences among the subframes used by participants at different positions in the system. Location, topic, and support or opposition to the movement all affect the use of frames. The variation in framing is apparent when each independent variable is examined graphically as a bivariate relationship.

School or Policy

The distinction between stories about schools and stories about policy is most pronounced. Only one of the 19 stories about schools framed charters in competitive terms. Of the 37 stories about policy, the framing was competitive nearly twice as often as it was complementary (see fig. 7.1).

Local, District/State, and National

When the split between school- and policy-based stories is modified to examine differences in framing among stories that describe different geographic scales, that is, stories about local, district/state, and national contexts, the results also match expectations (see fig. 7.2). Local stories, which were often about schools but also included community efforts unassociated with any particular school, used complementary frames in 22 out

FIG. 7.1.
Framing of Charter Schools: Stories about Schools Compared to
Stories about Policy (N=56)

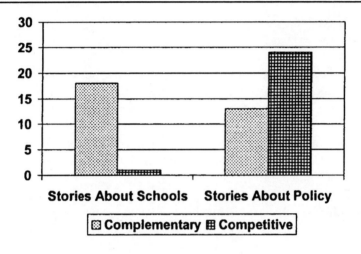

FIG. 7.2.
Framing of Charter Schools: Stories by Geographic Scope
(N=56)

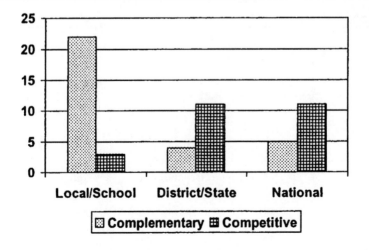

of 25 cases. State/district and national stories were much more likely to use competitive frames. Eleven of 16 state/district stories and 11 of 15 national stories used competitive frames.

Pro and Con

The variation in frames from stories where a pro- or anticharter emphasis could be determined was also illustrative (see fig. 7.3). Procharter stories were roughly evenly split between complementary and competitive frames, with 11 complementary articles compared to 12 competitive. The neutral stories were more likely to be complementary, with 20 complementary and 8 competitive stories; while all 5 of the articles identified as anticharter used a competitive frame.

While the bivariate relationships between framing and each of the independent variables are compelling, some readers may wonder how the preceding analysis addresses the effects of possible collinearity or whether each of these effects is significant when all other factors are held constant. For the interested reader, appendix A includes raw frequencies. Multivariate analysis is complicated by a lack of variance in two of the independent variables. This lack of variance reflects the expected results, but to such an extreme degree that multivariate analysis is problematic.

FIG. 7.3.
Framing of charter schools: Stories for, against, or neutral about charter schools (N = 56)

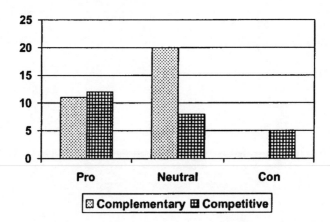

Discussion

It is not surprising to those familiar with school reform that people involved with individual schools prefer to focus on their accomplishments and efforts to meet student needs rather than their fights with outside entities. While school leaders are involved in the same conflicts described in many of the district- and state-based stories, they rarely see an advantage in emphasizing that conflict. Ironically, this emphasis on a complementary frame at the school level may not be due to any distaste for market mechanisms by progressives. Instead, the existence of a market in education may drive school leaders to avoid the appearance of conflict as a marketing strategy. Perhaps the need to retain and attract families creates a counterpressure that prevents schools from engaging in conflictual politics and competitive frames— as well as the expansive politics Schattschneider would predict. Schools need to attract parents and persuade them to send their children. While people may join organizations and engage in acts of protest based on frustration and anger with a failing system, they are likely to pause and ask how a school is doing at teaching kids before they enroll their child. Conflict and fiery school leaders willing to battle the system may harm efforts to market schools to parents of small children looking for safe and effective learning environments. In districts where the traditional schools are in dismal shape, perhaps a competitive frame may be sufficient and effective. In many other settings it may be incumbent upon school leaders to explain what their school does well if they are to survive in education markets.

At the district and state level there is no such pressure encouraging actors to avoid conflict-oriented media attention. When charter supporters at the state level frame the movement in terms of competition, they can do so without painting an individual charter school's success as coming at the expense of other public schools' resources.

A Growing Emphasis on Competition

It is also not surprising that opponents, especially those on the Left, characterize charter schools in the way that is least attractive to traditional supporters of public education on the Left. The competitive frame, then, may be as useful to charter opponents trying to scare people on the Left as it is to people on the Right who are trying to convince conservatives that charters are a step toward market-based education systems. This could make the competitive frame useful to more of the actors engaged in policy debates, perhaps signaling a long-term shift toward a more unitary and competitive

description of the movement. The competitive frame may come to dominate the movement because it is useful to both liberal opponents and conservative charter supporters. The complementary frame remains preferable
to school leaders. But these people are more focused on operations and less
interested in shaping media coverage, policymakers' understanding, and
public attitudes toward the movement as a whole. In the long run, the parties interested in shaping the public's perception of charter schools through
the media may have more influence on that perception than the people
running schools.

The potential dominance of a competitive frame among policy discussions about charter schools could make it more difficult for individual
school operators to create the schools they want within the public school
systems. If charters are considered to be primarily pieces of a broader
school choice agenda, based on a criticism of failing public systems, people
within the education establishment who would support complementary
schools could become opponents. Even charter proposals that are designed specifically to serve students that local districts find difficult to
teach—or charters operating in inexpensive and innovative facilities in districts with crowded schools—could find increasing resistance from school
boards, teachers' unions, parent organizations, and community-based organizations. In state legislatures former Democratic supporters could
change their position if they see charters used to further other forms of
school choice or to criticize traditional public schools.

The competitive frame's ascendancy could also discourage would-be
charter founders from pursuing the strategy in the first place. Progressive
educators in many communities may be interested in pursuing innovative
teaching strategies that could be implemented with fidelity and rigor in a
charter setting. These educators may envision schools that are designed to
serve the students they see most in need in their local district. But if the
charter movement is classified as a competitive reform designed to pressure the existing schools by drawing away resources, and historical allies
on the Left also use this characterization, many charter proposals may
never be written.

A puzzle emerges from the national- and state-level policy entrepreneurs who support charter schools in the media, but who do so using a
frame that charter school operators would rather avoid and that charter
opponents welcome. This raises questions about the agenda and tactics of
some of the social movement organizations putatively supporting the charter school movement. Perhaps individual schools are immune from the
negative publicity that comes with framing the movement as a critique of
public education. Or perhaps the larger choice agenda pursued by many

Appendix A

Table 7.1.
Frequencies from Article Codings

			Complementary Percent	Competitive Percent	N
School	Local	Pro	100	0	5
		Neutral	100	0	12
		Con	0	100	1
	District/State	Pro	—	—	0
		Neutral	100	0	1
		Con	—	—	0
	National	Pro	—	—	0
		Neutral	—	—	0
		Con	—	—	0
Policy	Local	Pro	50	50	2
		Neutral	100	0	4
		Con	0	100	1
	District/State	Pro	25	75	8
		Neutral	50	50	4
		Con	0	100	3
	National	Pro	38	63	8
		Neutral	17	83	7
		Con	—	—	0

Note: The data present a lack of variance in two of the independent variables, as all anticharter stories are framed competitively and 18 out of 19 school-based stories use a complementary frame. This lack of variance reflects the expected results, but to such an extreme degree that multivariate analysis is problematic.

of the conservative policy organizations that dominate debate at the national level leads them to willingly jeopardize support for charter schools from some people, to gain support for other versions of school choice from different audiences. To put it succinctly, conservative charter advocates may choose to alienate potential supporters of charter schools on the Left because it can help them expand support for other forms of choice among their constituencies on the Right.

The challenge to the charter school movement, regardless of actors' philosophical backgrounds, is to reconcile the competitive and complementary aspects of the movement in ways that broaden support for the movement and strengthen the likelihood that charter schools will succeed. It is not necessary that one frame "win," or that people within the charter school movement make up their minds and decide what charter schools are supposed to do or be. Instead, people who care about creating better schools that reflect and serve all our children should carefully consider how we define these schools and their roles.

People on the Right have little to lose by supporting charter schools. For them, creating individual schools that complement our public school systems on the way to generating competition with vastly expanded school choice is a win-win scenario. There are those on the Left who believe the larger systems require drastic change. Growing numbers of progressives see choice as one mechanism that may promote the structural changes needed to better serve the students whom the status quo fails to serve now. But many people on the Left are not interested in or are even opposed to more choice. They are rightly concerned about the potential impact of unfettered competition on our public school systems, and they are sensitive to criticism from traditional allies in labor and among the education establishment. For these people the competitive aspects of charter schools are an unfortunate addition. But forsaking the potential of charter schools because of this conflict would be even more unfortunate. With careful design and stewardship, competition may eventually further many progressive goals. Not only would the Left lose the chance to create more schools that serve children, but it would also play a greatly diminished role in shaping how the charter school movement and other forms of school choice are constructed and understood.

Notes

1. The term *traditional public school* is not meant to imply that the pedagogical or curricular services of nonchartered public schools are less creative than charter schools. For the purposes of this chapter, the term is strictly meant to describe public schools that do not have charters and that operate under the control and ownership of local school districts.

2. While beyond the scope of this chapter, the master frame of competition may play a larger role in the broader school choice movement, including efforts to enact voucher legislation. The competitive frame may provide opportunities for a cycle of protest to expand to include other forms of school choice.

3. For histories of the beginning of the charter school movement see Nathan, 1996; Budde, 1996; and Johnson and Medler, 2000. For a listing of the state charter school laws, see Johnson and Medler, 2000.

4. At the national level, both the NEA and the AFT initially embraced the concept of charters, but under a weak version that did not compete with the

traditional system. The AFT went as far as to embrace the Rhode Island charter school law as a model charter law, despite the fact that its passage had failed to generate a single charter school after four years (Nathan, 1996). In state legislatures the AFT lobbies strongly against charter legislation or works to change it from a competitive to a complementary role.

5. Some observers might question the significance of the divisions within the charter movement by pointing to the relative coherence of the demands the charter school movement places on state leaders. Charter school associations, resource centers, and advocates generally push for additional financial resources, help with facilities, and protection from hostile or capricious actions by district administrators. While the subframes reflect conflicting characterizations of the purpose and context for charter schools, they do not necessarily lead to disagreements about the details of implementation by participants. This has allowed for a growing network of charter school associations and support organizations to emerge that serve and speak collectively for the charter schools on issues that cut across the subframes. Under both subframes, the policies and resources required to create viable charter schools are basically the same, and the charter school movement can speak with relative coherence about many of the policies needed to further both versions of the movement, even if the actors disagree about broader goals.

6. The initial coding by location distinguished between district and state issues (which may still be relevant in most states). However, in the District of Columbia the state and district functions are generally combined, so for this analysis the location of the story was divided into three categories: school, district/state, and national.

References

Berliner, D., & Biddle, B. (1995). *The manufactured crisis: Myths, fraud, and the attack on America's public schools.* Reading, MA.: Addison-Wesley.

Bierlein, L. A. (1995). *Existing charter school laws: Analysis of "stronger" components.* Mimeograph.

Bierlein, L. A. (1996). *Charter schools: Initial findings.* Denver, CO: Education Commission of the States.

Budde, R. (1988). *Education by charter: Restructuring school districts.* Andover, MA: Regional Laboratory for Educational Improvement of the Northeast and Islands.

Budde, R. (1989, March). Education by charter. *Phi Delta Kappan, 70*(7), 518–520.

Budde, R. (1996, September). The evolution of the charter concept. *Phi Delta Kappan,* 72–73.

Center for Education Reform (1999). *The national charter school directory: 1998–1999.* Washington, DC: Author.

Center for Education Reform (2003). *The national charter school directory, 2003.* Washington, DC: Author.

Chubb, J., & Moe, T. (1990). *Politics, markets and America's schools.* Washington, DC: Brookings Institution Press.

Dale, A., & DeSchryver, D. (Eds.). (1997). *The charter school workbook: Your roadmap to the charter school movement.* Washington, DC: Center for Education Reform.

Egan, T. (2002, April 5). Failures raise questions for charter schools. *New York Times,* A15.

Finn, C. E., Jr., Manno, B. V., & Vanourek, G. (2000). *Charter schools in action: Renewing public education.* Princeton, NJ: Princeton University Press.

Friedman, D., & McAdam, D. (1992). Collective identity and activism: Networks, choices and the life of a social movement. In A. M. Morris & C. M. Mueller (Eds.), *Frontiers in social movement theory* (pp. 156–173). New Haven, CT: Yale University Press.

Hassel, B. (1999). *The charter school challenge: Avoiding the pitfalls, fulfilling the promise.* Washington, DC: Brookings Institution Press.

Jennings, W., Premack, E., Adelmann, A., & Solomon, D. (1998). *National study, 1998, A comparison of charter school legislation: Thirty-three states and the District of Columbia, incorporating legislative changes through October 1998.* Berkeley, CA: RPP International.

Johnson, J., & Medler, A. (2000). The conceptual and practical development of charter schools. *Stanford Law and Policy Review, 11*(2).

Kolderie, T. (1990, November 1). *Beyond choice to new public schools: Withdraw the exclusive franchise to public education.* Washington, DC: Progressive Policy Institute.

Kolderie, T. (1996). The charter idea: Update and prospects, Fall 1996. St. Paul, MN: Public Services Redesign Project.

Kolderie, T. (2002, Fall). Telephone interview with author.

Kozol, J. (1991). *Savage inequalities: Children in America's schools.* New York: Crown.

Manno, B. M., Finn, C. Jr., Bierlein, L., & Vanourek, G. (1998, March). How charter schools are different: Lessons and implications from a national study. *Phi Delta Kappan, 79*(7), 489–498.

McAdam, D., Tarrow, S., & Tilly, C. (1996). To map contentious politics. *Mobilization, 1*(1), 17–34.

McAdam, D., Tarrow, S., & Tilly, C. (2001). *Dynamics of contention.* Cambridge: Cambridge University Press.

Moe, T. M. (2001). *Schools, vouchers, and the American public.* Washington, DC: Brookings Institution Press.

Murray, F. J. (2002, February 21). Voucher debate tied to balance: Involves charter, religious schools. *Washington Times,* A3.

Nathan, J. (1996). *Charter schools: Creating hope and opportunity for American education.* San Francisco: Jossey-Bass.

National Commission on Excellence in Education (1983). *A nation at risk: The imperative of educational reform*. Washington, DC: U.S. Department of Education.

Peterson, P. E., & Hassel, B. (1998). *Learning from school choice*. Washington, D.C: Brookings Institution Press.

Reichgott-Junge, E. (2002, Fall). Telephone interview with author.

Rofes, E. (1998). *How are school districts responding to charter laws and charter schools?* Stanford and Berkeley, CA: Policy Analysis for California Education.

RPP International. (1998). *A national study of charter schools: Second-year report*. Washington, DC: U.S. Department of Education.

Schattschneider, E. E. (1960). *The semi-sovereign people*. New York: Holt Rinehart Winston.

Shanker, A. (1988a, March 31). Address at the National Press Club.

Shanker, A. (1988b, July 10). Where we stand. *New York Times*, E7.

Snow, D., & Benford, R. (1992). Master frames and cycles of protest. In A. M. Morris & C. M. Mueller (Eds.), *Frontiers in social movement theory* (pp. 133-155). New Haven, CT: Yale University Press.

Stryker, S. (1992). Identity competition: Key to differential social movement participation? In S. Stryker, T. Owens, & W. White (Eds.), *Self, identity, and social movements* (pp. 21-40). Minneapolis: University of Minnesota Press.

Tilly, C. (1978). *From mobilization to revolution*. Reading, MA: Addison Wesley.

Wells, A. S., Lopez, A., Scott, J., & Holme, J. J. (1999, Summer). Charter schools as postmodern paradox: Rethinking social stratification in an age of deregulated school choice. *Harvard Educational Review*, 69(2), 172-204.

Wohlstetter, P., & Griffin, N. C. (1997a, March). Creating and sustaining learning communities: Early lessons from charter schools. 1997 Annual Meeting of the American Educational Research Association. Chicago, IL.

Wohlstetter, P., & Griffin, N.C. (1997b). First lessons: Charter schools as learning communities. *CPRE Policy Brief*. Philadelphia: Consortium for Policy Research in Education.

CHAPTER 8

School Choice through a Foucauldian Lens: Disrupting the Left's Oppositional Stance

STACY SMITH

Introduction

You can't talk about school choice without talking about markets. A quick look at titles in the school choice literature provides a case in point. Whether it's the exuberant advocacy of choice in John E. Chubb and Terry M. Moe's *Politics, Markets, and America's Schools* (1990) or the skeptical warnings of Jeffrey R. Henig's *Rethinking School Choice: Limits of the Market Metaphor* (1994), the [neo]liberal ideal of the laissez-faire market frames school choice debates. In my own work to date I've noted that a certain market rhetoric—including terms like *competition, entrepreneur, consumer,* and *manager*—both exemplifies and constrains debates surrounding one specific form of choice, charter schools. I have argued that preoccupation with what Henig calls the "market metaphor" results in some overlooked democratic potentials of charter school reform, namely: (1) equalized access to choice, (2) more inclusive and participatory decision making in the public education arena, and (3) localized accountability (Smith, 2001).

As I was formulating these arguments I began to hear and read about Michel Foucault's notion of governmentality, his attention to contemporary forms of neoliberalism, and related work highlighting the concept of an "enterprise culture." I suspected that my assertions about the implications of the market rhetoric surrounding charter schools could be enhanced by a closer look at this literature. Thus, I turned to the governmentality literature with the goal of exploring how ideas about markets shape our conceptions of and our discourse about school choice.

Moreover, I turned to Foucault because I wanted to explore tensions between democratic potentials I see within the school choice movement—potentials that intrigue me because they appear to be in keeping with Leftist goals of social justice and equality—and my discomfort with being aligned with political stances and rhetoric employed by the Right. The school choice movement presents a bit of a political oxymoron because the traditional roles of political players are reversed: Rightist advocates of choice are activists for change and Leftist opponents of choice are defenders of the status quo. Foucault is an ideal theorist to draw upon in order to complicate taken-for-granted divisions between the political Right versus the Left. Foucault famously defied political characterization: he refused to label himself in interviews or to agree to the labels imposed by others. Precisely because he defies easy characterization, and because his methodology brings into bas-relief political discourses and ideologies in order to better understand and critique them, Foucault's work informs a critical investigation of the school choice movement.

Foucault's concept of governmentality has to do with "the conduct of conduct," or practices of government, ranging from governance of one's self to governance of specific populations of subjects. According to Foucault scholar Colin Gordon (1991) governmentality refers to:

> [a] rationality of government . . . a way or system of thinking about the nature of the practice of government (who can govern; what is governing; what or who is governed), capable of making some form of that activity thinkable and practicable both to its practitioners and to those upon whom it was practiced. (p. 3)

The concept of governmentality is usefully applied to the charter school movement because it offers an analytical tool for exploring the political rationalities framing school choice models. Governmentality provides a framework for thinking about how public education is governed under the rubric of school choice, how choice is practiced, and how various subjects are constituted within the choice arena.

Philosopher of education James Marshall (1996) explains that Foucault is interested in exploring regimes of discourses and practices, or power/knowledge, that permit certain statements to emerge and be legitimated as truth. In the context of school choice, attention to discourses and practices helps to reveals the particular rationalities legitimating the "truths" of public education. Thus, Foucauldian analysis of governmentality helps to unpack preponderant claims to truth such as "the Left opposes school choice" or "charter schools are private schools with public funding" by problematizing binary distinctions between Right and Left and public and private, among others. Furthermore, attention to discourses and practices surrounding school choice reveal ways in which a specifically neoliberal rationality shapes and legitimates possibilities for what counts as "public education."

In this chapter I draw upon Foucault's notion of governmentality to argue that schooling is not a public versus a private enterprise, but rather a location for ubiquitous techniques of government. I suggest that a careful look at the positions advanced by proponents and opponents in relation to the school choice movement reveals two simultaneous processes: the creation of choice discourses that reflect a neoliberal rationality and the creation of advocates and opponents as subjects of this rationality. These processes are dialectical and self-perpetuating; in other words, the processes both constitute subjects and instantiate discourses as regimes of truth. Moreover, the dual processes are fraught with contradictions in that they exhibit both oppressive and emancipatory elements.

Because the rhetoric surrounding school choice is full of contradictory potentials, and because the movement is in a nascent stage where it is impossible to determine what the actual, empirical outcomes of choice will look like, I find that I am ambivalent about choice. I consider myself a member of the Left in relation to public education because I am concerned with ends of social justice such as equality and fairness; I am also concerned that institutions of public education be governed democratically and that they prepare young people for democratic public life. Thus, this chapter is in many ways an exploration of myself as a subject of school choice discourses. The chapter is part of an ongoing effort to create my position within the movement as one of a public intellectual offering critique and acting to realize emancipatory potentials. My approach is Foucauldian in the sense that it is an exploration of the present and the future, a project of naming what is and what might be. In an essay entitled "What is Enlightenment?" Foucault (1984) advocated what he called a "critical ontology." He explained,

> The critical ontology of ourselves . . . must be conceived as an attitude, an ethos, a philosophical life in which the critique of what we are is at one and the same time the historical analysis of the limits imposed on us and an experiment with the possibility of going beyond them. . . . (p. 319)

Our ideas about the present and future influence what actually comes into being. My fear is that the democratic and emancipatory potentials of the school choice movement will be undermined by the totalizing discourses of a neoliberal rationality.

Thus, this chapter targets the self-defined Left within the public education arena. I urge those who view themselves as Leftist opponents of school choice to carefully consider their oppositional stance in light of Foucault's emphases on totalizing discourses and networks of power and resistance. It is my hope that drawing attention to these dynamics will disrupt the potentially totalizing effects of a neoliberal rationality by making thinkable, and therefore possible, Leftist political subjectivities and stances in relation to school choice that are more nuanced and complex. On my reading, Foucault's notion of governmentality calls for attention to local practices and the specificity of how power operates through these practices. Moreover, his challenge to the Left to demonstrate courage and political inventiveness provides us with impetus to not only critique relations of domination but, consequently, to identify and implement relevant strategies for action.

With these goals in mind I explore the question here, What are the limits imposed on us by the neoliberal rationality framing school choice and how might we move beyond them? In the sections that follow, I answer this question by beginning with a brief explication of Foucault's inquiry into the notion of governmentality. I outline his use of the term, the research literature that has grown out of this line of inquiry, and neoliberalism as one particular manifestation of a governmental rationality. In the second part of the chapter I describe the school choice movement in the United States as exemplary of a neoliberal rationality and warn against the totalizing effects of this rationality, particular for Leftist critics of school choice. Finally, in the last section I attempt to disrupt the neoliberal rationality that frames school choice by offering strategies for counterconduct and resistance centered around liberal theory's public/private binary and attention to localized practices of power.

Governmentality

In the late 1970s Foucault gave a series of lectures at the Collège de France in Paris concerned with his research into themes of security, territory, and population. In his February 1978 lecture entitled "Governmentality" Foucault set out to "begin making an inventory of this question of governance"

(p. 87). He traced the relationship between the triumvirate of sovereignty/discipline/governmentality from the Middle Ages through the rise of early classical liberalism. Within this complex set of concepts he defined the term *governmentality* most straightforwardly as:

> the ensemble formed by the institutions, procedures, analyses, and reflections, the calculations and tactics that allow the exercise of this very specific albeit complex form of power, which has as its target population, as its principal form of knowledge political economy, and as its essential means apparatuses of security. (p. 102)

According to Foucault's genealogical approach to the history of governmentality, sovereignty was transformed from that of the prince as exercised over individual subjects into the power of the modern state over populations of subjects. These transitions were paralleled by shifts from regimes ruled by structures of sovereignty to techniques of government, and from a "reason of state" to an "art of government" followed by a "governmentalization of the state."

The concept of governmentality addresses the intersection between forms of government and forms of political subjectivity. An individual's political subjectivity is in relation to the specific power relations within a given political order. For example, as Graham Burchell (1991) explains:

> Governed individuals may be identified by their governors as members of a flock to be led, as legal subjects with certain rights, as children to be corrected and educated, as part of a natural resource to be exploited, or as living beings who are part of a biological population to be managed. In each case the subjective self-identity of governed individuals presupposed or required by the exercise of political power will be different. (p. 120)

Foucault's notion of governmentality urges political theory beyond a theory of the state in at least two ways: because of the array of forms of governance that it draws attention to, and because the state is viewed as an institution without a universal essence, but rather as an institution whose function changes in relation to the practices of government being employed (Burchell, 1991, p. 120; Gordon, 1991, p. 4). According to this view, governmentality helps to define the state, but is not limited to its boundaries.

Following Foucault's 1978 lecture on governmentality, a consequent lecture series extended his original assessment of the rise of governmentality in the Middle Ages to the particular forms of governmental rationality posed by both classical liberalism, and then more recent forms of neoliberalism. According to Gordon's (1991) interpretation, Foucault was intrigued by, if not enamored with, contemporary manifestations of liberalism within modern Western societies. Foucault traced the liberal rationality of government according to individuals as economic subjects of interest (homo economicus) from Adam Smith's conception of the "invisible hand" that guides the laissez-faire market through neoliberal market models in modern Western societies. Liberal democratic theory, of both the classical and neoliberal varieties, tends to posit a private realm beyond the reach of the state and a public realm where state apparatuses regulate decision making and implementation based upon legitimate authority derived from the consent of the people. But Foucault's analysis reveals numerous ways in which the actual practices of government and techniques of governance operate on both sides of this binary. And, in doing so, it draws into question the concept of what is public, or controlled by the government or state, in modern liberal democratic contexts.

A Foucauldian reading in terms of governmentality posits liberalism as a political rationality that values individual preferences and choices based upon self-interest. Classical liberalism, of the Adam Smith "invisible hand" variety, presupposes economic market relations as spontaneous and natural phenomena. The purpose of government is then viewed as protecting the economic realm so that it can function to its optimal capacity without interference from the social or political realms. Classical liberalism, therefore, represents a rationality of government predicated on "the active meaning of *laissez-faire*, the devising of forms of regulation which permit and facilitate natural regulation" (Gordon, 1991, pp. 19–20). In other words, the basic objective of a classical liberal art of governance is to use state intervention and regulation in order to keep economic processes secure from interference. In this manner, public interests are best realized. As Burchell (1991) explains, the notion of laissez-faire involves the unrestricted pursuit of individual interests which spontaneously converge in the production of the general or public interest (p. 127).

In the later governmentality lectures, Foucault turned to the contemporary manifestation of this rationality, namely neoliberalism, as it had arisen and was practiced in three Western, postwar countries: West Germany, France, and the United States. Whereas some accounts of the distinction between classical and neoliberalism simply mark a chronological break, or a historical revival of liberal precepts, Foucault's genealogical account provides a conceptual demarcation between the two forms, which is more accurately described as a reinvention. Like the revivalist accounts,

Foucault's review of postwar neoliberal thought acknowledges radical challenges to the system of the welfare state, including emphases on market forces and a minimalist state. But, according to Gordon (1991), Foucault's account of neoliberalism as a particular governmental rationality highlights the novel governmental meaning that neoliberalism brings to the idea of market regulation. Within the postwar neoliberal rationality the market is no longer viewed as a natural social reality. Rather, it is seen as an artificial game, therefore making it necessary for governments to intervene so as to make possible the very existence and function of markets. As Gordon explains, "To enable competition to function in the real world, a certain framework of positive institutional and juridical forms is required . . . a capitalist system" (pp. 41–42).

Foucault's analysis of neoliberalism as a governmental rationality illuminates how it is both a reclamation and a revision of classical liberalism. While neoliberalism restores the classical emphasis on the free market and a minimalist state, the lines between the economic, social, and political become blurred. Thus, individual choice is touted as a fundamental human faculty to be exercised in all realms of interaction; economic man is subject to manipulation, from government among other forces; and the minimalist state may be small but strong nevertheless, and exercise substantial control over the market. These attributes of neoliberalism as a peculiarly contemporary model of governance call attention to a proliferation of techniques of governance and modes of subjectification.[1]

The growing body of literature that stems from Foucault's "Governmentality" essay sheds light on such techniques of governance, that is, how government is practiced, in a variety of localities. Following Foucault, the governmentality literature highlights the question of how practices of government inside the state, or driven by the state, relate to practices of government that are not based upon the state's authority. According to O'Malley, Weir, and Shearing (1997), this literature proceeds from Foucault's claim that "we live in the era of 'governmentality,'" tends to view government as a "decentered process," and is concerned with illuminating specific practices of government wherever they occur. These researchers consider the governmentality literature a valuable asset to sociological work. They contend:

> Not only does it provide a theoretical elaboration which potentially opens everyday and institutional programmes and practices for critical and tactical thinking, it also provides a considerable array of empirical work in terms of which interventions can be examined and thought out. (p. 503)

Thus, the notion of governmentality and related scholarship provides a framework for analyzing how school choice policies, as programs of
government within the public education arena, are formulated and articulated within particular political rationalities. Foucault's notion of governmentality encourages an analysis not only of the *practices* deployed by the
school choice movement, but of the construction of individuals as certain
types of *subjects* within and in relation to the movement. I contend that
scholarship stemming from Foucault's notion of governmentality urges
those on the Left to interrogate educational policies in terms of their contradictory potentials for both freedom and domination. Elaborating the
link between a neoliberal rationality and the school choice movement will
suggest avenues for empirical research as well as inform the tactical thinking and political interventions of those on the Left who are active in the
school choice arena.

Thus, the remainder of this chapter explores how neoliberalism
frames the school choice movement and its techniques of government.
While Foucault highlights the potential for a neoliberal rationality to encourage political inventiveness within public education reform, his
method also challenges us to beware of ways in which neoliberalism may
be translated into technologies of governance within education that will
simply reproduce, or even worsen, existing inequalities.

Neoliberalism and School Choice

Within the governmentality literature Burchell (1991) describes the thrust
of Foucault's line of questioning regarding the constitution of subjects:

> How, Foucault asks, through the operation of what practices of government
> and by reference to what kind of political reasoning, have we been led to
> recognize our self-identity as members of those somewhat indefinite global
> entities we call community, society, nation, or state? (p. 119)

In this section I adapt this question in order to conduct a Foucauldian
analysis of how school choice is formulated and articulated within the context of neoliberalism, and of how a neoliberal rationality frames the creation of particular subjects in relation to the school choice movement. My
exploration of the dialectical relationship between the mobilization of
school choice discourses and subjects of these discourses reveals a neoliberal rationality that posits binary dualisms between the public and private

sectors, between democratic and market-driven forms of decision making, and between the political Left and the Right.

Discourses surrounding the choice movement mimic and perpetuate these divides and delimit the forms of subjectivity that are formed in relation to the movement. For instance, the discourse of school choice as a privatizing mechanism enmeshes the movement within a free market characterized by pressures of competition, entrepreneurialism, and efficiency. In this context, participants within the choice movement are constituted as particular sorts of subjects such as consumers, clients, and entrepreneurs. And even to the extent that critics from the Left challenge these forms of subjectivity, they are formed as subjects solely in opposition to neoliberalism. They conceive of choice as market-driven, and therefore as antidemocratic. Thus, the neoliberal rationality that informs and is informed by the school choice movement in the U.S. threatens to operate in a totalizing fashion that threatens to preclude opportunities for the sort of political inventiveness that Foucault found alluring. Although advocates and critics alike are shaped by, operate within, and perpetuate the boundaries of discourse framed by a neoliberal rationality, some arguments posed by the muted voices of a pro–school choice Left suggest Foucauldian strategies for "counter-conduct and resistance" (Gordon, 1991, p. 5).

The New Right: School Choice through Voucher Schemes

The unique connection between neoliberalism and school choice in the United States dates back to Milton Friedman's advocacy of vouchers, first championed in the 1950s and then in his book *Capitalism and Freedom* (1962). In this classic text of contemporary neoliberalism, Friedman advocates a voucher plan whereby the government pays for schooling but does not provide it. Friedman's call for vouchers is ensconced within, indeed marks the beginning of, a neoliberal tradition that gained a stronghold in the United States and other advanced Western democracies late in the twentieth century. In the following passage Henig (1994) describes the rise of a perspective that has come to be referred to as the "New Right" in a diverse array of Western countries including the United Kingdom, New Zealand, and the United States, among others:

> Not only in the United States, but in much of the world, dissatisfaction with the growing apparatus of government has sparked a privatization movement. Its goals are to shrink the public sector by selling government-owned assets

and contracting with private firms to provide public services, and to replace
large social-welfare "helping" agencies with simpler voucher-type programs
that encourage recipients to help themselves. (p. 5)

The New Right's agenda is clearly linked with neoliberalism through
the shared tenet that market forces can solve domestic social problems
more reliably than government planning. The New Right tends to identify
centralized systems of government, or "big government," as problematic
because, in its view, centralization benefits interest groups that provide
services and are, therefore, better able to exert pressure at governmental
centers and secure their own interests in the policy-making process. The
solution articulated by the New Right in response to this problem is in the
form of purchasing power. This position advocates a return of consumer
power to individuals, or parents in the case of school choice and public education. This is because individual interests are more directly represented
via market relationships. It is posited that such consumer sovereignty will
lead to greater equity because the greater power that officials and professionals exercise in centralized systems of power is diminished (Peters and
Marshall, 1996, pp. 84–85).

Henig (1994) explains how the "market metaphor" is applied to
school choice. The neoliberal stance of the New Right informs the argument that market pressures should be introduced into educational decision making. Choice shifts the distribution of authority among existing
interests—from bureaucratic arms of the state to families. Whereas in the
government arena elected officials, public bureaucracies, and organized interests groups are central players, in the market-based arena the personal
preferences of children and parents will have a more prominent place. In
addition, market pressures from competition will stimulate efficiency, innovation, responsiveness, and improvement (Henig, 1994, pp. 4–5). This
neoliberal commitment to market forces as mechanisms for achieving both
efficiency and equality is evidenced most forcefully in school choice proponents' calls to reform public education through voucher plans that will
allow families to leave failing public schools.

Although Friedman first made his case for vouchers in the 1950s, the
strength of a mutually enforcing link between neoliberal rationality and specific school choice policies did not gain force until the late1980s, particularly
with Chubb and Moe's publications (1988, 1990; see Brighouse, 2000, pp.
25–28; Henig, 1994, pp. 5–6). Nevertheless, the reasoning behind many
policies is still articulated by Friedman's reasons for a voucher model. Friedman's case for vouchers is based on the premise that the market will do a better job of allocating resources, such as educational opportunities for

students and salaries for teachers, than does the existing system of public schooling. Chubb and Moe (1988, 1990) extended and popularized the case for vouchers through their study of the different organizational structures of schooling within the public versus private sectors. These pro–school choice academics characterized the public sector in terms of democratic politics, hierarchical control, bureaucracy, and large, heterogeneous groups of constituents and the private sector in terms of market-based decision making, individual interests, and small, fairly homogeneous groups of consumers, namely students and parents. Chubb and Moe (1988) concluded in the initial publication of their study that the market mechanisms of exit, voice, and autonomy make the marketplace preferable to direct democratic control of public education. They argued that "the key to school improvement is a shift away from direct democratic control [toward] some sort of voucher system" (p. 1085).

Chubb and Moe's research and their conclusions firmly rest on the premise that direct democratic governance and market pressures are polemical forces, or contradictory mechanisms for social control. They see hierarchy and bureaucracy as inherent to democratic control and argue that these attributes disallow school effectiveness. The institutional context of markets, on the other hand, would allow for decentralization of resources and choice, and therefore increase school effectiveness. Chubb and Moe do not discount democratic governance entirely. They call for some broad level of "democratic guidance" and, as Henig (1994) notes, they claim that the market is more democratic than democratic processes themselves (p. 5). Yet their position resonates with features common to the neoliberal rationality: suspicion of democratic governmental control, advocacy of a minimalist state role, and preference for the laissez-faire market as the best mechanism for regulation and allocation of resources. Their advocacy of market mechanisms echoes the neoliberal faith in market competition that David Boaz (1991) so succinctly captures in *Liberating Schools*:

> [E]ducational choice will lead, as if by an invisible hand, to the selection of the best ideas for educational improvement . . . not just those currently being tried by government schools but also new ideas that bureaucrats would never dream of and that entrepreneurs will naturally discover. (p. 49)

The Antichoice Left: Opposition to Markets

In typical debates about school choice, advocacy is commonly associated with the New Right and opposition with the Left from two different settings: an academic Left of university scholars and a professional Left comprised of teachers' organizations and unions (for example, the NEA, the AFT, their local affiliates, and other supporting organizations). All of these critics tend to dismiss choice because they see it as a privatizing force that is inherently antidemocratic and at odds with the idea of a public education. Leftist critics of decentralized reform efforts like school choice, such as Molnar in the United States and Peters and Marshall (1996, p. 76) in New Zealand, view a neoliberal rationality as spawning the commodification of education. They extend this argument that the norms of an "enterprise culture," fueled by the logic of the market, are at odds with democratic principles.

Like advocates of choice such as Chubb and Moe (1988; 1990), Leftist critics pose a stark polemic between democracy or the market. This polemic is highlighted in the following passage from choice opponent Alex Molnar's (1996) *Giving Kids the Business*:

> [T]he debate about public education cannot be understood by thinking only about schools. It is part of a much broader struggle: whether America will move in the direction of its democratic ideals, or be further ensnared in the logic of the market. . . . Over time, market values have eroded and debased the humane values of democratic civil society. Listen closely to the language that already fills discussions about school reform. It is the language of commerce applied to human relationships. Children are defined as "future customers," "future workers" and "future tax-payers." . . . When the logic of the market is allowed to dominate society, relationships are inevitably turned into commodities to be bought or sold. (p. 184)

In this passage Molnar clearly articulates many of the primary concerns of the antichoice Left: choice commodifies education and puts at risk democratic values such as fairness and equality.

In response to the New Right's view that market relations will best achieve democratic ends, Leftist critics of neoliberalism assert that the rhetoric of this position simply serves to mask unequal class relations under capitalism. Critiquing the predominance of what they call an "enterprise culture" framing education reforms in New Zealand, Peters, Fitzsimons, and Marshall (1999) assert:

> The valorisation of the notion of enterprise as a transformation of cultural values disguises such things as the coercive powers of the state and the promotion of values of competition and opportunism. Under enterprise culture the character of these attributes are dignified and sanitised by the rhetoric of enterprise. (pp. 4–5)

One attribute of an enterprise culture that they believe is sanitized by its rhetoric is increasing inequality, particularly along lines of race and gender (Peters and Marshall, 1996).[2]

Concerns such as those expressed by Molnar (1996) and Peters and Marshall (1996) problematize the ways in which a neoliberal rationality privileges market ends such as efficiency within the school choice movement. In so doing, they warn us to be wary of whether a neoliberal rationality will serve as a force of egalitarian transformation or further instantiate oppression. In addition, they point to processes within an enterprise culture, such as the "commodification" of education, that constitute subjects within the school choice movement as producers and consumers, possibly at the cost of the individual agency required for democratic action.[3]

Limits of the Neoliberal Rationality

While the arguments posed by the antichoice Left are framed in terms of critique and resistance, the radical potential of their stance as "counter-conduct" is constrained by the limits of the neoliberal rationality itself. Because the antichoice critique is framed almost wholly in response to the market metaphor as articulated and defended by the New Right, the subjectivity of Leftist activists is constituted as an oppositional one that is constituted through and by the discourses of neoliberalism, and therefore fails to disrupt the entrenchment of this particular political rationality. In *The Order of Things* Foucault (1973) claimed that Marxism was not in opposition to, but rather part and parcel of, the liberal humanist tradition. He stated:

> At the deepest level of Western knowledge, Marxism introduced no real discontinuity, it found its place without difficulty, as a full, quiet, comfortable and, goodness knows, satisfying form for a time (its own), within an epistemological arrangement that welcomed it gladly (since it was this arrangement that was in fact making room for it) and that it, in return, had no intention of disturbing and, above all, no power to modify, even one jot, since it rested entirely within it. Marxism exists it nineteenth century thought like a fish in water; that is, it is unable to breathe anywhere else. (p. 261)

In a similar manner, the oppositional identity of the antichoice Left is entrenched in the liberal tradition. Antichoice Leftists are creating themselves in opposition to neoliberalism, albeit unwittingly, rather than engaging in an altogether different discourse. Because the ways in which antichoice Leftists mobilize neoliberal discourses are manifestations of neoliberal rationality, their stance does not disrupt, but rather entrenches the predominance of neoliberal rationality and constrains other possibilities. Progressive analysis of the school choice movement according to the notion of governmentality, then, requires attention to practices of rule that complicate taken-for-granted boundaries between the democratic state and the liberal market. Governmental practices guided by a neoliberal rationality are not rejected carte blanche, but rather interrogated for their ability to achieve ideals of freedom and equality.

Disrupting the Limits of the Neoliberal Rationality Framing School Choice

Although Foucault claimed his project to be largely descriptive versus normative, Gordon (1991) claims that Foucault's research into governmentality reveals a positive interest in this neoliberal rationality. He speculates that Foucault was likely attracted to neoliberal models of the twentieth century because they most closely responded to his calls for inventiveness in political culture (pp. 6–7). On this reading:

> [Foucault] suggests that recent neo-liberalism, understood (as he proposes) as a novel set of notions about the art of government, is a considerably more original and challenging phenomenon than the left's critical culture has had the courage to acknowledge, and that its political challenge is one which the left is singularly ill equipped to respond to. . . . (p. 6)

I am interested in taking up Foucault's challenge to the Left to combine a critical project with one of political inventiveness that identifies novel and original strategies not only for critique and resistance, but for progressive forms of organization and governance of public education.

Leftist critics of neoliberal governmental programs often appear to want it both ways. We are quick to identify the hierarchy, inequality, and alienation often endemic to centralized governance implemented through bureaucratic mechanisms. Yet we are also suspicious of moves toward decentralization as mere ploys to further cement the power of the state and to disenfranchise marginalized populations. A carte blanche critique of choice by the Left overlooks aspects of the school choice movement that suggest grass roots activism and efforts at self-determination. To the extent that the critical position of the antichoice Left represents a totalizing discourse, it neglects gaps and fissures that empirical work can inform.

In addition to drawing upon empirical data in order to formulate our political subjectivities in relation to school choice, I want to also focus attention on the implications of the discourses surrounding choice. While I am sympathetic to many of the critiques advanced by the antichoice Left, I want to warn against the entrenchment totalizing antichoice discourse that precludes other possibilities. The oppositional identity of the antichoice Left is both based upon and further instantiates the distinction between a democratic public sector and a market-driven private sector that neoliberalism functions to naturalize. Because the subjectivity and positionality of the antichoice Left is so firmly entrenched within neoliberalism's political rationality, its liberatory or critical potential is constrained in two key ways. First, the oppositional stance takes for granted rather than problematizing the neoliberal binary between public/private or democratic versus market control. Second, the oppositional identity rejects the entire school choice movement rather than attending to the specific ways in which power operates within particular school choice policies. In this final section I will discuss each of these limitations in turn and attempt to expand the Left's range of options in terms of reform alternatives made possible and thinkable by the school choice movement.

Rethinking the Line between Public and Private

As I discussed earlier, neoliberalism's naturalized distinction between the public and private sectors, and between democratic and market-based control within each sector, pervades the school choice movement. Advocates of choice argue that the market is preferable to direct democratic control for allocating educational resources. Critics, on the other hand, view market mechanisms as antidemocratic, and therefore antithetical to the sphere of public education. Henig (1994), for example, warns that "the real danger of market-based choice proposals [is] that they will erode public forums in which decisions with societal consequences can democratically be resolved" (p. xiii).

Foucault's account of governmentality problematizes this polemic between democracy or the market in a number of ways. His attention to ubiquitous techniques of government, including the formation of selves as particular kinds of subjects, complicates strict distinctions between public and private. Specific techniques of governance, framed by broader governmental rationalities such as neoliberalism, rule conduct within both the public sector and private arenas, through the state as well as through families, and through subjectified identities including both "citizens" and "consumers." Hence, a focus on governmentality not only suggests that the empirical question, Is democracy or the market a superior allocative device? is insufficient, it also shifts the question to, How is conduct governed? This shift of focus opens up some hitherto squelched potentials for a progressive politics of school choice; namely, it opens space to hear muted scholars on the Left who advocate choice mechanisms and specific models that exemplify the ideal of political inventiveness that Foucault challenged the Left to imagine. Examining the constraints imposed by a neoliberal rationality encourages those on the Left to begin thinking about choice as a mechanism of democratic social organization versus laissez-faire economic association. Different organizational models highlight distinct normative ends—such as *democratic governance and community* structures seeking political and economic *equality* versus *capitalist economic enterprises* seeking individual and property *rights* and *efficiency*.

Choice as a Tool of Democratic Governance

Failure to recognize the multifarious vertical and horizontal ways that power operates across the public/private binary poses the potentially negative consequence for the antichoice Left that it will overlook the possibility that the market might serve as a mechanism for achieving democratic ends such as equality and community. The currently widespread perception that academic and professional educators on the Left are antichoice suggests that such possibilities are being actively silenced or ignored. I would argue that most people concerned with school choice who are outside of academe, and many within academe, are unaware that there is any Leftist support for school choice. But there is support for choice from the Left. And those Leftists who investigate choice look to it as a possibility precisely because they are interested in addressing inequality, particularly surrounding social class, race, and school funding.

Harry Brighouse (2000), in his book *School Choice and Social Justice*, draws attention to a group of scholars and economists including Samuel Bowles, Herbert Gintis, Christopher Jencks, and John Coons whom he refers to as "egalitarian defenders" or "Left-wing advocates of choice" (pp. 30, 182). These scholars are well known for their interest in and commitment to educational equity with specific interests in equal educational opportunity, school finance, and social reproduction through schooling, which dates back to the 1970s.[4] According to Brighouse, these egalitarian defenders of school choice link increased efficiency with greater equality:

"[P]recisely because it is more efficient, school choice makes educational equality easier to achieve" (p. 30). He draws particular attention to a model choice scheme intended to implement educational equality and offered as part of a cluster of Bowles's and Gintis's economic proposals to "recast egalitarianism." The voucher scheme, which was initially proposed by Gintis (1995), and then further elaborated in his work with Bowles (Bowles and Gintis, 1996), stipulates that all vouchers must be worth the same amount and that participating schools cannot accept additional tuition beyond the amount of the voucher. Thus, the scheme would have an equalizing effect because families from all income levels would have similar access to a variety of schooling options.[5]

Thus, egalitarian defenders of choice share with the New Right neoliberalism's market rationality for achieving dual ends of efficiency and equality within the sphere of public education. But these proschool choice Leftists offer a subtle yet crucial difference to the argument for choice advanced by the New Right. The egalitarian defenders of school choice do not simply view choice as a mechanism for market allocation of resources, but rather view market allocation as a mechanism of democratic governance. Leftist economist Gintis (1995), for instance, suggests the use of the market in public education "as an instrument of rather than an alternative to democratic policymaking" (p. 510). Within this egalitarian recasting of choice, as in Foucault's emphasis on governmentality, the question is not simply an empirical one surrounding whether the market or democratic governance will yield more equitable results. Rather, this Leftist model of choice demonstrates recognition of Foucault's insights regarding neoliberalism: governance takes place by and through the market. The question then becomes, how can market allocation be governed democratically, and with democratic outcomes?

Choice as a Tool for Building Democratic Community

It seems that for many on the antichoice Left the possibility that the market might achieve ends of equality is obscured by the New Right's emphasis on efficiency. Similarly, the possibility that democratic forms of social and political relationships might arise within the context of neoliberalism is often overlooked due to emphases on commodities, competition, and consumption. Peters and Marshall (1996) critique neoliberal policy reform in New Zealand according to arguments similar to those offered by anti–school choice Leftists in the United States. Yet they offer a nuanced approach to policy analysis that leaves room for identifying ways to engage in policy making in neoliberal contexts that are "consonant with a commitment to community and democracy" (p. 16). Specifically, they call for "genuine" democratic community to replace what they identify as an "impoverished sense" of community within neoliberal discourse.

Within the context of their critique of an enterprise culture, which I discussed earlier, Peters and Marshall (1996) are concerned that, for political reasons concerning the self-limiting state, an impoverished sense of community and community subjects is being constructed within neoliberal policy discourse. They fear that neoliberal discourses and policies will give rise to a "hollow" notion of "community" comprised of "merely an aggregate of autonomous individuals acting out of enlightened self-interest" (p. 19).

Peters and Marshall (1996) apply "Foucault-type questions" in order to problematize the notion of "community" as it is deployed in neoliberal policy initiatives that propose to move away from the model of the welfare state toward privatized approaches to the provision of public social services (p. 21). What is noteworthy about Peters and Marshall's (1996) use of Foucauldian analysis is that while they are clearly suspicious of neoliberal calls for community, they do not throw the baby out with the bath water. Instead, they are interested in drawing upon Foucault in order to both critique existing policies and to identify alternative strategies for resistance to totalizing or dominating aspects of neoliberal discourses.[6] Thus, unlike many members of the anti–school choice Left in the United States who critique choice but fail to suggest alternatives, they outline a carefully formulated, positive vision for change.

Peters and Marshall (1996) outline four broad policy fronts intended to provide a basis for moving toward a community-based social policy: 1) the devolution of control and decision making to local communities; 2) the democratization of local communities: increased participation and better representation; 3) the coordination and integration of community services; and 4) education: community prevention, planning, and promotion (pp. 44–50). Each of these general policy fronts includes features endemic to the school choice movement in the United States. For instance, I have argued elsewhere that charter school reform has the potential to localize, democratize, and make more participatory and inclusive decision making in the public education arena. Moreover, I have argued that the organizational structure of charter schooling coordinates educational interests and services in a manner that parallels associative democracy (Smith, 2001).[7]

Thus, Peters and Marshall's (1996) call for genuine democratic communities, and the specific criteria they provide for achieving such communities, suggests that Leftist opposition to school choice in the United States could be channeled differently. Rather than simply opposing school choice as monolithically privatizing and consumer oriented, Leftists in the United States might draw upon their model for implementing community-based social policy to develop a more nuanced approach to the school choice movement. Such an approach would not abandon the critical role of the Left—the importance of which is stressed by critics of the governmentality literature such as Kerr (1999) and O'Malley, Weir, & Shearing (1997)—but would supplement this role with an emphasis on resisting the totalizing effects of neoliberal discourses by identifying and supporting community-generating aspects of choice models that exemplify a democratic versus impoverished sense of community.

In sum, Foucault's account of governmentality challenges Leftists to explore ways in which the school choice movement might invent new models for configuring and bridging the public and private spheres of education. Stalwart critics of privatized market relations are concerned about issues such as fairness and equality in part because they view the private realm as beyond the scope of governmental regulation. But they are failing to attend fully to the ways in which governance takes place in a dialectical, up-down fashion at a number of levels that complicate a strict public/private binary—for example, self and self, private interpersonal relations, relations within social institutions and communities, and relations concerned with political sovereignty (Gordon, 1991, pp. 2–3). Foucault's analysis of contemporary neoliberalism suggests at least two things for those skeptical of the privatizing aspects of school choice. First, that the state should be interrogated for its practices of governance and should not be naively viewed as the protector of public goods or marginalized interests. Second, that there is no such thing as a fully privatized market society because the market depends upon governmental activism for its very existence. Thus, Leftist concern with privatization per se is misplaced. Instead, the Left should be concerned primarily with how power operates in localized practices, versus totalized movements, and the specific implications of these practices in terms of normative criteria of democratic participation, equality, and community.

Attending to How Power Operates within Localized Practices of School Choice

Scholars and activists on the Left need to be vigilant against constraining our subjectivity based only on an oppositional identity in response to school choice. This does not mean that we refrain from critique, but rather that we apply Foucauldian-like suspicion of the totalizing effects of discourse to our own actions and regimes of truth. Foucault would not be interested in valorizing any one form of governmental rationality or organization, be it the welfare state model of a big bureaucratic government machine or the neoliberal model of market competition. Instead, Foucault would stress attention to relationships of domination and resistance as they manifest themselves in the actual practices of governance at the local level, including the level of individual subjectification vis-à-vis social movements. Currently, many Leftist activists who care passionately about public education are resisting school choice reform because they reject neoliberal values, such as the primacy placed upon self-interest and efficiency, and because they lump all choice strategies together as equally exemplary of such values. A Foucauldian approach to school choice reform would view the movement neither as a panacea nor as a Pandora's box. Rather, his critical methodology encourages us to look for gaps and fissures within the discourse surrounding choice as one way to be vigilant against forms of domination within the movement. In this manner the Left can reconfigure the discourse of choice and open possibilities beyond the downsides it identifies with neoliberalism as an alternative to cynicism, nihilism, or simply defending the status quo.

As O'Malley et al. (1997) advocate:

> [E]ven a politics that seeks to maximize the possibilities for contestation should, in co-operation with extra-academic organizations, think out the kinds of political and social conditions that would facilitate contestation and make room for diversity, help locate and define targets and intervention, and assist in the development and refinement of strategies for confronting or interrogating problematic regimes and technologies. (p. 504)

Such an approach to the school choice movement will not only guard against the constraints imposed by a neoliberal rationality, it will urge Leftists to employ theoretical critique to guide concrete political action in localized contexts. For example, in my own work I am exploring the question of whether it is possible to make a principled distinction between two distinct forms of school choice: vouchers and charters. My approach to this question shares Foucault's concern with asking how power operates in society. Thus, my inquiry requires attention to concrete practices in terms of how governance is taking place and how power is operating within both models. I need to ask, for instance, how are voucher schemes versus charter laws affecting power relations in public education? Many proponents of school choice see charters as a step toward vouchers and applaud the privatization of education. Foucault's notion of governmentality suggests to me that we resist the characterization of charter reform according to this naturalized schematic progression. Instead, like Peters and Marshall (1996) who developed criteria for assessing whether particular educational policies in New Zealand are consistent with principles of democracy and community, Leftists concerned with school choice in the United States must develop and apply relevant criteria in order to assess the desirability of specific policies. Aims of democratic social justice provide Leftists with starting points for developing such criteria.

As I undertake such work, I have begun to identify broad distinctions between vouchers versus charter schools—including democratic participation inclusive of teachers, parents, and students; equalized opportunities for middle- and low-income families; and accountability mechanisms—that lead me to reject the former and support the latter. The important point here is that the generalized critique that school choice is privatizing does not provide those of us on the Left with an all-or-nothing proposition. Rather, the implications of specific forms of choice, both "public" and "private," must be scrutinized by assessing how power operates within situated contexts and localized practices of governance.

In conclusion, Foucault's approach to governmentality suggests that the oppositional stance of the antichoice Left undermines attention to localized practices of school organization and governance that will both reveal social reproduction of inequalities and inform liberatory strategies of counter-conduct and resistance. Attention to the specificity of state charter laws, particular charter policies at state and district levels, and charter school practices within situated contexts will allow the Left to assess how power works in its particularities—not only in terms of how the state exercises authority, but also in terms of how microtechniques of power rule day-to-day behaviors and practices. We may then be able to advance more nuanced stances regarding school choice policies and to recognize more widely that Foucault's call for political inventiveness is already being realized in the growing grassroots movement of charter schools.

Notes

1. This interpretation of Foucault's work on governmentality in general and neoliberalism in particular is the subject of noteworthy debate. Many scholars

of governmentality view Foucault's genealogy of liberalism—in terms of the particular forms of government and political subjectivity that it calls forth—as one of his more provocative lines of inquiry within this strand of his research. While some view this as a fruitful line of inquiry (Gordon, 1991; Burchell, 1991), others claim that the treatment of neoliberalism within the governmentality literature falls short of the emancipatory potential offered by Foucault's larger intellectual project (O'Malley, Weir, and Shearing, 1997; Kerr, 1999).

2. Similar concerns are articulated by scholars in the United States who are concerned that school choice will further entrench racial segregation and class stratification among schools. See, for example, Moore and Davenport (1990), Margonis and Parker (1995), Fuller and Elmore (1996), and UCLA Charter School Study (1998).

3. Yet these Leftist arguments also presume that simply identifying choice as a market phenomenon reveals that it is an inappropriate mechanism for distributing educational opportunities. In *School Choice and Social Justice*, Harry Brighouse (2000) points out that opponents of choice often proceed from the assumption that "the very language of efficiency echoes the language of business and industry from which the world of education is supposed to keep a respectable distance" (p. 30). But this assumption needs to be defended. Critics of the market need to articulate more fully their reasons for finding ends like efficiency and commodification problematic. Brighouse argues, "[T]he commodification charge is unconvincing, not because choice does not commodify education, but because some degree of commodification of education is both unavoidable and unobjectionable" (p. 48). He also contends that efficiency claims should not simply be dismissed as inappropriate, but either proven false or demonstrated "that they are gained at the expense of other more fundamental values" (p. 31). After careful philosophical analysis—Brighouse's project is to evaluate the burgeoning school choice movement according to the principles of autonomy and equal educational opportunity—he concludes that arguments for and against choice are each overzealous; neither side's case is definitively compelling in light of these two principles. But he contends that choice policies may, in fact, do better than existing models in achieving equality; in his view the question cannot be resolved theoretically, but becomes an issue for empirical study. Therefore, he urges opponents of choice to do more than simply criticize and thereby provide de facto support for the status quo, which is fraught with inequalities. Skeptics of choice must advocate alternative reforms that address equity issues.

4. See Jencks (1970), Coons and Sugerman (1978), Gintis (1995), and Bowles and Gintis (1996).

5. Brighouse adapts and further develops the voucher model proposed by Gintis (1995) and Bowles and Gintis (1996). See Brihgouse (2000, ch. 9).

6. Peters and Marshall's (1996) application of Foucault's concept of governmentality suggests that they do not share the optimistic reading of neoliberalism as an example of political inventiveness advanced by Gordon and

Burchell and discussed above. Rather, they interpret Foucault's work on govern-mentality to suggest a more critical approach to "the liberal normative framework of autonomy, rights, and freedom" (pp. 21–22). In the following passage they de-scribe what they think it means to undertake a Foucauldian analysis, in terms of the concept of governmentality, of public choice theory in neoliberal contexts: "When we begin to apply Foucault's analysis of the development of notions of power as gov-ernance to the realms of social policy, what we have is a general philosophical/his-torical critique of the liberal normative framework, and a series of cautions against the way in which the policy sciences . . . can serve simply to drive social control mechanisms deeper into social fabric" (p. 32). In their view, Foucault's critique of neoliberalism as a governmental rationality simply serves to reveal how relations of domination are entrenched through discourses, governmental policy, and policy research espousing the liberal tenets of market competition and consumer choice.

I suspect that Foucault would be wary of Peters and Marshall's call for "gen-uine" community. The notion of a genuine democratic community is just as po-tentially totalizing, and thereby constraining on freedom, as are calls for genuine freedom vis-à-vis the laissez-faire market. But this drawback is easily addressed by applying the "Foucault-type questions" that these authors ask of neoliberal policy discourse to their own policy schemes surrounding democratic communities and community subjects. In other words, their normative framework must be subject to an interrogation of techniques of governance and their implications for freedom and equality.

7. In my work in this area I am drawing on a model of associative democ-racy as advanced by Cohen and Rogers (1992) and more recently by Cohen (1996).

References

Boaz, D. (1991). *Liberating schools: Education in the inner city.* Washington, DC: CATO Institute.

Bowles, S., & Gintis, H. (1996). Efficient redistribution: New rules for markets, states, and communities. *Politics and Society, 24,* 397–342.

Brighouse, H. (2000). *School choice and social justice.* Oxford: Oxford University Press.

Burchell, G. (1991). Peculiar interests: Civil society and governing "The system of natural liberty." In G. Burchell, C. Gordon, & P. Miller (Eds.), *The Fou-cault effect: Studies in governmentality* (pp. 119–150). Chicago: University of Chicago Press.

Chubb, J. E., & Moe, T. M. (1988). Politics, markets, and the organization of schools. *American Political Science Review, 82*(4), 1065–1087.

Chubb, J. E., & Moe, T. M. (1990). *Politics, markets, and America's schools.* Wash-ington, D.C.: Brookings Institution.

Cohen, J. (1996). Procedure and substance in deliberative democracy. In Seyla Benhabib (Ed.), *Democracy and difference: Contesting the boundaries of the political* (pp. 95–119). Princeton, NJ: Princeton University Press.

Cohen, J., & Rogers, J. (1992). Secondary associations and democratic governance. *Politics and Society, 20,* 393–473.

Coons, J., & Sugerman, S. (1978). *Education by choice: The case for family choice.* Berkeley, CA: University of California Press.

Foucault, M. (1973). *The order of things.* New York: Vintage.

Foucault, M. (1978/1991). Governmentality. In G. Burchell, C. Gordon, & P. Miller (Eds.), *The Foucault effect: Studies in governmentality* (pp. 87–104). Chicago: University of Chicago Press.

Foucault, M. (1984). What is Enlightenment? In Paul Rabinow (Ed.), *The Foucault reader* (pp. 32–50). New York: Pantheon Books.

Friedman, M. (1962). *Capitalism and freedom.* Chicago: University of Chicago Press.

Fuller, B., & Elmore, R. E., with G. Orfield (Eds.). (1996). *Who chooses? Who loses?: Culture, institutions, and the unequal effects of school choice.* New York: Teachers College Press.

Gintis, H. (1995). The political economy of school choice. *Teachers College Record, 96,* 492–511.

Gordon, C. (1991). Governmental rationality: An introduction. In G. Burchell, C. Gordon, & P. Miller (Eds.), *The Foucault effect: Studies in governmentality* (pp. 1–51). Chicago: University of Chicago Press.

Henig, J. (1994). *Rethinking school choice: Limits of the market metaphor.* Princeton, NJ: Princeton University Press.

Jencks, C. (1970). *Education vouchers: A report on financing education by payments to parents.* Cambridge, MA: Center for the Study of Public Policy.

Kerr, D. (1999). Beheading the king and enthroning the market: A critique of Foucauldian governmentality. *Science & Society, 63*(2), 173–202.

Margonis, F., & Parker, L. (1995). Choice, privatization, and unspoken strategies of containment. *Educational Policy, 9,* 375–403.

Marshall, J. (1996). *Michel Foucault: Personal autonomy and education.* Dordrecth, The Netherlands: Kluwer Academic.

Molnar, A. (1996). *Giving kids the business.* Boulder, CO: Westview Press.

Moore, D. R., & Davenport, S. (1990). School choice: The new improved sorting machine. In W. L. Boyd & H. J. Walberg (Eds.), *Choice in education.* Berkeley, CA: McCutcheon.

O'Malley, P., Weir, L., & Shearing, C. (1997). Governmentality, criticism, politics. *Economy and Society, 26*(4), 501–517.

Peters, M., & Marshall, J. (1996). *Individualism and community.* London: Falmer Press.

Peters, M., Fitzsimons, P., & Marshall, J. (1999, March). *Postmodern science and the new theology of the curriculum: A poststructuralist critique.* Invited paper presented at the meeting of Curriculum Theory Project, Louisiana State University, Baton Rouge, LA.

Smith, S. (2001). *The democratic potential of charter schools*. New York: Peter Lang.

University of California at Los Angeles Charter School Study. (1998). *Beyond the rhetoric of charter school reform: A study of ten California school districts*. Los Angeles: Author.

CHAPTER 9

Charter Schools as the Counterpublics of Disenfranchised Communities: Pedagogy of Resistance or False Consciousness?

ERIC ROFES

Nearly seven of ten newly created charter schools seek to realize an alternative vision of schooling, and an additional two of ten were founded especially to serve a special target population of students. Four of ten public schools report that they converted to charter status in order to gain autonomy from district and state regulations.

—U.S. Department of Education,
The State of Charter Schools, Third-Year Report

Parents of students with disabilities enroll their children in charter schools and other schools of choice because they believe those schools are more effective at meeting individual student needs, keeping parents informed, and providing mainstreaming options, and because they are dissatisfied with the bureaucracy of regular public schools and the stigma attached to special education.

—U.S. Department of Education,
Charter Schools and Students with Disabilities

During the 1970s and 1980s, a group of eminent education historians, theorists, and economists produced work arguing that systems of schooling in the West functioned as one of the primary mechanisms for the reproduction of stratified social and economic classes (Bowles and Gintis, 1976; Greer, 1976; Katz, 1971). These writers described—often in meticulous detail—how the organization, processes, and everyday educational practices of systemized schooling ensured the replication of privilege

245

and disadvantage, channeling students into paths defined in large part by the education and occupation of their parents and the color of their skin. This generation of academic researchers argued that a complex convergence of structures, practices, ideologies, and policy decisions colluded to ensure the transmission of capital, privilege, and resources within existing socioeconomic class and racial trajectories. As the debates about education reform, school choice, and charter schools intensify during this first decade of the twenty-first century, it may be a useful moment for contemporary researchers and policymakers to step back and consider recent reform initiatives through the lens of educational theorists who have examined social and cultural reproduction through schooling.

One of the most prominent (and provocative) sociologists who has produced a massive oeuvre focused on the reproduction of inequities through schooling is Pierre Bourdieu. His work in this area is broad, complicated, and often difficult reading for people unaccustomed to dense social theory. It is not likely that many American charter school founders, advocates, or opponents have read his books and essays. Yet his writings on educational theory and the reproductive nature of schooling speak directly to current debates within educational reform in the United States. Bourdieu grappled with at least three matters central to charters: the ways in which various forms of capital are produced and reproduced; the manner in which pedagogical systems such as schools serve as the machinery of reproduction for social inequities; and the complex nature of choice and the sociopolitical function of distinctions.

What happens when we examine the United States' charter schools movement through the lens of Bourdieu's critique of systems of schooling? What pitfalls and possibilities might his theories allow us to see in this decade-old form of decentralized education? And how might Bourdieu's thinking about the limitations of systematized schooling, his views about the transmission of social, cultural, and educational capital, and an examination of the politics of distinction that lies at the heart of his work be put to the service of proponents of charter schools?

This chapter brings together one contemporary school reform initiative with the insights of one educational theorist concerned with social reproduction through schooling. While charter advocates often cite the desire to puncture reproduction cycles in schooling as their primary motivation for embracing charters, such discussions are often wildly undertheorized. The chapter lays out aspects of Bourdieu's thinking that are especially pertinent to charter schools, focusing on key concepts that are useful to think on when one considers charters, choice, and public education. Next, I bring Bourdieu's theorizing into dialogue with U.S. charter schools, seeking applied ways of using Bourdieu to benefit at-risk students and interrupt a cycle of social reproduction through schooling. Finally, I take a step back from the data and the theory and suggest ways in which the charter school initiative might be understood as an attempt to break the stranglehold of systematized education, rupture the culture of schooling that reifies the status quo, and link choice with new forms of schooling in an attempt to resist continuing patterns of social inequality. Here I draw especially on the work of Stephen Nathan Haymes (1995) and his discussion of the social and cultural significance of urban place making for Blacks in the United States.

How Is Capital (Re)produced in Schools?

In writing about the reproductive function of schooling in *Reproduction in Education, Society and Culture*, Bourdieu's 1970 book written with Jean-Claude Passeron, Bourdieu summarizes their project:

> *Reproduction* sought to propose a model of the social mediations and processes which tend, behind the backs of the agents engaged in the school system—teachers, students and their parents—and often *against their will*, to ensure the transmission of cultural capital across generations and to stamp pre-existing differences in inherited cultural capital with a meritocratic seal of academic consecration by virtue of the special symbolic potency of the *title* (credential). Functioning in the manner of a huge classificatory machine which inscribes changes within the purview of the structure, the school helps to make and to impose the legitimate exclusions and inclusions which form the basis of the social order. (pp. ix–x)

Bourdieu's central analysis of systems of pedagogy criticizes bureaucratized forms of education for privileging elite forms of capital and reproducing—sometimes subtly and covertly through the deployment of unseen and unacknowledged methods he refers to as "symbolic violence"—current socioeconomic stratification. Because the organization, interactions, language, and curriculum of systematized schooling mirror and affirm the "habitus" ["an acquired system of generative schemes objectively adjusted to the particular conditions in which it is constituted" (Bourdieu, 1977, p. 95)] of privileged classes, the success of elite students is essentially guaranteed, even while appearing to the individual to be the result of hard work and persistence. The social capital that privileged students bring into the classroom—what has been broadly identified as "the resources accruing from membership within social networks" (Schaefft and Brown, 2000)—is an exact match with the sort of capital that the school is seeking to inculcate. At the same time, students from poor backgrounds struggle and fail, in large part due to the mismatch between their social capital, as embedded in their habitus, and that of the school. While Bourdieu sees dominated classes as being "beaten before they start" (Bourdieu, 1984a), he sees the elite, in the words of one critic, confusing what they have learned for what they are born with (Jenkins, 1992). A system of reproduction hence is misrecognized as meritocracy.

This is captured powerfully in Peter W. Cookson, Jr. and Caroline Hodges Persell's study of elite private boarding schools, *Preparing for Power* (1985):

> Privilege must appear to be earned, because the only real justification for inequality is that it is deserved—as payment for sacrifices, the powerful must endure in the name of the common good. Thus the prep rite of passage aims not only to transform individuals into a collective identity, but also serves to legitimate the maintenance of privilege. To achieve this end, the prep school administrators and teachers must tame their high-spirited, hedonistic charges both in the sense of demanding outward conformity and in the deeper sense of internalizing the school's value system. (p. 125)

At the same time that elite students have entered into a game where their success is virtually guaranteed, Bourdieu and Passeron explain the lose/lose situation faced by members of dominated classes because school officials refuse to confront the core power-based reality that circumscribes their relations:

> Blindness to what the legitimate culture and the dominated culture owe to the structure of their symbolic relations, i.e. to the structure of the relation of domination between the classes, inspires on the one hand the 'culture for the masses' programme of 'liberating' the dominated classes by giving them the means of appropriating legitimate culture as such, with all it owes to its functions of distinction and legitimation . . . ; and on the other hand the populist project of decreeing the legitimacy of the cultural arbitrary of the dominated classes as constituted in and by the fact of its dominated position, canonizing it as 'popular culture.' (Bourdieu and Passeron, 1977, pp. 23-24)

Here Bourdieu points to the two approaches school systems have used in working with children from poor families, the "dominated" classes: (1) providing them with the means of accumulating the cultural capital of elites; or, (2) providing them with curriculum focused on their own cultures ("popular culture"). In the former case, Bourdieu argues, the dominated classes achieve only limited success because their habitus is unable to easily take in and incorporate the cultural capital of the elite. In the latter, they are inculcated with a type of cultural capital that is not valued by the culture at large. This seems to point to a no-win situation for advocates for children from poor families seeking to use public education as a means of breaking cycles of poverty.

How Do Systems of Pedagogy Reproduce Inequality?

Bourdieu and Passeron (1977) write, "All pedagogic action is, objectively, symbolic violence insofar as it is the imposition of a cultural arbitrary by an arbitrary power" (p. 5). They understand "pedagogic action" as including "diffuse education," which occurs informally and through exchanges with "all educated members of a social formation or group," "family education," which occurs when the family unit serves as the transmission source for the culture, and "institutionalized education," through formal institutions—such as schools—of the culture.

　　These sources of pedagogic action are problematic to Bourdieu and Passeron because they usually serve simply "to reproduce the cultural arbitrary of the dominant or the dominated classes" (p. 5). Because to their minds sources of pedagogic action "always tend to reproduce the structure of the distribution of cultural capital among these groups or classes, thereby contributing to the reproduction of the social structure" (p. 11), the authors offer little opportunity for social transformation, individual agency, or progressive education reform. Their highly deterministic diagnoses of reproduction through schooling seem to offer little hope for people committed to putting schools to the service of progressive social change.

　　While *Reproduction* is focused specifically on systems of education in France, in the introduction to the 1990 edition Bourdieu points out similarities with schooling in the United States:

> [W]e now know that, in America, no less than in Europe, credentials contribute to ensuring the reproduction of social inequality by safeguarding the preservation of the structure of the distribution of powers through a constant re-distribution of people and titles characterized, behind the impeccable appearance of equity and meritocracy, by a systematic bias in favor of the possessors of inherited cultural capital. (p. xi)

Hence in Bourdieu's perspective, inherited cultural capital can be understood as the necessary ticket to success is school (and life). Schools do not serve to promote mobility; instead they function to provide certification for the cultural capital of privileged students. While most of Bourdieu's major writing on education focuses on higher education (1984b, 1990), his work with Passeron (1977) and his discussion of education in *Distinction* (1984a) encompass the entire spectrum of schooling in France, from infancy through adult education.

By utilizing this understanding of the ways in which systems of pedagogy reproduce inequality, are we able to move beyond Bourdieu and Passeron's pessimistic vision and suggest ways in which alternative forms of organizing schooling might benefit the life chances of poor children? Is it possible to puncture their deterministic vision and suggest ways in which schools might become sites of resistance? Such a project seems like the logical next step, yet Bourdieu's work on the issue of choice does not lend itself to easy answers to these questions. Yet perhaps people working on school reform as a strategy for advancing the life chances of poor children might find some helpful guidance contained in Bourdieu's complex understanding of distinction and choice.

What Role Can Choice Play in Resisting the Reproduction of Inequality?

Writing with Passeron, Bourdieu has strongly condemned educational systems he considers to function as simple, mechanistic copying machines for social reproduction. He sets forth his criticism succinctly in the introduction to the 1990 edition of *Reproduction*:

> In any given social formation, the dominant educational system is able to set up the dominant pedagogical work as the work of schooling without either those who exercise it or those who undergo it ever ceasing to misrecognize its dependence on the power relations making up the social formation in which it is carried on. . . . (p. 67)

Here Bourdieu and Passeron argue that parents and children within school systems do not even consciously or formally need to consent to the reproduction work of schooling—their movements through years of schooling, explicit and implicit choices, and the everyday home and school practices, culminate in effectively replicating existing power relations and solidifying the child's original position in the overall scheme of things.

Yet despite his powerful critique of the educational system and machinery of schooling, it is unlikely that Bourdieu would have thought favorably about any mechanism that would move Western systems of education closer to a free market system of enhanced school choice. Indeed, Bourdieu theorizes choice as perhaps the most central mechanism by which symbolic violence occurs; to him it is the social practice by which dominated populations ensure their continual domination, without their dominators having to make use of coercion, force, or overt forms of enforcement. For Bourdieu, distinctions and choices appear innocent, arbitrary, and apolitical, while actually they are the essential building blocks of social reproduction.

Bourdieu's six-hundred-page book *Distinction* (1984a) can be read as an exposé on the illusionary nature of choice, taste, and cultural distinctions. While the data used in this book emerges from a field outside of schooling—the high arts and popular culture—the book elegantly deconstructs the process of distinction making and the practice of choice to show how what we believe to be personal aesthetics and tastes are tightly linked with social class position and inherited cultural capital. The book is a full frontal assault on Kant's writings on innate cultural taste, laying bare the complicated workings behind what appear as simple choices based on an innocent preference. What many of us typically see as innocent and genetically triggered preferences or biologically constituted tendencies ("I just happen to like music by Sting"), are actually performances of class position.

Bourdieu drives this home in one of the book's few passages focused on schooling. In discussing how academic certification is actually a process of reifying the cultural capital of the elite, he writes:

> This process occurs at all stages of schooling, through the manipulation of aspirations and demands—in other words, of self-image and self-esteem—which the educational system carries out by channeling pupils towards prestigious or devalued positions implying or excluding legitimate practice. (1984a, p. 25)

Bourdieu is not talking only about much-critiqued mechanisms such as tracking or ability grouping here. He is highlighting more subtle practices and invisible processes by which the capital of students and their internalized habitus are either reinforced or undermined, valued or devalued, rewarded or punished, in schools. Yet even when parents and students attempt to navigate strategically through the educational system, the system succeeds imperceptibly at squelching their opportunities for advancement:

In the present state of the system, the exclusion of the great mass of working-class and middle-class children takes place not at the end of primary schooling but steadily and impalpably, all through the early years of secondary schooling, through hidden forms of elimination such as repeated years (equivalent to a deferred elimination); relegation into second-class courses, entailing a stigma that tends to induce proleptic recognition of scholastic and social destiny; and finally, the awarding of devalued certificates. (p. 154)

Hence Bourdieu again paints a discouraging portrait of the possibilities for poor and working-class students to successfully gain mobility through the educational system. This is especially true, as he indicates in great detail, because of the way individuals' desires and expectations shift subtly and unconsciously to match the possibilities offered people of their cultural capital within the larger social structure ("subjective expectations of objective probabilities"). Bourdieu shows how processes that funnel entire classes of people into certain social positions go unrecognized, in part because the individual members of these classes are encouraged to personalize the process and internalize blame:

It goes without saying that the adjustment between objective chances and subjective aspirations that is thereby established is both more subtle and more subtly extorted, but also more risk and unstable. Maintaining vagueness in the images of the present and future of one's position is a way of accepting limits, but it is also a way to avoid acknowledging them, or to put it another way, a way of refusing them. But it is a refusal in bad faith, the product of an ambiguous cult of revolution which springs from resentment at the disappointment of unrealistic expectations. Whereas the old system tended to produce clearly demarcated social identities which left little room for social fantasy but were comfortable and reassuring even in the unconditional renunciation which they demanded, the new system of structural instability in the representation of social identity and its legitimate aspirations tends to shift agents from the terrain of social crisis and critique to the terrain of personal critique and crisis. (1984a, p. 156)

Bourdieu's critique of the free market paradigm in all fields is that it encourages cultural production to embrace mediocrity, or, in his terms "leveling" or "homogenization of standards" (1996, p. 26). In fact, unlike neoliberal theorists in education, he believes excellence is more commonly achieved outside of market demand:

Today, on the contrary, the market is accepted more and more as a legitimate means of legitimation. . . . Audience ratings impose the sales model on cultural products. But it is important to know that, historically, all the cultural productions that I consider . . . the highest human products—math, poetry, literature, philosophy—were all produced against market imperatives. (1996, p. 27)

One critic has noted, "Bourdieu's sociology of culture is . . . a sociology of cultural consumption, the uses to which culture is put, and the manner in which cultural categories are defined and defended" (Jenkins, 1992, p. 130). This insight begins to suggest why school choice would have been problematic for Bourdieu: Bourdieu appears profoundly skeptical about individuals' explanations and understandings of their own actions and the reasoning they offer for their choices, cultural consumption, or tastes. He would be the first to deploy terms such as *false consciousness* (although the term he utilizes is *misrecognition*) to describe the acceptance by some progressives and communities of color of school choice and educational alternatives such as charter schools. Bourdieu would see poor people of color choosing a community-based charter as ensuring their children's bleak future. While aiming to assist their life chances, the opening up of school choice options serves simply as a mechanism for the dominated classes to guarantee their own domination.

To Bourdieu, charter schools and other forms of school choice may simply be yet another mechanism for allowing poor people to believe that they've found a way to give their children the kind of education that might forward their life chances, while in actuality, they remain trapped in their class position. Yet is it possible for others to make use of Bourdieu's work to suggest ways in which charter schools might be the mechanism needed to ensure that these children receive a strong education without taking on the cultural capital, values, and personal characteristics of the dominating class? Might the charter school experiment be more about attempting to move beyond the limited options Bourdieu identifies and create an alternative system of public schooling that advances the life chances of poor children without distancing them from their familial and community values?

Charter Schools as a Choice Mechanism that Educates and Empowers

Placing the educational theories of Bourdieu alongside charter schools in the United States raises a range of interesting questions. On the one hand, Bourdieu's critique of the reproductive nature of vast school bureaucracies might suggest that a reorganization of public schooling is needed in order to offer possibilities for resistance. After damning the curriculum, pedagogy, culture, and organization of systems of schooling for reproducing existing class divisions, one might think that an innovative and new sector of schools with greater autonomy from the apparatus of reproduction (the district), and increased school-site control over the curriculum, pedagogy, and culture, along with new forms of decentralized governance, might be what is needed to spur mobility for children from poor and working-class families.

Indeed, studies of charter schools suggest that these are precisely the populations that are being served disproportionately in charter schools (U.S. Department of Education, 1998). Authors of a national study of charter schools wrote:

> Our best estimate is that six out of ten charter schools are not racially distinct from their surrounding district. About three out of ten are much more likely to enroll students of color than their surrounding district. Similar findings hold for low-income students. (U.S. Department of Education, 1998, section 4)

Furthermore, the study found, "At least 32 charter schools serve more than two-thirds African-American students, 13 serve more than two-thirds Native American children, 22 have more than two-thirds Hispanic students, and eight serve more than 50 percent students with disabilities" (section 4c). Are these populations initiating the formation of new schools and enrolling heavily in charters because they share Bourdieu's belief that large public systems of schooling simply funnel their students into programs and eventually jobs that reproduce the status quo? And if so, does this portion of Bourdieu's analysis suggest that legislation granting charter schools greater authority over curriculum, pedagogy, governance, and culture is critical to charters functioning as sites of resistance to the status quo?

Some states have specifically targeted neighborhoods and populations with their charter school and community schools initiatives. For example, "With the expansion of the program . . . to districts in 'academic emergency' Ohio's community school program became specifically focused on raising student achievement and providing more educational choices within the public system to parents and students in Ohio's urban and low-performing districts" (Ohio Community School Center, 2000, p. 2). Yet other state charter policies—including Arizona and California, the two states with the greatest number of charter schools—do not create incentives for poor and working-class communities to initiate charters. Likewise the U.S. Public Charter School program has awarded its grants intended to support charter start-up efforts, with no distinction concerning a school's socioeconomic background.

On one level, many people think about parent dissatisfaction with traditional district schools from an individualistic frame: these parents opt to withdraw this child from this school for this specific and individualized reason. And it is likely that many parents would also identify their choice decisions in this way. Yet is it possible to think about the exodus of specific collectivities of families from traditional district schools in a broader and more collective manner? Does the social reproductive nature of U.S. schooling serve as a catalyst for African American and Native American families to come together collectively and create charter schools to better serve their children? Can at least some sectors of charter schools be seen as points of resistance to an otherwise replicative machine called public education?

The Max Weber in Bourdieu might answer yes, but Bourdieu's body of work goes considerably beyond Weber's critique of bureaucracy as an engine of stability and social reproduction. Bourdieu's powerful microanalysis of choice indicates that he sees it primarily as a way for the dominated classes to participate agreeably in their own domination and take the work off the shoulders of the dominators. He sees this occurring within systems of education, when students elect to choose certain classes and not others, acquire high rates of absenteeism, and participate in educational tracks that direct them away from up-class opportunities. Bourdieu has summarized the pitfalls of choice in this way:

> Like every sort of taste, it unites and separates. Being the product of the conditioning associated with a particular class of conditions of existence, it unites all those who are the product of similar conditions while distinguishing them from all others. And it distinguishes in an essential way, since taste is the basis of all that one has—people and things—and all that one is for others, whereby one classifies oneself and is classified by others. (1984a, p. 56)

While Bourdieu has been widely considered to be a sociologist who aims to "integrate agency within structure" (Robbins, 1998), his sense of the possibilities of realizing mobility through agency seems quite limited, especially in his writings about schooling. In fact, it is at this juncture that one must interpret Bourdieu's writings on schooling as either stuck in a hopelessness about reproduction, or open to alternative forms of school organization spearheaded by democratic collectivities of citizens. Yet couldn't what Bourdieu sees as the "taste" that both "unites and separates" also be conceptualized as mass collective action?

It is likely Bourdieu would have seem the traditional class-reifying dynamics occurring within systems of school choice, including charter schools. The data we have on charter schools and parental choice provide us with a wide range of explanations parents offer for choosing specific charter schools. The U.S. Department of Education's study of charter schools (1998, exhibit 5-6) found the following responses to be the most common when charter school leaders were asked, "How powerful is this feature in attracting parents and students to your school?"

- Nurturing environment
- Safe environment
- Value system
- Quality of academic program
- Small class size
- High standards for achievement
- Specialized curriculum focus

Yet Bourdieu would likely understand these explanations as examples of "misrecognitions." He would argue that families have been driven from traditional district schools—and been kept from enrolling in the elite schools of the district—through a process of aligning their "subjective expectations to objective probabilities." Essentially, their enrollment in the charter school might be seen as the final mechanism that ensures the reproduction of class status for their child.

There is another way Bourdieu's sociology might be utilized as a way to theorize charter schools. It seems critically important, absent a profound social and economic transformation in the United States, that we develop a form of public education capable of stepping outside the overwhelming drive toward consistently reproducing the status quo. This involves considering charters from a different Bourdieuean lens: as mechanisms of resistance rather than as the machinery of reproduction. The charter movement might be seen as a movement that encompasses both the "despair" and the "hope" Bourdieu writes so much about (see Cookson and Berger, 2004). Charter schools may be seen as new forms of collective action, contemporary innovative structures of political work.

In Bourdieu's pessimistic worldview, if there is going to be any possibility at all of significant mobility occurring for the working class and poor, it would require a mass exodus from current bureaucratized forms of education and the formation of a new sector of public education that is freed from the rigid bureaucracy. This seems to be occurring in charter schools:

> The majority of charter schools are newly created, and most such schools are founded to realize an alternative vision for schooling or to serve a special target population of students. The primary reason pre-existing public schools convert to charter status is to gain flexibility and autonomy from their districts or by-pass various regulations. (U.S. Department of Education, 1998, section 5)

Bourdieu believes such a shift would then lead to the creation of a new assemblage of organizations engaged in pedagogical work determined to puncture existing systems of stratification. He argues that we need new structures of schooling that respect indigenous cultures in the everyday scholastic culture of schooling. Yet now that we have hundreds of such charters in the United States (U.S. Department of Education, 1998, section 4), would he argue that these schools simply furnish students with an enhanced form of a type of capital that will not be valued by the world at large?

Bourdieu has also argued that social structures are not permanently fixed, that they are subject to transformation through collective action. One critic summarized Bourdieu's perspective: "Objective structures are not only identifiably *structured*: they are identifiably *structuring*. In other words, observed structures can and should be seen as constituting and dynamic, not static" (Grenfell and James, 1998, p. 11).

This is precisely where charter schools offer possibilities but also dangers. For charters to function as sites of resistance, they have to accomplish two challenging tasks: they need to ensure that students develop strong academic skills and they need to do so without transforming their students into mindless adherents to the dominant culture. Thus we would be aiming to ensure the basic skills of poor children without mindlessly loading them with the social and cultural capital of the affluent, even as they become adept at working with that precise social and cultural capital. This demands that children receive not only skills and capital from their K–12 schooling, but also a critical consciousness about the ways power circulates, cultural groups and communities are valued and devalued, and capitalism functions as a colonizing force.

Much would be demanded from the leaders of the charter school movement, were these new schools to truly become sites of resistance. Charters would have to continue to combat the drive to grant them titular independence, while forcing them under the smothering oversight of the broader educational regime through standardized testing, enforced curricula, required hiring of certificated teachers, and increased programmatic regulation. The "Animal Farm" moment that is currently faced by charters around the country—where they are being both overtly and subtly driven to adopt practices, structures, and values of the larger, dominant field of public education—would have to be thoroughly exposed and resisted. Charters might also need to acquire the self-conscious awareness of their identities as resistant organizations, aiming to transform the trajectories of their students, and inculcate this specific identity into their students, parents, and faculty members.

Bourdieu clearly was aware of the difficulties associated with creating progressive organizations and forms of public education. He understood how what appears to be emancipatory might actually turn out to function as a dominating force:

> One of the paradoxes of what is called the 'democratization of schooling' is that only when the working classes, who had previously ignored or at best vaguely concurred in the Third Republic ideology of 'schooling as a liberatory force,' actually entered secondary education, did they discover schooling as a conservative force, by being relegated to second-class courses or eliminated. (1984, pp. 143-144)

A breed of resistant charter schools might be able to work strategically with the cultural capital of pupils from dominated classes, and they might simultaneously be able to value and affirm their preexisting cultural capital, but provide them with the tools and the educational capital to acquire and work with elite forms of cultural capital in a critical way. In some ways, this harkens back to Lisa Delpit's discussions of equipping students of color to grapple with the mainstream "culture of power," rather than providing them with an education in their home culture and no keys to unlock the culture that controls the vast resources and opportunities (1995). It also requires a Freirean focus on praxis and critical consciousness (1970, 1993) and a sense of Frantz Fanon's "pedagogy of resistance" (1986). As Henry Giroux (1983) has shown, critical pedagogy is key—in a pragmatic and profound way—to providing marginalized communities with the collective understandings needed to create social change.

Stephen Nathan Haymes, in his landmark book *Race, Culture, and the City: A Pedagogy for Black Urban Struggle* (1995), argues for "the necessity of developing a pedagogy of Black urban resistance" which is embodied in what he dubs a "pedagogy of place." Haymes moves the discussion of marginalized groups working collaboratively to create specific urban sites to a deeper level; he shows "how Black urban communities resist White supremactists' urban meanings and urban forms by constructing alternative images and representations of place" (p. 9).

Using Haymes's thinking as a lens through which to view charter schools, much of the appeal of charters to communities of color is rooted in the fact that "place making is tied to the idea that places are significant because we assign meaning to them in relation to our specific projects" (p. 10). The conceptualization and creation of a charter school becomes one of increasingly few sites where communities of color can collaboratively make an independent meaning from an educational venture. It can also be a site for the production of authentic cultural identities linked to long-held community values, historical understandings, and social norms. As Haymes writes, "In a sense, black settlement space is the location from which urban blacks construct alternative experiences of time, space, and interpersonal relationships or community, as alternative culture to that of white supremacist capitalist patriarchy" (pp. 13-14). Furthermore, Haymes shows that creating charter schools may be more central to Black communities than White, because "it is in the context of 'place making' that blacks form their individual and collective identities as blacks" (p. 72), while mainstream American culture affords Whites the same opportunity.

Haymes shows how the creation and preservation of a "black public sphere is . . . the basis for building a community of resistance." He draws on Nancy Fraser's work (1991):

> Subaltern couterpublics have a dual character. On the one hand, they function as spaces of withdrawal and regroupment; on the other hand, they also function as bases and training grounds for agitational activities directed toward wider publics. It is precisely in the dialectic between these two functions that their emancipatory potential resides. (p. 69)

This may explain the strong appeal that charters have for communities of color: they offer the potential to create pockets of resistance to White supremacy and produce alternative Black identities. As Haymes notes, "The public sphere is not only an arena for the formation of discursive opinion; it is an arena for the formation and enactment of social identities; it is the arena that allows one to speak in one's own voice" (p. 113).

Hence, using new thinking about the functions of counterpublics, we might reconceptualize the emancipatory potential of charter schools. Students might emerge from these charters on a different trajectory than often cited in charter debates: one that has inculcated in them multiple forms of cultural capital, a new understanding of the social capital of their home community, and a critical pedagogy of resistance. This opens the possibility that choice and agency might create new sites of pedagogy that resist the reproduction of inequality. It also suggests that charters offer the opportunity to interrupt entrenched patterns of social reproduction.

References

Bourdieu, P. (1977). *Outline of a theory of practice.* Cambridge: Cambridge University Press.

Bourdieu, P. (1984a). *Distinction: A social critique of the judgment of taste.* Cambridge: Harvard University Press.

Bourdieu, P. (1984b). *Homo academicus.* Stanford, CA: Stanford University Press.

Bourdieu, P. (1990). *In other words: Essays towards a reflexive sociology.* Stanford, CA: Stanford University Press.

Bourdieu, P. (1996). *On television.* New York: New Press.

Bourdieu, P., & Passeron, J. (1990). *Reproduction in education, society and culture.* London: Sage.

Bowles, S., & Gintis, H. (1976). *Schooling in capitalist America.* New York: Basic Books.

Cookson, P. W., Jr., & Berger, K. (2004). *Expect miracles: Charter schools and the politics of hope and despair.* Boulder, CO: Westview Press.

Cookson, P. W., Jr., & Persell, C. H. (1985). *Preparing for power: America's elite boarding schools.* New York: Basic Books.

Delpit, L. (1995). *Other people's children: Cultural conflict in the classroom.* New York: New Press.

Fanon, F. (1986). *The wretched of the earth.* New York: Grove Press.

Fraser, N. (1991, Spring). Rethinking the public sphere: A contribution to the critique of actually existing democracy. *Social Text.*

Freire, P. (1970, 1993). *Pedagogy of the oppressed.* New York: Continuum.

Giroux, H. (1983). *Theory and resistance in education: A pedagogy for the opposition.* South Hadley, MA: Bergin and Garvey.

Greer, C. (1976). *The great school legend: A revisionist interpretation of American public education.* New York: Viking.

Grenfell, M., & James, D. (Eds.). (1998). *Bourdieu and education.* London: Falmer.

21

y. (95. *e, culture, and the city: A pedagogy for Black urban struggle.*
Albany: State University of New York Press.
Jenkins, R. (1992). *Key sociologists: Pierre Bourdieu.* London:Routledge.
Katz, M. (1971). *Class, bureaucracy, & schools: The illusion of educational change in America.* New York: Praeger.
Ohio Community School Center. (2000, April 10). Comments on the first-year community school implementation report by the Legislative Office of Educational Oversight. Columbus, OH: Author.
Robbins, D. (1998). The need for an epistemological "break." In M. Grenfell & D. James (Eds.), *Bourdieu and education* (pp. 27–51). London: Falmer.
Schaefft, K., & Brown, D. (2000). Social capital and grassroots development: The case of Roma self-governance in Hungary. *Social Problems, 47*(2), 201–219.
U.S. Department of Education. (1998a). *A national study of charter schools.* Washington, D.C.: Office of Educational Research and Improvement, U.S. Department of Education.
U.S. Department of Education (1998b). *Charter schools and students with disabilities.* Washington, D.C.: Office of Educational Research and Improvement, U.S. Department of Education.
U.S. Department of Education (1999). *The state of charter schools third-year report.* Washington, D.C.: Office of Educational Research and Improvement . U.S. Department of Education.

Conclusion:
Toward a Progressive Politics of School Choice

ERIC ROFES AND LISA M. STULBERG

Introduction

For over two decades, liberal and progressive voices in education in the United States have been effectively put on the defensive in policy debates focused on American public schools. Conservative social critics success-fully have manipulated data on student achievement to argue that there is an all-out crisis in public education and that our nation has lost its competitive edge due to the failings of our public school system. From the era of "A Nation at Risk" to the current "No Child Left Behind" moment, arguments put forward by these social critics and scholars from the fields of business, political science, law, economics, and education have tapped successfully into our nation's anxieties about security, economic stability, and our identity as Americans and transformed both the way the public thinks about schooling and its votes on educational issues.[1]

The Left has attempted to respond to conservative critics by producing evidence showing that public schools are doing well by America's children and that the crisis construct has been used to distract attention from other important issues, like the growing disparity in wealth in the United States and the failure of our nation to adequately fund public education (Berliner and Biddle, 1996; Rothstein, 1998). They have argued that there is no authentic crisis or that public schools may not be perfect, but are performing better than they ever have and that public schools remain successful engines of social mobility. Perhaps because it has been put on the

263

defensive, the Left has backed away from the work of its own revisionist historian-theorists in the 1960s and 1970s, which demonstrated the powerful ways in which public schools function to reproduce inequality (see Bowles and Gintis, 1976; Carnoy and Levin, 1985; Katz, 1971, 1985; Spring, 1972, 1975). This body of literature still looms large and presents vexing challenges to all of us who hope to see equity and economic redistribution through the power of the state.

When we speak of "progressives" or "the Left," we do so with a kind of self-consciousness that acknowledges the imprecision of our language and the tremendous shifts occurring in words like *conservative, liberal,* and *progressive* over the past two decades. We define ourselves as progressives because we believe that fundamental structural and cultural changes need to take place in order to approach the vision of a multicultural democracy in our nation and that these changes will require the radical reenvisioning of solutions to most social problems. We separate ourselves from liberals, who tinker with policies but essentially leave in place the central regimes of power that maintain the status quo: capitalism, White supremacy, and patriarchy. Instead, as self-defined progressives, we look toward big-picture changes that will bring about profound transformations that will improve the life chances of those marginalized in our nation: poor and working-class people, communities of color, gays and lesbians, and women and girls. We also ally ourselves with social movements that are aimed at sweeping shifts that redistribute our nation's resources and create more sustainable forms of living. We draw on the political vision of radical historian and true optimist, Howard Zinn (1994), who distinguishes between "liberal" and "radical" in his work, contending that a liberal is "a believer in the self-correcting character of American democracy." He writes, "I was a radical, believing that something fundamental was wrong in this country . . . something rotten at the root. The situation required not just a new president or new laws, but an uprooting of the old order, the introduction of a new kind of society— cooperative, peaceful, egalitarian" (p. 173).

We believe that, contrary to what many progressive voices in education argue today, there *is* a crisis in education, but that it is far narrower and focused than the crisis imagined by the Right. We share in the Left's general analysis that the bulk of American public schools do a good job of preparing students for participation in democracy and successful employment in a changing workplace. But there are significant discrepancies here. We believe that American public schools are still significantly failing to serve low-income students and students of color, and it is these students who particularly lose out in current schooling debates and politics.

Just as the debate over the success or failure of American schooling is unhelpful in the way it either proclaims premature victory or condemns American schools to certain and stubborn failure, so, too, the debate over school choice is generally too dichotomous, simplistic, and staid. As progressives, we not only implicate the Right here, we implicate our colleagues and friends on the Left as well. For those on the Left who care about social justice and equality and believe that public schools have a significant role to play in social movements and in equalizing life chances for all students, it is time for a new kind of conversation about—and new action on—school choice.

What Is School Choice?

While today advocacy groups ask educators and ordinary citizens the simple question of whether or not they support or oppose "school choice," our nation has embraced various forms of school choice for a very long time, we just have not usually identified it by this specific name. Almost one hundred years ago, when courts ruled that families had the right to opt out of the local public education and independently fund their child's education through private schooling, the legal precedent was established in this nation that all children did not have to attend a common public school (Potter, 1967, p. 388). Studies have shown for years that middle- and high-income parents use various strategies—ranging from residential choice to requests for specific teachers; to tracking; to the deployment of social and professional contacts as references for their children—to ensure their children are placed in the best possible public schools.[2]

It seems that when choice is enacted by elite populations, our society tacitly approves and asks few questions. When choice is enacted by poor populations, many raise questions of ethics, effects on our vision of democracy, and the impact on the student achievement of children from low-income families. We have a problem with this dynamic, which we have seen again and again in our young careers as education professors.

On one idealistic level, we endorse a vision of a "common school" that has never been fulfilled in this nation. This vision involves the creation of systems of public education that aggressively work to bring a mix of students into the same classroom, refuse to track them by ability grouping, and work assiduously to create social options that do not encourage segmentation by race, ethnicity, or sex. These schools would need to be truly multicultural, and not simply work to "include" children of color and children of diverse religious backgrounds into school cultures and curricula that are generically White, Protestant, and middle class. These schools would also need to find ways to be consonant with the cultural background and values of all their students and to ensure that power and decision making rest in the hands of adults from a range of backgrounds and cultures. It would clearly be a huge challenge to create such institutions for the masses of children in American public schools. But when we dig into the literature on the problematic dream of a common school in our nation, this is what we believe would fulfill a progressive vision. More homogenous school communities, that truly have autonomy and resources to build and sustain schools that serve them, also fulfill this progressive vision.

Absent significant movements by progressives to place barriers on the school choice options utilized by elite populations, we believe equity is best achieved by ensuring that poor people are provided access to public school choice options. This should be achieved by supporting public school choice options for children from poor families and communities. This does not mean that we fully endorse all mechanisms and processes that fall under the rubric of school choice. In fact, we believe that a major problem facing educational policymakers today is that the term school choice is bantered about in a manner that obfuscates rather than illuminates, and that fails to do justice to the full panoply of activities that take place in some kind of choice format. We cannot think of examples of respected educational leaders who are fully prochoice or antichoice on all possible options, yet we are constantly asked to put our own politics into one of these very narrow categories. Instead of embracing meaningless terms, we believe one is best guided by a vision that incorporates one's values and beliefs about public education's mission, and then opts to either support or oppose specific choice *strategies* or choice *mechanisms* commensurate with this vision.

Policymakers need to have a deep and public conversation about the full range of school choice options—formal mechanisms (including charter schools, vouchers, controlled choice, postsecondary, magnets, interdistrict, intradistrict, private "scholarship" programs, private and parochial schools, and homeschooling), structural mechanisms (such as real estate segmentation, residential choice, choice by default due to transportation, and tracking), and stealth mechanisms (parental requests for specific teachers, divorced families choosing a student's primary residency based on schools, sibling choice, or teacher/child choice). If people declare that they oppose school choice, do they truly oppose all of these mechanisms? Why do some of us oppose certain forms of choice but not other forms?

Those of us on the Left have frequently embraced the 1960s feminist slogan, "The personal is political." At the same time, we have noticed that progressives within the field of education (and perhaps beyond) seem to look the other way when colleagues on the Left take advantage of various choice options for their own children, even as they participate in campaigns decrying school choice for others. What would it look like if advocates for charter schools or other forms of school choice put their resources into examining the schooling practices of key academic researchers, public officials, and advocacy group leaders who oppose charters for exacerbating stratification in our schools? We argue that such personal decisions are profoundly political and believe that such an examination might uncover a gap between the political positions and rhetoric of many (although not all) progressive leaders and the school choice practices in which they engage. We wonder why the Left has not more aggressively challenged its own members who send their children to private schools, lobby professional colleagues to win acceptance of their children into elite public schools of choice, and move out of urban centers and into suburbs to fulfill their perceived parental duty of sending their kids to "good" schools?[3]

We know why the Left has not challenged such practices: because progressives generally accept that fulfilling one's parental responsibilities trumps all other ethical and moral obligations and, at times, we feel as if we would not want to begrudge progressive parents this opportunity. When it comes to parenting practices, we allow for a wide range of activities that we might challenge at the policy level, because parents supposedly have the best interests of their children in mind. Yet, who has the best interests of democracy in mind? Who has the best interests of the children from poor families in mind? School choice allows progressive people with means to feel as if and say that they support public schools by sending kids to magnets, charters, or exam schools—mobilizing all forms of their elite capital to gain access for their children to "good" schooling. Residential choice, too, rarely gets criticized by people who support public schools, yet it is perhaps the most insidious way in which the status quo becomes replicated through the system of schooling.

In fact, we believe the dynamic we describe—whereby elite populations publicly oppose choice while simultaneously utilizing choice—is how the status quo gets replicated. It is one key way in which the reproduction of elite forms of capital get passed from one generation to another in class- and race-based populations. We allow middle- and upper-class families to maneuver, use all possible forms of capital, and assuage any guilt they have by defaulting to the "good mother" syndrome, yet, until recently, our nation has not allowed poor people to do the same and to start their own schools.

Imagine if our nation simply reversed current practice and decided to halt all choice options currently utilized by the middle and upper class and only permitted choice options for poor families. Imagine if, all of a sudden, elite families—including presidents, governors, senators and members of Congress, as well as academics—were barred from paying to send their children to private or parochial schools, prevented from making phone calls and marshalling social networks to assure their children's acceptance into specific high-achieving magnet or public exam schools, and were given the choice to move to the suburbs or the "good" urban neighborhoods, but their children were not promised slots in their neighborhood schools. Imagine if the children of those families with the greatest means and the greatest educational capital were the ones we placed in crumbling school buildings with the least-prepared teachers assigned to classrooms with huge teacher-student ratios. On the face of it, this seems like the most equitable way to distribute limited educational resources: shouldn't the children from communities with a long-standing history of dropouts and school failure receive the strongest and best funded schooling?

As the debates about school choice flare, we believe there is a paucity of critical thinking about choice on all sides of the issues. The Right often elides all forms of choice, refuses to look closely at racial and class implications of various choice options, and adopts a simple-minded "It's a free country" attitude toward public education. The Left—driven by the unions—characterizes the few choice options available to poor families as a step backward, as part of a trend toward individualism and privatization and as evidence that the state has opted out of its responsibility to ensure free public education to all. We argue that a truly progressive position on school choice would promote deeper and more critical thinking about all choice options and advocate for significantly expanded options for low-income families.

The History of School Choice and the Left

The Left today generally offers the same arguments against school choice reforms that it did a generation ago. In this, it is important to understand the Left's historical relationship with school choice politics and policies. School choice has always been threatening to a Left that has been defined by a focus on unionization, civil rights, and an unproblematized vision of desegregation as the primary strategy for racial justice. This Left, rather than a progressive Left that provides a systemic critique of public schooling and recognizes the need for fundamentally new institutional forms, dominates the history of school choice policy and politics in the United States.

As noted in Lisa Stulberg's chapter in this collection, the concept of school choice initially connoted rejection of the *Brown v. Board of Education* decision of 1954. Many southern states used language of choice to evade school desegregation (Henig, 1994; Rossell, 1990; Wells, 1993). Richard Kluger (1975), in his classic work on the *Brown* decision, writes that after the Supreme Court put responsibility for school desegregation in the hands of the local district courts, many of the states were able to devise plans that ostensibly met the requirements of *Brown* and *Brown II* but that, in practice, maintained racial segregation. Many southern courts, initially, took their cues from a 1955 South Carolina court's response to the *Brown* mandate. South Carolina district judge John Parker wrote:

> Nothing in the Constitution or in the [*Brown*] decision of the Supreme Court takes away from the people the freedom to choose the schools they attend. The Constitution, in other words, does not require integration. It merely forbids discrimination. It does not forbid such discrimination as occurs as the result of voluntary action. (quoted in Kluger, 1975, p. 752)

Kluger (1975) argues that, using language of choice and preference, Judge Parker "set a standard for evasiveness by school districts throughout the South" (p. 751). Southern states instituted so-called "freedom of choice" plans, which in theory allowed individual White and African American students the option to choose their schools. But, in practice, freedom of choice plans maintained racially separate schools, as few African American students, and virtually no White students, participated in these programs (Kluger, 1975; Wells, 1993).[4] In addition, a form of private school choice came to be associated with southern evasion of school desegregation. A number of southern states financed new private "academies" that were only open to White students. These private options allowed White students, with the support of public money via tax credits and forms of vouchers, to leave the public schools and guaranteed that they could remain in racially segregated educational institutions (Henig, 1994).

Eventually, these choice plans were struck down by federal courts and the Supreme Court, in the 1968 *Green v. County School Board of New Kent County, Virginia* decision (see, for example, Kluger, 1975; Rossell, 1990; Wells, 1993). By the early 1970s, in fact, school choice began to gain a new and positive connection to school desegregation and, therefore, the support of liberals. As Jeffrey R. Henig (1994) writes, "Later, beginning in the 1970s, the practice of educational choice came to be associated with efforts to *integrate* schools" (p. 101). As discussed in Stulberg's chapter, this new association came through magnet schooling and other "voluntary" desegregation plans, particularly in the North. Amy Stuart Wells (1993) points out that while much of the South achieved relatively significant school desegregation after the 1968 *Green* decision, northern school districts made slower progress through the 1970s by relying on "small, voluntary, choice-oriented transfer plans" (p. 72).

Another aspect of the Left's historical relationship with school choice is that it has focused very narrowly on forms of school choice that support or detract from school desegregation, like the freedom of choices plans after the *Brown* decision or the magnet school plans designed to promote voluntary school integration and to keep White families in urban school districts. But, even with this focus, liberals have downplayed the politics and effects of residential choice: a more personally damning endeavor that hits White liberals much closer to home.

Gary Orfield (1996), in a piece on the connection between school segregation and residential segregation, argues that there was a short period when the issue of residential segregation and White flight from cities was taken seriously as a matter for public policy. But, he writes, "In just two years from 1974 through 1976, the facts of white flight changed from an issue the civil rights forces used to try to obtain more far-reaching school desegregation orders to an issue opponents used to defeat desegregation" (p. 314). Since the mid-1970s, he argues, residential segregation has been naturalized, such that it is seen as a form of choice by both Whites and families of color— something "mysterious" that is "an innocent result of private choices"— rather than as a product of past and present housing discrimination policies and practices (1996, pp. 292, 293). This, he argues, has allowed courts to throw up their hands when faced with a school desegregation suit, reasoning that courts can play no role in impacting the individual private residential choices that so effect the demographics of public schools. Orfield writes that continued housing discrimination and legacies of past discrimination frame and constrain individual choices. He also finds, citing 1994 data, that when asked to express these choices, while Whites increasingly support residential integration, "whites still prefer lower levels of integration than blacks" (p. 319).

Recent census data also show that White people typically live in more segregated areas than people of color.[5] White liberals have had little to say about White choice to abandon cities and city public schools. Yet it is this form of school choice that most significantly impacts the demographics of the schools. It is this form of choice that liberals who care about desegregation should pay primary attention to—both in their professional agendas and their personal lives—if they truly want to achieve integrated schooling (Orfield, 1996).[6]

Finally, and relatedly, the traditional Left has historically opposed a form of school choice that ostensibly threatens teacher and administrator union control: community control. As discussed in Stulberg's first chapter in this volume, this form of choice, which gives a local community choice and control over curriculum and programming, personnel, and budget, has been vehemently opposed by teachers' unions since the 1968 confrontation between the New York City United Federation of Teachers and the African American and Latino community in Ocean Hill-Brownsville, Brooklyn.[7] The movement for public school community control in New York City was the catalyst and inspiration for a number of public and private community school movements: initiatives for schools that had significant autonomy from public school governance and that had the freedom to define and meet the needs of a wide range of communities. Those on the traditional Left have generally opposed these initiatives. Liberals, in the name of desegregated schooling, oppose these schools as regressive and balkanizing. Liberals, in the name of unions, opposed these schools as threats to teacher power and professionalism and due process.

One historical example illustrates the way in which those on the Left have ignored residential choice as an issue impacting schooling while opposing community control in urban areas like New York City. The head of the teachers union in New York City, the United Federation of Teachers (UFT) in the 1960s, Albert Shanker was a civil rights supporter and desegregationist.[8] He also was one of the earliest architects of the charter school concept.[9] He led the virulent fight between the teachers union and community control activists in Brooklyn and Harlem, which resulted in a series of citywide teachers' strikes in 1968. During this contentious struggle, community control advocates in the November 1968 issue of the SCOPE Bulletin ran the headline "Shanker's Children Go to School in a Suburban District with Community Control!" detailing the Shanker family's move to Putnam County, New York (Cunningham, 1968). The December issue followed up by detailing a number of ways in which Putnam Valley parents (the Shankers included) had controls over their schools that were routinely denied to New York City parents. This piece highlighted the extent to which Shanker exercised both choice and control over the schooling of his children while opposing these for New York City students. This "Open Letter" to Shanker ended, "Why did you choose a school system with local control for your own family, but deny it to the children of New York City? Could it be because many of us are Black or Puerto Rican or poor?" (Open Letter, 1968, p. 8).

This historical story reveals liberals who envision school choice as a barrier to school desegregation, while, at the same time, they ignore the kind of choice that most significantly impacts the demographics of city schools: residential choice. This history also reveals a labor Left that envisions school choice as a threat to teacher job security and professional control of schools. These are the same arguments against charter schools that resonate with unions and Left academics today. Yet these arguments are outdated and in need of overhaul. They simply do not speak to the social justice concerns that the Left claims guides its scholarship and activism. To do this, we must understand some of the critiques of public schooling that have come from those on the Left who have not been included among the civil rights establishment, the unionists and the desegregationists.

Revisionist Critique of Public Education as Large Bureaucracy

The revisionist critique of public schooling in America looms large in our thinking about charter schools as a useful reform initiative. We were both graduate students at Berkeley exploring charter schools as a new reform initiative in the mid-1990s when we began reading this body of literature. It spoke to us about core questions we had been struggling with as we considered the field of education and the ability of schooling to further the life chances of children from poor and marginalized communities: Why did so many children from poor communities of color find failure in public schools that were supposedly in place to better their life chances? What was it about the nature of schooling—or what we had come to know as the culture of schooling—that presented these children with formidable barriers? How did we explain the test scores, dropout rates, and literacy levels of Black and Latino students?

This literature spoke to us quite powerfully. From the mid-1970s to the mid-1980s, a group of conflict theorists explored schools as fundamental sites of economic and political battles.[10] These scholars asserted that not only did public schools have a limited capacity to serve race and class equality, they actually perpetuated and legitimated existing inequalities. It was, in fact, their primary purpose to do so within

American capitalism. If schools were reproducing social stratification, they were not failing, but rather succeeding in their role.

Neo-Marxist theorists Samuel Bowles and Herbert Gintis argued, in their groundbreaking 1976 work, *Schooling in Capitalist America*, that capitalist class division and stratification drove public schooling, such that the job of American public schools was to reproduce and legitimize an enduring class structure. As "part of the web of capitalist society" (Bowles, 1977, p. 137), Bowles and Gintis (1976) argued, "schools are constrained to justify and reproduce inequality rather than correct it." (p. 102).They asserted a neat fit between schooling and the economy, such that schooling shuttled lower- and working-class students into lower- and working-class jobs and groomed middle- and upper-class students for professions and leadership positions. Despite the "façade of meritocracy" (p. 103) presented by schools and the faith that Americans put in schools for social mobility, there was little chance that schools could or would assuage racial and class inequalities.

Martin Carnoy and Henry M. Levin later nuanced this understanding of the reproductive function of schooling, adding that schools did not only shuttle students into the economic positions of their parents, they also provided opportunity for rupture of existing power relations. Carnoy and Levin (1985) argued that American public schools were actually more egalitarian, both in terms of access and results, than most American institutions. While schools did maintain and reproduce capitalist class relations, to do so was not their only role. Rather, American schools produced both stratified workers within a capitalist system and citizens within a democracy. "The tension between reproducing inequality and producing greater equality," they argued, "is inherent in public schooling." Through these contradictory functions, schooling was the "product of conflict between the dominant and the dominated" (pp. 27, 50). Schools were dynamic institutions that provided a political terrain on which struggles for social change could be fought and won.

The work of historian Michael Katz also had a profound influence on our thinking about charter schools and school choice. His work illustrates how the essential nature of schooling in America has changed little since the 1880s and that the large bureaucracies governing urban schools have themselves been a central mechanism for reproducing the status quo. In *Class, Bureaucracy, and Schools: The Illusion of Educational Change in America* (1971), Katz closes his powerful critique of the social reproductive nature of schooling with four suggestions for reformers that we take seriously in our thinking about reform in contemporary American schools:

(1) "Educational reformers should begin to distinguish between what formal schooling can and cannot do. They must separate the teaching of skills from the teaching of attitudes, and concentrate on the former" (p. 142). Not only is this an attempt to narrow the charge and scope of schooling to objectives that can be more readily fulfilled, but it is an acknowledgement of the powerful ways in which broader regimes of power—for example, advanced capitalism—constrain the possibilities of public schooling as currently constituted. (2) "The reformulation of educational purposes cannot be accomplished within current educational structures. Bureaucracy, as I hope I have made clear, is more than a form of organization; it is the crystallization of particular values. . . . Any radical reformulation of educational objectives . . . requires a radical restructuring of educational forms" (p. 144). (3) Schooling should be voluntary rather than compulsory, and the "abolition of compulsion should be accompanied by radical changes in educational structure," so that youth are able to engage in meaningful activities suited to their goals, interests, and cultural settings (p. 147). Katz suggests here that a shift away from compulsory schooling must be accompanied by the creation of alternatives suited to the opportunity structures and educational needs of poor youth—we must fit schooling into the trajectory of their real lives. These days, these alternatives might include new forms of schools of choice, community-based learning centers, and web-based learning opportunities. (4) "Decentralization should include a shift of power to teachers and students, away from administrators, as well as to local communities. . . . [F]or decentralization to bring about improvements, the teacher as well as the school must be liberated" (p. 146).

Katz (1972) elegantly illustrates that this nation had the potential to organize schooling in various ways outside of the bureaucratization that is often naturalized and defended as "the only way" today. In the early years of the republic, various distinct models vied with one another to become the primary model for public education. Katz highlights "paternalistic voluntarism" (p. 25), "democratic localism" (p. 32), and "corporate voluntarism" (p. 37), historic models that are in fact ways of characterizing different forms of charter schools in the present moment. While these models existed 150 years ago, they lost out to a form of organizing schooling that is heavily bureaucratized and that actually functions to limit alternative models of school governance, philosophy, and pedagogy.

Katz's work lays bear the fact that the organization of schooling in America was driven by a purpose outside of traditional skills development and knowledge acquisition:

Public school systems existed to shape behavior and attitudes, alleviate social and family problems, and reinforce a social structure under stress. The character of pupils was a much greater concern than their minds. . . . In both their strengths and their limits, school systems, with their emphasis on equal access and unequal rewards, their fictive meritocracy, and their bureaucratic organization of experience, became miniature versions of America's social and political order. (1987, p. 21)

Katz's (1987) work also offers key lessons to the charter school movement. First, he argues that the organization of schooling is neither politically neutral nor inconsequential to social reproduction. Instead, he sees "administrative arrangements" as inherently linked—and falling out from—the overall mission of public schooling. This is because school reform emerges from "contradictions between the schools and the social order" (p. 122), an insight which provides a powerful lens from which to consider charter schools. Second, Katz shows how the creation of robust and democratic processes at the local level stand the best chance of improving achievement yet stand the worst chance (historically) of finding a home in public education. He writes, "Despite its limits, reform that begins by empowering parents and teachers to change their own schools and stresses the possibility of effective education for everyone represents a radical break with the past" (p. 129). And third, he grasps some of the critical distinctions between public and private when speaking of education and shows how, historically, "a variety of types of schools existed before the creation of public educational systems." He believes, furthermore, that successful reforms are usually reforms "undertaken at the level of the individual school" rather than throughout an entire system (pp. 132-134).

Katz (1987) writes, "[T]he challenge is to formulate theory that understands schooling as a process shaped by history, great social forces, and particular contexts" (p. 127). We attempt to do precisely that in this volume. We do so because we believe Katz offered a challenge over a dozen years ago when he wrote:

If it can overcome political resistance, avoid the isolation of schooling from its social context, restrain the temptation to blame individuals, and overcome the limits of past research and theory—and these are great though not insurmountable challenges—then a commitment to effective schools represents a creative response to failure, indeed a genuine and welcome initiative within American education. (1987, p. 129)

Additional Critiques of the Current Constitution of Public Schooling

Along with those who assert a strong connection between American public schooling and the needs of American capitalism and the nation-state are those who take public schools to task for maintaining inequalities by producing and reproducing achievement gaps between White students and students of color (see, for example, the collection by Jencks and Phillips, 1998). In addition, there is also another important critique of urban schooling raised particularly by scholars and activists of color. This critique is founded on deep disappointment in and anger about American schooling's past and simultaneous optimism about and vision for what schools can and should become. These academics, educators, and activists argue that public schools undermine the cultural integrity of their communities and cause students of color to either resist (and become a school-failure statistic) or comply (and begin a process of assimilation). In our own work in and with schools, and in building our own vision for how schools of choice can be part of movements for social justice, we draw inspiration from this scholarship as well.

This critique has a history in those who have seen American public schools as literally killing students and communities of color. White urban educator and activist Jonathan Kozol wrote in 1967 that the school that was crumbling around his African American students in Boston—a school in which White teachers ranged from apathetic to abusive—was bringing "death at an early age" to its students. African American community control activists and the community school boards in Harlem and Brooklyn in the late 1960s likened the educational status quo to genocide, and Jewish writer I. F. Stone drew an analogy between the German Holocaust and the New York City school system's treatment of African Americans (see Parent/Community Negotiating Committee of I.S. 201, 1966; quotations by activists included in Perlstein 1994, pp. 314–315; Statement by the Ocean Hill Governing Board, quoted in Ferretti, 1969, p. 304; Stone, 1968). Similarly, the administrator of the community district in Harlem, Charles E. Wilson (1968), asserted that the current schooling system is "so unworkable that it commits unnumbered murders each and every day under the heading of 'public education'" (p. 405). For these activists, then, school change—particularly change in school governance and control—was an urgent matter of survival (see Fantini, 1970; McCoy, 1968; Seabrook, 1967; Van Deburg, 1992; Vann, 1970).

Some current African American scholars and school builders also believe that public schools deplete African American communities. Yet they envision that the institution of the school has been and can be a tool for individual transformation, cultural development and transmission, and community and political power. This focus, particularly by African American independent school theorists and practitioners, calls for an alternative school governance structure that allows African American leaders and communities to control schools through which they have the freedom and power to define and meet their children's and communities' needs. Mwalimu Shujaa (1994), an academic and independent school founder, writes that American public schools are designed to serve and reproduce dominant cultural, economic, and political interests, as is school reform: "Schooling reforms are not intended to produce fundamental changes in the role schooling plays in reproducing both the value system of the politically dominant culture and the social ordering that serves its elites" (p. 22).

Shujaa asserts, instead, that schools by and for African American communities can only teach and support an alternative "cultural and political worldview" when they are built and controlled by African Americans (p. 16, quoting a piece that he coauthored with African American independent school leaders Carol D. Lee and Kofi Lomotey). It is through his distinction between education and schooling that Shujaa can be extremely pessimistic about and critical of public schooling and, at the same time, hand schools an optimistic heavy political and social charge. He writes, "I foresee no change in this situation that does not involve African-Americans taking control of our own education. When education is strategically differentiated from schooling, there is no reason this cannot be done" (p. 32).

Shujaa has been joined by other leaders of African American independent school movements in his anger and frustration with public schools and school reforms and his belief that schools will only truly preserve and strengthen African American communities when they are community controlled. Haki Madhubuti (1994), an African American independent school founder and activist in Chicago, writes in the foreword to Shujaa's 1994 book, "When it comes to the education of African-American children, rats are biting at the doors, floors, desks and gym shoes of the nation's public schools." He continues, "The rat I speak of is white supremacy (racism) manifesting itself freely in the structured and systemic destruction of millions of unsuspecting children and their parents" (pp. 1–2; also see Lomotey, 1992).

Another critique of public schooling by African American scholars is one grounded primarily in heavy skepticism about traditional civil rights reforms, like school desegregation, and their ability to transform schooling. Legal scholar Derrick Bell, for instance, in his first book of parables, *And We Are Not Saved*, wrote that school desegregation plans have benefited public school districts as a whole, White urban communities, and White students. Through one parable, "The Chronicle of the Sacrificed Black Schoolchildren," Bell writes that urban school leaders implement racial desegregation plans that bring political legitimacy, money, and resources to their district, often at the expense of African American teachers and educational leaders, schools, and students, whom he calls the "the casualties of desegregation" (1987, p. 107). While Bell does not believe that change is impossible within the public school system, he writes that only a focus on governance will bring significant change to the schooling experience of African American students. He argues that "giv[ing] blacks meaningful access to decision making" and "desegregating not the students but the money and the control" is "a prerequisite to full equality still unattained in many predominantly black school systems" (1987, pp. 112–113; also see Bell, 1981, 1989). Writing of a 1987 proposal by a group of African American parents and leaders in Milwaukee to carve out a separate district of nine schools that would be independently governed and almost entirely African American, Bell (1989) asserts that this kind of focus on African American control of public schooling and participation in school decision making takes up where *Brown v. Board of Education* and a focus on school desegregation left off: "The Milwaukee manifesto is simply the next logical step in the continuing effort by black people to obtain effective schooling for their children" (p. 139).

Finally, some African American scholars and practitioners offer their critique in the hope that schools can become vibrant places of democratic and community engagement. Through a focus on democratic decision making in schools, they, like Shujaa and Bell, also focus on school control as an important piece of public school reform. One of our teachers and mentors, education activist and professor Pedro A. Noguera, is highly critical of current public schooling and its record of educating low-income students and students of color. But he also believes that it is important not to give up on public schools as educational and community institutions. In a 1994 article entitled "More Democracy Not Less: Confronting the Challenge of Privatization in Public Education," Noguera writes that privatizing public education through voucher plans has the dangerous potential of depleting a public school system that is "one of the few remaining viable social institutions that can be relied upon to address a variety of social issues" and that "continue[s] to offer one of the only sources of mobility to poor and working-class people in a society that remains stratified by race, class, and gender" (pp. 238, 245–246). Citing the 1960s New York City public school community control movement as an example, Noguera urges a focus on democratic decision making: including parents, educators, students, and local communities in the process of building and maintaining their public schools.

African American education activists and scholars add an important critique and an important hopeful vision of public schooling. Within the damning view that public schooling is listless, broken, and dangerous—that it is literally decimating African American communities—is the broad vision of schooling as a potential site of community-building, democratic participation, personal transformation, and political and social activism. Shujaa, Bell, Noguera and others all focus on alternative school governance as a key piece of building school institutions that can be vibrant, healthy, viable centers of democracy, scholarship, and community life.

African American educators are not alone in their critique of or hope for the contemporary organization of public schooling. They are joined by Latino, Asian American and Pacific Islander, and Native American educators and scholars who find similar problems deeply entrenched in American public education (Carger, 1996; Locust, 1988; Pank and Cheng, 1998; Reyhner, 1992; Valdes, 1996; Valencia, 1991). Additionally, feminist and queer studies scholars have raised questions about the effects of the current way of organizing public education on girls and gender-nonconforming children and youth (American Association of University Women, 1992; Harris, 1997; O'Connor, 1995; Rofes, 1995; Sadker and Sadker, 1994; Thorne, 1993).

The answer from the Left, typically, has been that we have to root out racism, sexism, and homophobia in the schools, but that the current way schooling is constituted is basically sound. We believe otherwise. While we certainly support the rooting out of racism, sexism, and homophobia by educators, we believe that because such changes meet formidable challenges, additional solutions must be offered alongside this work. These must include attention to the relationship between schooling and other institutions and the impact on systemic inequalities, and a focus on governance and the building of new school institutions as meaningful forms of empowerment for many communities. Stephen Nathan Haymes has shown how place making and community building are social practices out of which marginalized populations construct and negotiate new identities. Haymes (1995) writes:

I will argue that culture is a constitutive element in urban redevelopment itself. Furthermore, within this context, I will advance the idea that culture
plays an integral role in the production of space, particularly in terms of its
textual and visual representations and how such representations are the
meaningful basis for constructing "homeplace." This means then that it is
in the context of "place making" that blacks form their individual and collective identities as blacks. (p. 72)

One of us recently attended a meeting called by a national gay and lesbian policy center to probe educational policy matters. In the briefing
paper sent in advance of the meeting, the sponsoring organization discussed school choice fully within the framework of the Left that we describe
above. Clearly the group—historically closely tied to unions—maintained
major concerns about breaking with the Left's public position of blanket
opposition to school choice and discussed choice with little nuanced understanding of the diversity of mechanisms that actually occur under this
rubric and little sympathy for families advocating for choice.

At the same time, the opening speaker at the meeting was a man who
successfully sued his rural school district for the abuse he suffered as a boy
because he was perceived to be gay. In a powerful and painfully graphic
speech, this man told his story of being spat upon, stalked, raped, and uri-
nated upon through middle school and high school, with very little response from school authorities. His story also discussed the various ways
he availed himself to limited school choice options as ways of continuing
his education and finding less violent school experiences. His poor farm-
ing family managed to send him to parochial schools for a few years.
He ran away to a city and attended public schools in a new district. His
parents offered to drive him out of the district to yet another school.

When the powerful speech ended, he was asked his view of school
choice, given that it is such a controversial area among progressives. Without hesitation he explained that school choice was a lifesaver for him and
that he was committed to making it available to other suffering youth.

Clearly the theoretical political stand of another progressive organization—this one a gay and lesbian think tank—was in stark contrast to the
needs and perspectives of even their own constituency.

Charters as Response to These Critiques

We understand the charter school initiative in the United States as a direct
response to the progressive critics of public schooling discussed above.
While we do not support all charter policies or admire the philosophies,

cultures, and teaching practices of all charter schools, we do believe that embedded within the charter mechanism is a tool that the Left should be putting to use in the full service of its long-term stated commitment to the education of children from poor families and families of color. The simplistic and bifurcated discourse surrounding charter schools that has evolved over the past decade is useful to no one. We need to rupture the ping-pong back-and-forth debates that characterize all charters and the charter school movement itself in universalizing ways. We need to step beyond the "all charters or no charters" polarization. The very prominence of this discourse demonstrates a kind of laziness on the Left—as if the Left will not distinguish between types of charters, various charter policies, and the diverse constituencies of various charter movements. This laziness serves only to retain the status quo and reify a system of public education that we believe works for many middle- and upper-class families, but that serves simply as a holding pen for the children of the poor. Breaking beyond this status quo thinking seems critically important if we are to ensure educational equity for all.

Once we trouble the discourse and complicate our analyses, we are able to talk about various charter *strategies* and craft a particular charter strategy that meets the values and vision of progressive educators. Charters are not simply a market-driven response; they are a response to huge, bureaucratized systems of public schooling that create homogenized curricula that covertly transform people of diverse cultures into a bland mainstream norm; a system that continues to create five-thousand-student high schools that are incapable of fostering community and promoting authentic and equitable partnerships between young people of various racial and class backgrounds. Charter schools are also a response to the current system of public schooling that continues to reproduce profound inequalities a half-century after *Brown*. Charters might just be the most important mechanism progressives can use to create an alternative vision of schooling that is more student centered, community based, and life affirming.

This collection asks people to consider whether democracy and democratic processes might look different in 2004 than they looked earlier in our nation's history, and even earlier in our lifetimes. How much authentic experience with participatory democracy might parents and students actually feel as they attempt to engage in dialogue with the school boards of large urban districts? How do the bureaucratization of schooling and the entrenchment of rigid unionism, which have failed to tackle the stubborn barriers that keep poor children from school success, raise serious and profound questions about the ability to consider public schools governed through truly democratic processes? Between the massive scale, the historic and rigid rules, and the competing demands of various interest groups that might deprioritize the improved education of poor children in favor of what they see as more compelling interests (such as teacher job security), we believe that few current participants in public education debates and decision making would argue that robust and democratic processes prevail.

The process of proposing, creating, and ensuring the healthy functioning of a charter school, to us, creates greater and more authentic experiences with democracy than participation in large, bureaucratized districts. While we neither diminish nor deny the undemocratic features of some charter policies and some charter schools, we also see in other charters a robust potential for reinvigorating participatory democracy. We see this in the endless meetings attended by participants from diverse communities, perspectives, and locales that are the building blocks of opening many charter schools. We find democracy in the meaningful ways in which faculty, parents, and students form community, struggle to establish ground rules, and forge uneasy compromises on matters of great importance. Charters look to us like real sites in which democracy can be built, created, and contested.

These features of charters are some of the reasons why both of us endorse specific charter policies and charter schools, while we remain firmly opposed to school vouchers.

Our Own Concerns about Charter Schooling

We strongly believe that charter schools can be part of progressive movements for social change, democratic engagement, and community building. We strongly believe that charter schools can be part of strategies to close the race- and class-based achievement gap. We strongly believe that charter schools can be exemplary educational communities, rich with innovation. We both know of schools like this—that we would not hesitate to recommend to children whom we love, that we admire as truly the best examples of public schooling. But we are not uncritical of charter schooling as a "movement," and we, too, have our doubts about the reform as it has been put into practice. Often, supporters of charter schools are unwilling to acknowledge the dangers and drawbacks of the reform. But this unwillingness is not a sign of strength. Rather, we must acknowledge our own doubts and work to meet them. Toward that end, we offer here a few of the concerns that we have about the charter school movement as it currently exists.

First, some charter opponents write that charter schooling is a form of privatization, though perhaps a stealthier one than vouchers. We agree, in part, with this assessment. In general, charter schools do represent, as Robert C. Bulman and David L. Kirp (1999) write, "new public-private hybrid" models that "challenge the public-private paradigm that defines so much of the politics of school choice" (pp. 52, 60). This is particularly true in the arena of funding and sustainability, where charters can bring significant privatization. For-profit companies, like Edison, may have an edge in gaining charter approval in some large cities (See, for example, Hart and Zuckman, 1998. For examples of private industry's inroads into public schooling, see Ascher, Fruchter, & Tserne, 1996). At the same time, in most states, for-profits run a small portion of the existing charter schools (Rhim, 1999). They have a corporate model of education that is a well oiled and well funded (though not yet profitable and as yet unproven in terms of achievement) machine. They can raise capital and exploit political connections in ways that many parent and community groups vying for charter schools cannot. Grassroots groups may turn to them because funding is scarce. This leads to the feeding of public money to private industry. So, too, charter schools provide an opportunity for the state to slough off some of its financial responsibility to public schools onto private donors (UCLA Charter School Study, 1998; Wells, 1999), all while appearing to grant a kind of magnanimous autonomy to individual schools. Current charter school arrangements necessitate private subsidy of public schooling, since most charter schools must supplement their state funds in order to survive. Charter school leaders, too, must be creative about the partnerships they form, as many rely on in-kind donations of food, supplies, labor, and other services to stay afloat (UCLA Charter School Study, 1998; Wells, 2002b). These necessary alternative sources of support for charter schools lighten the load for the states, which, by granting yet underfunding charters, can lessen the public price of educating their children. These issues concern us, and they have policy implications for charter schooling, which we discuss below. But they do not cause us to abandon the promise and possibility of charter schooling.

Nor do these concerns about the ways in which charter schooling represents school privatization draw us into the slippery slope argument that says that supporting charter schools will ultimately and necessarily result in opening the door to vouchers—or lead us to the analytically lazy argument that vouchers and charters are virtually indistinguishable reforms. We understand the progressive equity arguments in support of vouchers.[11] We believe that it is hypocritical for parents who can afford private school choice to deny it to low-income parents. We understand that it is often utter exhaustion and frustration that leads urban parents to throw their hands up at their local public schools and envision that vouchers provide an escape from these failing schools. But we do not support educational vouchers as they currently exist. We do not believe that they—at $2,250 or $5000 or even $10,000 or $12,000 apiece[12]—provide a real choice for parents stuck in failing urban schools and we believe, like Noguera cited above, that there is inherent value to the publicness of schooling. But we do not believe that supporting charters jeopardizes public schooling or necessarily paves the way for a slip toward a large-scale voucher movement. We also believe that, in some critical ways, charter schools provide increasing numbers of people with an authentic experience with public democracy in action (Smith, 2001). One of our reasons for opposing vouchers is that they may provide an individual family with choice but do nothing to expand access to a publicly constituted democracy.

Second, we take seriously the critique that charter schools in some places sustain and perpetuate educational inequalities (Wells, 2002b; Wells, Lopez, Scott, & Holme, 1999). In some cases—not most—charters do "cream" the top of whatever communities they serve. In other cases, they have shown limited commitment to serving the needs of students of with special needs. We also know that charter schools have informal ways of counseling students out, though they are required by law to serve any student that walks in the door. Some charter schools and state laws have received attention for this, particularly as it pertains to special education and students with disabilities (Stoneman, 1998). The ways in which charter schools fail to serve some students, and the extent to which they may draw more involved parents or stronger students, deserve further study. But these questions do not diminish our support for the charter strategy. We know of schools that also attract students who are below district averages on standardized tests, schools that draw parents who are the most dissatisfied with their district schools because these schools are not working for their children. Charter schools thus do provide an option for students who are traditionally the most underserved by district schools. In addition, we believe that any "creaming" or informal counseling out that occurs in charter schools is cause for policy attention, not cause for eliminating the reform. We also know that such practices are linked to all forms of public school choice, not solely charter schools.

Third, we have experienced and are quite skeptical of the strange bedfellows that charter schooling produces. We are uncomfortable being in bed with the Right on charter schools. As discussed in this collection's first chapter, strong charter school supporters include the Walton family, which supports vouchers and which runs the Wal-Mart chain that has been the subject of a number of race and sex discrimination, harassment, and antilabor lawsuits in recent years. Charter supporters also include Clint Bolick's Institute for Justice, which opposes affirmative action and has worked, in the name of school choice, to overturn court-ordered school desegregation (see Stulberg's chapter in this collection; and on Wal-Mart lawsuits see, for example, Abelson, 2001; Egelko, 2001; S. Greenhouse, 2002; Karp, 1996; Tinsley and Harris, 1999). Walton and Bolick, not to mention George W. Bush, John E. Chubb, and Terry M. Moe, and any number of Republicans and conservatives, are not among those with whom we would like to stand in support of charter schools. But their support does not preclude a progressive vision for charter schooling. We have met enough charter school practitioners with progressive politics, committed to social justice and equal schooling, to know that Walton et al. may be wealthy, well-connected, and vocal charter proponents, but they do not speak for the movement as a whole. In fact, we have wondered whether, while the Right may take the lead on advancing charter legislation, the Left provides the bulk of the creative leaders putting in place actual charter schools.

Fourth and finally, we have a significant concern about charter school funding and the role of the state. We believe that the role of the state should be to redistribute capital, such that poorer schools and school districts receive *more* public money than their wealthier counterparts. This is not how school funding has worked historically, as funding tied to local property taxes, even with a statewide funding floor, has resulted in "savage inequalities" between low-income and wealthy districts (Kozol, 1991). Charter schools inherit these inequalities, as charter funding often mirrors district funding. This means, as Wells and her colleagues at UCLA found, that charter schools, particularly in urban areas, are often under-resourced (UCLA Charter School Study, 1998; Wells et al., 1999. For a discussion of charter school funding issues, also see Sugarman, 2002). We believe that the current charter school funding system is not enough. Charter legislation must allow states to give more money to schools that truly need it. Charter school funding must be progressive and be weighted toward low-income communities.[13]

We believe that it is important to acknowledge and act on these concerns. These are the critiques often raised by those who oppose charter schools. These are the critiques that some charter school zealots ignore or dismiss out-of-hand. We voice these concerns as part of our support for the charter school reform. We raise these issues in order to strengthen charter schooling—to make it more viable, more equitable and redistributive, and more worthy of support by political progressives. We call on progressive charter leaders to come together soon and create structures and mechanisms that will troubleshoot these challenges and maximize the opportunities for utilizing chartering for the progressive advancement of public education.

What the Left Has Not Done

In charter school work, the scholarship and politics of the Left have significant shortcomings. If there were a robust and rigorous discussion on the Left about charter schooling, we would be happy to join it. But it does not thus far exist. There are a number of things that the Left has failed to do in the current charter school debate. This Left is now primarily defined by unions, some education activists and scholars who act and write in a civil rights tradition, and some progressive publications, like *Rethinking Schools*. We view ourselves as part of this Left and value the work of our colleagues here, but we seek to create a Left that is alive and open to rethinking key positions, not lost in an earlier era. We hope this book inspires an active debate within the Left on charter schools, school choice, and the most effective ways to promote equality.

What we see as the "Old Guard Left" has excelled at diagnosing the problems of American schooling: continued educational inequality between cities and suburbs, White students and students of color, and wealthy and low-income families and communities; and a willful lack of interest on the part of policymakers, politicians, and many career educators to work toward true, sustained educational equality for all. But the Left has been bankrupt on solutions and resistant to new ideas. The Left's only answer to the problems it poses is to stutter—or to fall back on old remedies. This Left relies primarily and narrowly on integration as a strategy of equal educational opportunity. Yet while it supports racial integration, it rarely focuses on true multiculturalism and multiracial/ethnic coalition building and power sharing.

Wells, for instance, is one of the most nuanced and thoughtful of the liberal charter opponents. But she and other activists and scholars on the education Left remain stuck on school solutions of a generation ago (along with Wells's work cited here, also see Elmore and Fuller, 1996; Frankenberg and Lee, 2003; Fuller, 2000a, 2000b; Orfield, 1998; Wells and Crain, 1997). They remain committed to the idea that school integration, by race

and class, is still the primary answer to educational inequality. As they criticize charter schooling for its "segregative effects" (Wells, 2002b, p. 15),
they still do not take a critical view of school desegregation as a strategy for
equal educational opportunity (see Frankenberg and Lee, 2003). They do
not take seriously the costs of desegregation for some students, families,
and communities of color or for community-based institutions. They do
not fully acknowledge the benefits of alternative school strategies that
focus on self-determination for communities of color, like independent,
community-based, community-controlled schools (see, for example, Siddle
Walker, 1996; Sowell, 1974, 1976). Finally, at the same time that the Left
criticizes charter schooling for its ostensible impact on school segregation,
it has not been critical enough of the major form of school choice: residential segregation. The Left's opposition to school choice seems to come
only when poor communities begin to have choices. Why has the education Left been relatively silent on White flight from urban centers and
middle-class abandonment of city public schools? Why have union leaders and liberal educators and scholars said so little about where they live
and where they send their own children to school?

    This Left also offers no strong focus on true multicultural coalition
building. These kinds of genuine partnerships require hard work, trust,
openness, and the willingness to make mistakes. There has thus far been little patience on the current Left for the work needed to build these coalitions. The Left has not been a voice for authentically multicultural schools,
in which power and decision making are truly shared. At the end of her
most recent collection on charter schools, Wells (2002a) includes a two-
and-a-half page conclusion entitled "Envisioning a More Progressive
Agenda." She rightly writes specifically about funding equality, a policy
focus on poor communities and schools, and the building of integrated
schooling through a "coalition of more progressive, equity-minded reformers" (p. 178). But who on the current Left is effectively doing this work?
What would it look like to take bell hooks's view of the revolutionary and
transformative potential of airing rather than stifling difference, allowing
disagreeing rather than seething silence, and power sharing rather than
tokenism? She writes about feminist and antiracist movements in a way that
we believe we should apply to our thinking about school movements:

> Moving away from the notion that an emphasis on sameness is the key to
> racial harmony, aware feminist activists have insisted that anti-racist struggle
> is best advanced by theory that speaks about the importance of acknowledg-
> ing the way positive recognition and acceptance of difference is a necessary
> starting point as we work to eradicate white supremacy. (1992, p. 13)

And:

> It is a utopian dream to imagine that white women will divest of white su-
> premacist thinking in isolation without critical engagement and dialectical
> exchange with non-white peers. It is concrete interaction between groups
> that is the proving ground, where our commitments to anti-racist behavior
> are tested and realized. (1995, pp. 104–105)

These are challenges that the Left should take seriously.

School choice plans have always been threatening to liberalism. The
Left now sees school choice as a challenge to the liberal agenda of civil
rights, desegregation, and unionism. But this Left confuses these liberal
strategies with strategies for radical social change. In contrast to these
voices, we, as progressive scholars and activists, look rather to options that
will radically transform American education and will work to decimate
long-standing social inequalities. We believe that it is more radical to ask
the tough questions, be honest about our doubts about school choice, and
engage in difficult work—sometimes finding ourselves in this work with
those with whom we have very little in common politically.

Most of all, though, we believe that it is more radical to remain hopeful about the potential of public education than it is to be chronically discouraged and passively nihilistic. We believe that this is the role that the
Left can and should play. We have many role models here. Bill Ayers (actually a charter school skeptic), offers damning critiques of the indifference
and stagnation of many public schools (see, for example, Ayers, 2001). But
he also remains infectiously hopeful about the possibility of schooling. He
writes, in *To Teach*, that teaching requires engagement with the world,
hope, love, and faith: "[P]eople teach as an act of construction and reconstruction, and as a gift of oneself to others. I teach in the hope of making
the world a better place" (2001, p. 8). Paulo Freire (1970), too, in *Pedagogy
of the Oppressed*, amidst his analysis of schooling as a tool of oppression,
as "the exercise of domination" (p. 59), offers an alternative vision of liberatory and transformative "problem-posing" schooling. "Problem-posing
education," he writes, "is revolutionary futurity" (p. 65).

What the Left Should Do to Build a Progressive Politics
of School Choice

Guided by the hope of education scholars and activists like Ayers and Freire,
we offer here our vision of what progressives can and should do to begin to

build a politics of school choice that includes support for charter schools and some other forms of public school choice. This list is not exhaustive. But it is a start.

First, progressives should reject either/or, choice/no choice, integration/separatism, public/private dichotomies. This dichotomizing impulse is not politically helpful and does not make for rigorous and nuanced scholarship. It makes more sense to speak of charter *strategies*, of public and privatizing mechanisms and the relationship between them, of the interaction between integrationist and separatist tactics, and of the nuances and variation in school choice plans. It will take letting go of this dichotomizing for the Left to build responsible, rich, and useful school choice analyses and policy plans.

Second, as noted above and in Stulberg's first chapter, the Left must move beyond a desegregation framework to a more complicated race and class analysis of school choice. This requires a more complex understanding of race and class. In particular, it requires a shift in the way in which most liberal school choice scholars think and write about the construction of race. For this, scholars should look to the richest pieces of the literature to understand the ways in which race is lived and negotiated. There is a discourse on race, developed since the civil rights movement, that moves beyond an understanding of race as a social category that is fixed, static, and determined by institutional, social, and legal relationships. This scholarship sees race as an active set of strategies constantly being made and remade, negotiated, and redefined. In this scholarship, race is lived through an interaction of social structures and meanings, interpreted by individuals and communities, and mobilized strategically in various ways in different historical and social moments. Useful here, for the Left, is Michael Omi and Howard Winant's (1994) notion of *racial formation*. They argue for a dynamic understanding of race as an active and ever-changing intersection of structure and meaning:

> The effort must be made to understand race as an unstable and "decentered" complex of social meanings constantly being transformed by political struggle. With this in mind, let us propose a definition: *race is a concept which signifies and symbolizes social conflicts and interests by referring to different types of human bodies.* Although the concept of race invokes biologically based human characteristics (so-called "phenotypes"), selection of these particular human features for purposes of racial signification is always and necessarily a social and historical process. (p. 55, emphasis in original)

Their term *racial formation* captures the extent to which race is an active process: "We define *racial formation* as the sociohistorical process by which racial categories are created, inhabited, transformed, and destroyed" (p. 55). They write:

> From a racial formation perspective, race is a matter of both social structure and cultural representation.
>   [. . . .]
>   Racial projects connect what race *means* in a particular discursive practice and the ways in which both social structures and everyday experiences are racially *organized*, based upon that meaning. (p. 56, emphasis in original)

This understanding of race troubles the school choice debate, because it requires that scholars look not just to racial demographics and state policies that impact school segregation, but to the negotiations around school policy and structure, the racial meanings with which educators, parents, and students imbue the schools they build, and the historical specificity of particular strategies for racial justice in schooling in particular historical moments. These complexities of race, racial politics, and racial strategies usefully and importantly complicate and enrich the school choice debate, yet they are not even allowed into the existing discussion.

Third, progressives must also create a voice of the Left independent from and willing to be critical of unions.[14] The example of the West Oakland Community School, a charter middle school in Oakland, California, is instructive here. Marjorie Wilkes began her career at the New York City teachers' union, the United Federation of Teachers (UFT). She moved to Oakland to do school reform work and in 1996 she convened a group of friends and colleagues to begin plans to open a charter school. The group had a particular concern for low-income African American students in West Oakland, and it developed a charter school plan to serve these students in the West Oakland community. In the course of the charter application process, Wilkes, her co-founder and co-director Akiyu Hatano, and the WOCS founding group were called on a number of times to defend their school against the Oakland teachers' union's opposition to charter schools. Wilkes and others often expressed support and sympathy for labor organizing and the importance of teachers' unions, but they also refused to support the union when they believed it stood in the way of the education of low-income students and students of color in the district. Wilkes, Hatano, and others were able to create a vibrant and successful school for African American students in part because of their willingness to voice a critique of and vision for public schooling, in the name of equal educational opportunity, that was distinct and at odds with the local union (see Stulberg, 2001, chapter 4).

Finally, the Left must emphatically adopt strategies, including choice strategies, that further quality education and social justice and equality. This requires two things. First, progressives must keep the Left's social justice *vision* intact from forty years ago, but it must not be so rigid about *tactics*. In this new millennium, we cannot get stuck in 1960s tactics like school busing and a heavy reliance on the courts to open the way to progressive social change, even as we consider such court cases critical to this work. Even ardent integrationist and sociologist Orlando Patterson (1997) writes that the tactics for achieving school integration must be different now than they were forty, or even thirty years ago:

> Busing was an essential tool during the fifties, sixties, and seventies, when outright racism and unequal expenditures on schools were the central issues, and there are many areas of the country where this strategy is still essential. Today, however, it makes more sense in many cases to concentrate on those measures that will first integrate neighborhoods and occupations and let the integration of schools follow from them. (p. 190)

Residential integration, and resulting school integration, is just one tactic the Left might adopt. Others may not focus on integrating schools, but on building and supporting schools that allow communities of all kinds to define, meet, and institutionalize their needs through their schools.

To adopt strategies for successful and equal schooling, the Left also must move beyond obsessive critique. Bowles and Gintis provide a good model here. In 1976, in *Schooling in Capitalist America*, they offered one of the most expansive and enduring critiques of the role of public schooling in reproducing inequalities under American capitalism. They confirmed their analysis in a 2002 article entitled "*Schooling in Capitalist America* Revisited." Yet they articulated a hope for public schooling that many critics on the Left do not share. They wrote in 2002:

> We were then, and remain, hopeful that education can contribute to a more productive economy and a more equitable sharing of its benefits and burdens, as well as a society in which all are maximally free to pursue their own ends unimpeded by prejudice, the lack of opportunity for learning, or material want. (p. 1)

They also acknowledged that with their 1976 critique they had not offered sufficiently concrete suggestions for school change: "The more important shortcoming, we think, is programmatic. We avoided, for the most part, the question of what schools *should* be, focusing instead on what schools actually are and do." They continued:

> Although the book endorses the idea that radicals—even revolutionaries—must also be reformers, we provided little guidance to policy makers, teachers, or students who are seeking practical positive steps to bring about long-term improvements in educational structure and practice. (2002, p. 15)

They have now grappled with and turned to school choice reform as a concrete, viable, hopeful, and creative response to school inequities (see Bowles and Gintis, 1996; Gintis, 1995; and "Herbert Gintis on School Choice," 1998; also see Stacy Smith's chapter in this collection). They focus on capitalist entrenchment and the ways in which schools reproduce social inequalities, but they do not opt out of the discussion of the specific ways in which schools can mitigate these inequalities. Too many choice opponents on the Left do.

Conclusion

Our own vision for the future of school choice takes Bowles and Gintis as a given. As long as schools are embedded within capitalism, there are real limits to what schools can do to mitigate social inequality. But given capitalism, we cannot give up on schooling as a positive force for social change. Charter schools are not a replacement for structural school reform (see, for example, Fuller, 2000a, p. 24). But charter schooling and other forms of public school choice have an important role to play in making schools responsive, democratic institutions that can address and redress social inequalities. Charter schooling as a strategy allows us not to have to go to the "mushy middle"—a middle ground of inertia, tepid action, and tangled compromises. There is something to be said for creating autonomous schools based on one's vision and values by any means necessary.

Charter schooling is one of a number of public school choice strategies that may provide important school reform options. First, larger-scaled controlled choice plans, in which every family in a district chooses its schools but the market does not drive this choice, is one such option (for discussions of controlled choice plans, see, Carnegie, 1992; Wells, 1993; Wells and Crain, 1997; Willie, 1991). Controlled choice is not perfect. It does not eliminate the inequities among schools, it does not address funding issues, and it sometimes assumes equal knowledge and social and cultural capital among parents. But it allows for curricular diversity and a degree of racial and economic integration not found in traditional district schooling. Second, and often related to choice, teacher and parent empowerment is another strategy that can allow schools to be more responsive to community needs and interests and that creates schools that serve as vibrant community institutions.

As for charter schooling, we take up the challenge of Milwaukee voucher activist Mikel Holt (2000), who writes of school critics on the Left:

> While condemning parental school choice, often calling it part of a vast right-wing conspiracy, the Left offers no solutions for the abysmal failure of the public school system and the harm it has reaped [sic] on literally millions of minority and poor children. (p. 183)

We also take up the challenge of education writer Jonathan Schorr (2000), who argued in the *Nation* that progressives needed to end their disdain for charter schooling and join a movement that has social justice promise and could restore them to "the educational cutting edge":

> We have reached a curious pass when inner city parents look to right-wing billionaires and well-heeled corporations for help while Democrats and progressives get tagged as hypocrites and sticks-in-the-mud. But liberals need not abdicate their place on the educational cutting edge, and ought not be seen as defenders of bureaucracy and failure. Charter schools present an opportunity to do the right thing, politically and morally. There is a need here, as evidenced by the struggles of inner-city communities to start their own schools, and progressives ought to answer the call, giving their own flavor to the charter movement. People—and particularly educators—of conscience can lead by example, aiding in the creation of excellent, model schools. (np)

Schorr concludes his article with this call:

> A generation ago, progressives were the guardians of innovative education for children who needed education the most. Through helping to create superb independent public schools, they can return to their place in the vanguard. It's not just a politically savvy way to fight the enemies of public education. It's the right thing to do for children. (np)

Toward this end, we offer here some considerations that we believe the Left should take up in building truly progressive forms of school choice.

First, as we settle into the second decade of charter schooling, we believe that school choice mechanisms should be in the service of those whom the current system is not supporting. Charter legislation and policy making should prioritize low-income communities and schools, and funding should be delivered directly to those communities. This means, in part, that the Left needs to demand progressive, equitable funding for charter schools, such that charter schools in low-income communities receive more funding that their wealthier counterparts (see, for example, Wells, 2002a; 2002b). This also means that we need a concentration of urban strategies for schooling. Charter schools can be part of urban school reform, but not the entire vision.

Second, and relatedly, we need to not pit charter schools against other public schools. District and charter schools have many if not all of the same interests, and progressives who support charter schools should be part of a movement to make sure that charter school support serves the broader interest of public schooling. Funding is one piece of this. Since charter school funding is so closely tied to district funding, raising public funding in urban and other low-income districts will help all public schools. We should not see charters as having a separate constituency from district schools, nor should we use our support of charter schooling as a stand-in for a broader commitment to public school change. In fact, we would be surprised if those who have argued against additional financing of public schools and then founded charters have not had their minds changed about the profound ways in which education is shortchanged in our national and state budgets.

Third, while we strongly support many schools that focus on a particular racial/ethnic group of color, as part of an educational and political strategy, the Left could also push for true multiracial, mixed-income schools through policy. It could push for states to support charter schools that actively grapple with self-conscious multiraciality. This is something that Wells (2002a) advocates in her most recent collection: that states provide additional incentives for integrated schooling. Through this, the state can and should have a role in actively encouraging truly integrated schooling, while, at the same time, it can and should support schools for students of color that are effectively serving more racially/ethnically homogenous student bodies. But the state needs to ensure that multiracial schools are not simply schools that are still based primarily in White cultural constructs and values and that students of color attending these schools are not forced into painful choices about their identities and home values.

Fourth, we need to move to a value-added approach to school accountability that looks broadly to the difference that schools make in students' lives. This can give us a better idea of which schools are skilled at working with low-income students, which schools add value to students' lives and achievements, rather than simply holding up middle-class charter schools or middle-class district schools as the success stories.

Ultimately, the Left can throw itself into the new tools of school reform and harness those tools to social justice aims. Progressives can affect a radical break in the current discourse and politics of schooling. Instead, now, the Left has become—shamefully—the party of the status quo. Rather than throwing up our hands at the intractability of public school failures, and rather than contributing solely through critique, we can enter and guide the school choice debate so that charter schooling truly can become part of a new generation of more effective efforts to promote equality and justice for children from poor families and families of color and to open up American schooling to its full democratic potential.

Notes

1. For business, see Kearns and Doyle (1988); for political science, see Chubb and Moe (1990), as well as Peterson and Campbell (2001); for law, see Coons and Sugarman (1978); for economics, see Merrifield (2002) and Vedder (2000); for education, see Ravitch and Finn (1987), Finn (1993), and Viteritti (2001).

2. E.g., Brantlinger (2003). Also, a concise history of school choice can be found in Fusarelli, 2003, pp. 6–9.

3. A terrific new book by Adam Swift (2003) captures these dynamics and provides a helpful alternative. And see Fran Schumer's *New York Times* article entitled "School Choice: Where They Send Their Own," which reveals where President Bush, urban public school leaders Joel I. Klein and Paul Vallas, and education researchers and academics Diane Ravitch, Howard Gardner, and E. D. Hirsch, Jr. choose to send their own children to school.

4. Wells (1993) writes, "As a result of harassment by local whites and the tactics employed by state pupil-placement boards, by 1965 almost 94 percent of southern black students remained in all-black schools, and in several states only the slightest change had been made in the system of separate and unequal schools" (p. 66).

5. See, for example, Schmitt, 2001. Reporting on a study of 2000 census data done by SUNY Albany researches, Schmitt writes, "An average white person living in a metropolitan area, which includes city dwellers and suburbanites, lives in a neighborhood that is about 80 percent white and 7 percent black. . . . In

contrast, a typical black person lives in a neighborhood that is 33 percent white and 51 percent black" (p. A15). Also, on residential segregation, see Massey and Denton, 1993.

6. Orfield (1996) writes, "Lasting school desegregation requires either stable integrated housing or a plan that copes effectively with the patterns of spreading housing segregation" (p. 292).

7. See Stulberg's chapter in this volume, note 16, for citations on Ocean Hill-Brownsville and the community control movement.

8. Shanker had been a member of the Congress of Racial Equality (CORE), marched in Selma with Rev. Martin Luther King, and worked for integration in New York City schools (Mayer, 1969; Jacoby, 1998).

9. See Alex Medler's chapter in this collection.

10. See Karabel and Halsey (1977) for a discussion of the role of conflict theory in education research of the past fifty years (pp. 33–44).

11. See, for example, Flake, 1998; "We Cannot Afford to Wait . . . ," 1998; "Herbert Gintis on School Choice," 1998; Miller, 1999; Reich, 2000; Rauch, 2002. Miller (1999) calls for a voice of the "voucher left," as we call for progressives to support and lead the charter debates and movements: "Missing entirely from the debate is the progressive pro-voucher perspective. . . . [I]f urban children are to have any hope, the voucher left's best days must lie ahead."

12. See L. Greenhouse (2002), and its accompanying graphic (p. A17), for current spending in Milwaukee and Cleveland's voucher programs and Reich (2000) for his proposed voucher value.

13. This focus on funding equality is something that Wells (2002a), in her most recent work on charter schools, also supports (pp. 178–179). Also see Wells, 2002b.

14. The National Coalition of Education Activists (NCEA) is a new, hopeful organization here. It is not clear yet how closely it adheres to union stances.

References

Abelson, R. (2001, June 20). 6 women sue Wal-Mart, charging job and promotion bias. *New York Times*, C1.

American Association of University Women. (1992). *The AAUW report: How schools shortchange girls.* Washington, DC: American Association of University Women Educational Foundation.

Ascher, C., Fruchter, N., & Berne, R. (1996). *Hard lessons: Public schools and privatization.* New York: Twentieth Century Fund Press.

Ayers, W. (2001). *To teach: The journey of a teacher* (2nd ed.). New York: Teachers College Press.

Bell, D. (1981). Civil rights commitment and the challenge of changing conditions in urban school cases. In A. Yarmolinsky, L. Liebman, & C. S. Schelling

(Eds.), *Race and schooling in the city* (pp. 194–203). Cambridge: Harvard University Press.

Bell, D. (1987). *And we are not saved: The elusive quest for racial justice.* New York: Basic Books.

Bell, D. (1989). The case for a separate Black school system. In W. D. Smith & E. W. Chunn (Eds.), *Black education: A quest for equity and excellence* (pp. 136–145). New Brunswick, NJ: Transaction Publishers.

Berliner, D., & Biddle, B. (1996). *The manufactured crisis: Myths, fraud, and the attacks on American public schools.* New York: Perseus Publishing.

Bowles, S. (1977). Unequal education and the reproduction of the social division of labor. In J. Karabel & A. H. Halsey (Eds.), *Power and ideology in education* (pp. 137–153). New York: Oxford University Press.

Bowles, S., & Gintis, H. (1976). *Schooling in capitalist America: Educational reform and the contradictions of economic life.* New York: Basic Books.

Bowles, S., & Gintis, H. (1996, December). Efficient redistribution: New rules for markets, states, and communities. *Politics & Society, 24*(4), 307–342.

Bowles, S., & Gintis, H. (2002, January). Schooling in capitalist America revisited. *Sociology of Education, 75*(1), 1–18.

Brantlinger, E. (2003). *Dividing classes: How the middle class negotiates and rationalizes school advantage.* New York: Routledge/Falmer.

Bulman, R. C., & Kirp, D. L. (1999). The shifting politics of school choice. In S. D. Sugarman & F. R. Kemerer (Eds.), *School choice and social controversy: Politics, policy, and law* (pp. 36–67). Washington, DC: Brookings Institution Press.

Carger, C.L. (1996). *Of borders and dreams: A Mexican-American experience of urban education.* New York: Teachers College Press.

Carnegie Foundation for the Advancement of Teaching. (1992). *School choice.* Princeton, NJ: Author.

Carnoy, M., & Levin H. M. (1985). *Schooling and work in the democratic state.* Stanford, CA: Stanford University Press.

Chubb, J. E., & Moe, T. M. (1990). *Politics, markets and America's schools.* Washington, DC: Brookings Institution.

Coons, J. E., & Sugarman, S. D. (1978). *Education by choice: The case for family control.* Berkeley: University of California Press.

Cunningham, B. (1968, November). The Shankers in suburbia. *SCOPE Bulletin,* 3–4.

Egelko, B. (2001, June 20). Largest sex-bias suit filed; Damages sought from Wal-Mart. *San Francisco Chronicle,* C1.

Elmore, R. F., & Fuller, B. (1996). Empirical research on educational choice: What are the implications for policy-makers? In B. Fuller & and R. F. Elmore with G. Orfield (Eds.), *Who chooses? Who loses?: Culture, institutions, and the unequal effects of school choice* (pp. 187–201). New York: Teachers College Press.

Fantini, M. D. (1970). Community control and quality education in urban school system. In H. M. Levin (Ed.), *Community control of schools* (pp. 40–75). Washington, DC: Brookings Institution.

Ferretti, F. (1969). Who's to blame in the school strike. In M. R. Berube & M. Gittell (Eds.), *Confrontation at Ocean Hill-Brownsville: The New York school strikes of 1968* (pp. 283–313). New York: Frederick A. Praeger.

Finn, C. E., Jr. (1993). *We must take charge: Our schools and our future.* New York: Free Press.

Flake, F. (1998, Fall). More on school choice by the Rev. Floyd Flake. *School Voices,* 6(1), 20.

Frankenberg, E., & Lee, C. (2003, June). *Charter schools and race: A lost opportunity for integrated education.* Cambridge: Harvard University, Civil Rights Project.

Freire, P. (1970). *Pedagogy of the oppressed* (M. B. Ramos, Trans.). New York: Continuum.

Fuller, B. (2000a). Growing charter schools, decentering the state. Introduction to B. Fuller (Ed.), *Inside charter schools: The paradox of radical decentralization* (pp. 1–11). Cambridge: Harvard University Press.

Fuller, B. (2000b). The public square, big or small? Charter schools in political context. In B. Fuller (Ed.), *Inside charter schools: The paradox of radical decentralization* (pp. 12–65). Cambridge: Harvard University Press.

Fusarelli, L. D. (2003). *The political dynamics of school choice.* New York: Palgrave Macmillan.

Gintis, H. (1995, Spring). The political economy of school choice. *Teachers College Record,* 96(3), 492–511.

Greenhouse, L. (2002, June 28). Supreme Court, 5–4, upholds voucher system that pays religious schools' tuition: Ruling in Ohio case. *New York Times,* A1+.

Greenhouse, S. (2002, June 25). Suits say Wal-Mart forces workers to toil off the clock. *New York Times,* A1+.

Harris, M. (Ed.). (1997). School experiences of gay and lesbian youth: The invisible minority. Special Issue, *Journal of Gay and Lesbian Social Services,* 7(4). Binghamton, NY: Haworth Press.

Hart, J., & Zuckman, J. (1998, February 26). For-profit firms get 4 of 8 charters for schools. *Boston Globe,* B1.

Haymes, S. N. (1995). *Race, culture, and the city: A pedagogy for Black urban struggle.* Albany, NY: State University of New York Press.

Henig, J. R. (1994). *Rethinking school choice: Limits of the market metaphor.* Princeton, NJ: Princeton University Press.

Herbert Gintis on school choice. (1998, Fall). *School Voices,* 6(1), 12–13+.

Holt, M. (2000). *Not yet "free at last." The unfinished business of the civil rights movement: Our battle for school choice.* Oakland, CA: ICS Press.

hooks, b. (1992). *Black looks: Race and representation.* London: Turnaround.

hooks, b. (1995). *Killing rage ending racism*. New York: Henry Holt.

Jacoby, T. (1998). *Someone else's house: America's unfinished struggle for integration*. New York: Free Press.

Jencks, C., & Phillips, M. (Eds.) (1998). *The Black-White test score gap*. Washington, DC: Brookings Institution.

Karabel, J., & Halsey, A. H. (1977). Educational research: A review and an interpretation. In J. Karabel & A. H. Halsey (Eds.), *Power and ideology in education* (pp. 1–85). New York: Oxford University Press.

Karp, D. (1996, September 22). Wal-Mart loses suit over sexual harassment. *St. Petersburg Times*, 10B.

Katz, M. (1971). *Class, bureaucracy & schools: The illusion of educational change in America*. New York: Praeger.

Katz, M.(1987). *Reconstructing American education*. Cambridge: Harvard University Press.

Kearns, D., & Doyle, D. P. (1988). *Winning the brain race: A bold plan to make our schools competitive*. San Francisco: Institute for Contemporary Studies Press.

Kluger, R. (1975). *Simple justice: The history of Brown v. Board of Education and Black America's struggle for equality*. New York: Vintage Books.

Kozol, J. (1985). *Death at an early age: The destruction of the hearts and minds of Negro children in the Boston public schools*. New York: Plume Books.

Kozol, J. (1991). *Savage inequalities: Children in America's schools*. New York: Harper-Perennial.

Locust, C. (1988, August). Wounding the spirit: Discrimination and traditional American Indian belief systems. *Harvard Educational Review, 58*(3), 315–330.

Lomotey, K. (1992, Fall). Independent Black Institutions: African-centered education models. *Journal of Negro Education, 61*, 455–462.

Madhubuti, H. R. (1994). Cultural work: Planting new trees with new seeds. In M. J. Shujaa (Ed.), *Too much schooling, too little education: A paradox of Black life in White societies* (pp. 1–6). Trenton, NJ: Africa World Press.

Massey, D. S., & Denton, N. A. (1993). *American apartheid: Segregation and the making of the underclass*. Cambridge: Harvard University Press.

Mayer, M. (1969, February 2). The full and sometimes very surprising story of Ocean Hill, the teachers' union and the teachers strikes of 1968. *New York Times Magazine*, 18–23+.

McCoy, R. A. (1968, April). A Black educator assails the "White" system. *Phi Delta Kappan*, 448–449.

Merrifield, J. (2002). *School choices: True and false*. Oakland, CA: Independent Institute.

Miller, M. (1999, July). A bold experiment to fix city schools. *Atlantic Monthly, 284*(1), 15–18+.

Noguera, P. A. (1994). More democracy not less: Confronting the challenge of privatization in public education. *Journal of Negro Education, 63*, 237–250.

O'Connor, A. (1995). Who gets called queer in schools. In G. Unks (Ed.), *The gay teen* (pp. 95–104). New York: Routledge.

Omi, M., & Winant, H. (1994). *Racial formation in the United States: From the 1960s to the 1990s* (2nd ed.). New York: Routledge.

Open letter to Albert Shanker from very angry parents and children in New York City. (1968, Christmas). *SCOPE Bulletin*, 8.

Orfield, G. (1996). Segregated housing and school resegregation. In G. Orfield, S. E. Eaton, & the Harvard Project on School Desegregation. *Dismantling desegregation: The quiet reversal of* Brown v. Board of Education (pp. 291–330). New York: New Press.

Orfield, G. (1998, January 2). Charter schools won't save education. *New York Times*, A15.

Pank, V. O., & Cheng, L.L. (1998). *Struggling to be heard: The unmet needs of Asian Pacific American children*. Albany: State University of New York Press.

Parent/Community Negotiating Committee of Intermediate School 201. (1966, October 21). *Response to board of education "Proposals for improving education in schools in disadvantaged areas."* Mayors Advisory Panel Collection, box 14566, "I.S. 201" folder, Ford Foundation Archives.

Patterson, O. (1997). *The ordeal of integration: Progress and resentment in America's "racial" crisis*. Washington, DC: Civitas/Counterpoint.

Perlstein, D. (1994). *The 1968 New York City school crisis: Teacher politics, racial politics and the decline of liberalism*. Ph.D. dissertation, Stanford University.

Peterson, P. E., & Campbell, D. E. (Eds). (2001). *Charters, vouchers, and public education*. Washington, DC: Brookings Institution.

Potter, R. (1967). *The stream of American education*. New York: American Book.

Rauch, Jonathan. (2002, October). Reversing White flight. *Atlantic Monthly*. Retrieved October 24, 2002 from http://www.theatlantic.com/issues/2002/10/rauch.htm

Ravitch, D., & Finn, C. (1987). *What do our 17-year-olds know?* New York: Harper & Row.

Reich, R. B. (2000, November 6). The liverwurst solution. *American Prospect*, 11(23). Retrieved July 11, 2002 from http://www.prospect.org/print-friendly/print/V11/23/reich-r.html

Reyhner, J. (1992, October). American Indian cultures and school success. *Journal of American Indian Education*, 32(1), 30–39.

Rhim, L. (1999, April 22). Franchising public education: An analysis of the linkage of charter schools and private educational management companies. 1999 Annual Meeting of the American Educational Research Association

Rofes, E. (1995). Making our schools safe for sissies. In G. Unks (Ed.), *The gay teen* (pp. 79–84). New York: Routledge.

Rossell, C. H. (1990). *The carrot or the stick for school desegregation policy: Magnet schools or forced busing*. Philadelphia: Temple University Press.

Rothstein, R. (1998). *The way we were? The myths and realities of America's student achievement.* Washington, DC: Brookings Institution.

Sadker, M., & Sadker, D. (1994). *Failing at fairness: How our schools cheat girls.* New York: Touchstone/Simon & Schuster.

Schmitt, E. (2001, April 4). Analysis of census finds segregation along with diversity. *New York Times,* A15.

Schorr, J. (2000, June 5). Giving charter schools a chance. *Nation.* Retrieved April 6, 2002 from http://past.thenation.com/issue/000605/0605schorr.shtml

Schumer, F. (2003, August 3). School choice: Where they send their own. *New York Times,* section 4A, page 7.

Seabrook, L. W. (1967, October). School strike: Black teachers' group opposes union. *Harlem News,* 1(2), 1–2.

Shujaa, M. J. (1994). Education and schooling: You can have one without the other. In M. J. Shujaa (Ed.), *Too much schooling, too little education: A paradox of Black life in White societies* (pp. 13–36). Trenton, NJ: Africa World Press.

Siddle Walker, V. (1996). *Their highest potential: An African American school community in the segregated South.* Chapel Hill: University of North Carolina Press.

Smith, S. (2001). *The democratic potential of charter schools.* New York: Peter Lang.

Sowell, T. (1974, Spring). Black excellence—The case of Dunbar High School. *Public Interest, 35,* 3–21.

Sowell, T. (1976, Spring). Patterns of Black excellence. *Public Interest, 43,* 26–58.

Spring, J. (1972). *Education and the rise of the corporate state.* Boston: Beacon Press.

Spring, J. (1975). *The sorting machine: National educational policy since 1945.* New York: Longman.

Stone, I. F. (1968, Christmas). I. F. Stone (I. F. Stone's Weekly, Nov. 4). *SCOPE Bulletin,* 5.

Stoneman, C. (1998, Fall). New battlegrounds. *Rethinking Schools, 13*(1), 3.

Stulberg, L. M. (2001). *Teach a new day: African American alternative institution-building and the politics of race and schooling since* Brown. Ph.D. dissertation, University of California at Berkeley.

Sugarman, S. D. (2002, August 9). Charter school funding issues. *Education Policy Analysis Archives, 10*(34). Retrieved September 6, 2002 from http://epaa.asu.edu/epaa/v10n34.html

Swift, A. (2003). *How not to be a hypocrite: School choice for the morally perplexed parent.* London: Routledge.

Thorne, B. (1993). *Gender play: Girls and boys in school.* New Brunswick, NJ: Rutgers University Press.

Tinsley, J., & Harris, C. (1999, June 30). NAACP to talk with Wal-Mart execs; Wal-Mart says search of workers not racial. *Plain Dealer,* 1B.

UCLA Charter School Study. (1998). *Beyond the rhetoric of charter school reform: A study of ten California school districts.* Los Angeles: Author.

Valdes, G. (1996). Con respeto: Bridging the distances between culturally diverse families and schools. New York: Teachers College Press.

Valencia, R. R. (Ed.). (1991). Chicano school failure and success. New York: Falmer.

Van Deburg, W. L. (1992). New day in Babylon: The Black Power movement and American culture, 1965–1975. Chicago: University of Chicago Press.

Vann, A. (1970). "Community involvement" in schools. In N. Wright, Jr. (Ed.), What Black educators are saying (pp. 231–233). New York: Hawthorn Books.

Vedder, R. K. (2000). Can teachers own their own schools? New strategies for educational excellence. Oakland, CA: Independent Institute.

Viteritti, J. (2001). Choosing equality: School choice, the constitution, and civil society. Washington, DC: Brookings Institution.

We cannot afford to wait any longer: An interview with the Rev. Floyd H. Flake. (1998, Fall). School Voices, 6(1), 18–20.

Wells, A. S. (1993). Time to choose: America at the crossroads of school choice policy. New York: Hill and Wang.

Wells, A. S. (1999, August). Charter schools and the myth of the common school. 1999 Annual Meeting of the American Sociological Association.

Wells, A. S. (2002a). Conclusion: Envisioning a more progressive agenda. In A. S. Wells (Ed.), Where charter school policy fails: The problems of accountability and equity (pp. 178–180). New York: Teachers College Press.

Wells, A. S. (2002b). Why public policy fails to live up to the potential of charter school reform: An introduction. In A. S. Wells (Ed.), Where charter school policy fails: The problems of accountability and equity (pp. 1–28). New York: Teachers College Press.

Wells, A. S., & Crain, R. L. (1997). Stepping over the color line: African-American students in White suburban schools. New Haven: Yale University Press.

Wells, A. S., Lopez, A., Scott, J., & Holme, J. J. (1999, Summer). Charter schools as postmodern paradox: Rethinking social stratification in an age of deregulated school choice. Harvard Educational Review, 69(2), 172–204.

Willie, C. V. (1991, February). Controlled choice: An alternative desegregation plan for minorities who feel betrayed. Education and Urban Society, 23(2), 200–207.

Wilson, C. E. (1968, Fall). Lessons of the 201 complex in Harlem. Freedomways, 8(4), 399–406.

Zinn, H. (1994). You can't be neutral on a moving train: A personal history of our times. Boston: Beacon Press.

Contributors

Mary Jiron Belgarde is an associate professor in the Department of Language, Literacy, & Sociocultural Studies at the University of New Mexico. She teaches courses regarding the history, policy, and issues of American Indian education, multicultural education, and research. Her research interests include the performance and persistence of American Indian students in schools, rethinking the structures of schools for Indian students, and Indian self-determination in education. She is of San Juan and Isleta Pueblo descent.

Nina K. Buchanan is an educational psychologist and professor of education at the University of Hawaii at Hilo and codirector the university's Charter School Resource Center. She has coedited (with John F. Feldhusen) *Conducting Research and Evaluation in Gifted Education: A Handbook of Methods and Applications* (Teachers College Press, 1991). Her latest work has been in talent development through innovative high school programs. She is a contributing editor of *Roeper Review* and serves on the local school boards of the West Hawaii Explorations Academy and Wai Ola Public Charter Schools.

Robert A. Fox is a professor of physics in the Department of Physics and Astronomy at the University of Hawaii at Hilo where he serves as codirector of the Charter School Resource Center. Dr. Fox has completed a four-year term as an elected member of the statewide Board of Education and is former president of the University of Hawaii Professional Assembly, the union representing Hawaii's 2900 public university professionals. His current research interests include the effect of collective bargaining on Hawaii charter schools and the policy implications of the national school choice movement.

John B. King, Jr. is a codirector at Roxbury Preparatory Charter School in Boston. He previously taught high school history and civics at the City on a Hill Charter School in Boston and Saint John's School in San Juan, Puerto Rico. He holds a B.A. in Government from Harvard University and an M.A. in the teaching of social studies from Teachers College, Columbia University. Mr. King is currently pursuing a doctorate in education administration at Teachers College.

Melissa Steel King is a doctoral student in human development and psychology at the Harvard Graduate School of Education. She is investigating the relationship between academic achievement and interpersonal relationship skills, with a focus on low-income and minority communities. Her research includes work with the Harvard Family Research Project and with ASPIRE, a social and ethical awareness program in Boston public schools. Ms. King earned her master's in elementary education from Teachers College, Columbia University, and she has taught in public and charter elementary schools in New York and Boston.

Alex Medler is an independent education consultant who specializes in education policy, school choice, and charter schools. He worked for the U.S. Department of Education's Public Charter Schools Program (PCSP) from 1997 to 2001, serving as a policy analyst and later acting director. In addition to overall direction of the program, he served as the department's principal expert on charter schools, providing guidance on national activities to support and promote the charter school movement to the U.S. Secretary of Education. Prior to joining the Department of Education, he worked for the Education Commission of the States from 1992 to 1997. He earned his B.A. in politics from the University of California, Santa Cruz, and is presently studying for a Ph.D. in political science at the University of Colorado Boulder.

Eric Rofes is an associate professor of education at Humboldt State University. He presented his dissertation findings on the overall effects of charter schools on nearby school districts to a U.S. Senate subcommittee hearing on school choice and charters and has been quoted in *Education Week*, the *Philadelphia Inquirer*, and the *Wall Street Journal*. He has written about school choice for *Rethinking Schools*, *Dollars and Sense*, and *The Har-*

vard *Educational Review.* Dr. Rofes received his Ph.D. in social and cultural studies in education from UC-Berkeley's Graduate School of Education.

Stacy Smith is an associate professor of education at Bates College. She is the author of *The Democratic Potential of Charter Schools* (Peter Lang, 2001) and a number of articles on school choice. Her teaching and research interests include the growing school choice movement, democratic education, race and educational equity, and political philosophy.

Lisa M. Stulberg is an assistant professor of educational sociology in the Department of Humanities and Social Sciences in the Professions at New York University's Steinhardt School of Education. In 2001, she completed a doctoral dissertation in sociology at UC-Berkeley, on African American alternative school-building since the 1950s. She is currently working on a manuscript based on this work. As part of this research, she explored the way in which the politics of race and the politics of school choice intersect, particularly with regard to charter schools. Her interest in school choice also comes from her involvement as a member of the founding team of a charter middle school in Oakland, California, the West Oakland Community School.

Patty Yancey, is an associate professor in the Department of Education at Humboldt State University in Arcata, California. Her areas of focus at HSU are the visual and performing arts and multicultural foundations in elementary education. Prior to her position at Humboldt, she was an assistant professor and director of the Arts and Education Collaborative in the School of Education at the University of San Francisco. In 2002, she developed and piloted an arts-integrated K–8 multiple-subject teacher credential/M.A.T. program for the University of San Francisco, in partnership with the East Bay Conservation Corps Charter School. From 1996 to 1999, Dr. Yancey worked as an independent research consultant for the National Study of Charter Schools and Policy Analysis for California Education (PACE), visiting over thirty charter schools across the nation. In 2000, Peter Lang (New York) published a book of her case studies, *Parents Founding Charter Schools: Dilemmas of Empowerment and Decentralization,* chronicling the start-up sagas of two California charters. Dr. Yancey is also one of the contributing authors of *Inside Charter Schools: The Paradox of Radical Decentralization* (Harvard University Press, 2001).

Index

307